Please renew/return this item by the last date shown.

So that your telephone call is charged at local rate, please call the numbers as set out below:

	From Area codes 01923 or 0208:	From the rest of Herts:
Renewals:	01923 471373	01438 737373
Enquiries:	01923 471333	01438 737333
Minicom:	01923 471599	01438 737599

L32b

MILITARY OBLIGATION
IN
MEDIEVAL ENGLAND

MILITARY OBLIGATION
IN
MEDIEVAL ENGLAND

A Study in Liberty and Duty

BY

MICHAEL POWICKE
ASSOCIATE PROFESSOR OF HISTORY
UNIVERSITY OF TORONTO

OXFORD
AT THE CLARENDON PRESS
1962

Oxford University Press, Amen House, London E.C.4

GLASGOW NEW YORK TORONTO MELBOURNE WELLINGTON
BOMBAY CALCUTTA MADRAS KARACHI LAHORE DACCA
CAPE TOWN SALISBURY NAIROBI IBADAN ACCRA
KUALA LUMPUR HONG KONG

PRINTED IN GREAT BRITAIN

PREFACE

THIS book was written in the years 1954–8, although work done on articles in the previous six years has been incorporated in Chapters IV to VIII. For the original inspiration, and invaluable encouragement and criticism, I am deeply indebted to my senior colleague Professor Bertie Wilkinson. I have received much advice from my old teachers Sir Maurice Powicke and Sir Goronwy Edwards. On the twelfth and fourteenth centuries respectively I have learned much from Mr. J. O. Prestwich and Professor N. B. Lewis. The advice of many other scholars has helped, I hope, to keep me from falling into too many of the errors attendant on a work of this range.

On the financial side, I am indebted for grants in aid of travel and research to the University of Toronto, the Humanities Research Council of Canada, and the Social Science Research Council of the U.S.A.

M. P.

CONTENTS

INTRODUCTION

THERE is at present no connected account of the development of military obligation in medieval England, and it is to fill this gap that the present book has been written. Much significant work has been printed on this subject, but almost always in connexion with some special period or as part of a larger canvas. Thus, the student can turn to thorough studies of feudal levies in the twelfth and thirteenth centuries, of Edward I's armies, and of Henry V's recruitment for Normandy, besides excellent monographs or articles on particular campaigns; there are also general surveys of warfare, however unsatisfactory; but he will have to turn to William Stubbs or J. H. Ramsay, if not to older writers, for even a disconnected account of the whole process. New work on retaining fees, supply, naval organization, mercenaries, and particular wars is continually being undertaken, and much lies buried in manuscript in the libraries of graduate schools. Two important functions, then, can be discharged by this book. In the first place, it attempts to relate the whole story of the development of militia duty to general political and social history; and in the second, it contributes an analysis of the terms of military service which is primarily for the many workers in this and related fields: workers whose habitat ranges from Edinburgh to Albuquerque. It is in this provisional and utilitarian spirit that these pages have been penned.

The survey which follows is primarily concerned with the rights and duties of the subject rather than with the mechanics of the pay office or the technique of the soldier. In adopting this approach, there is a conscious effort to move away from that concern with administrative arrangements which has dominated the subject since the time of T. F. Tout. At the same time, it may be hoped that the vast increase in knowledge which Tout and his followers have made available has been proved relevant to the study conceived as part of the history of liberty.

The medieval trinity of king, nobles, and people provide the *dramatis personae* of the history of recruitment. Perhaps if we were to substitute 'government' and 'establishment' for the first two terms, this cast would fill the stage of modern British history too. It is in tracing the shifting relationship between these three estates that one of the chief fascinations of this subject lies. The king's duty and right to declare war, and to summon, lead, and direct armies was balanced by his dependence on the nobility for mounted warriors and on the local communities for his auxiliary and defence troops. Royal authority was only partially fortified by the existence, from the early eleventh century, of an expansible nucleus of household or professional warriors and by the possibility of hiring foreigners. In local defence forces, moreover, royal power was always either in the background, or modified by a process of consultation which acknowledged the dominance of local interests.

The role of the nobility as the principal suppliers of cavalry antedated and survived the brief period of classical feudalism. As thegns and five-hide warriors, they were the mounted infantry of the Anglo-Saxons. As feudal tenants-in-chief they introduced cavalry proper into English armies, which they dominated for 200 years. Finally, as recruiters of paid levies and as lords of indentured retainers, the nobility entered on their penultimate and possibly most influential period in English military history. Certainly it was in this third role that they obtained the greatest control over questions of peace and war, and first exercised their hitherto largely dormant power to endorse or reject the objectives of their monarchs. Moreover, the fact that the element of central organization in the last phase was at least as potent as in the earlier ones, lent urgency to the problems of both a stable monarchy and proper machinery of consultation.

The people (i.e. the non-nobles) in England were not mere instruments. Three features of their role emerge from a study of military obligation. First, they merged with the nobility through the intervening categories (according to period) of ceorls, yeomen, burgesses, esquires, and knights. From five-hide rule and fyrd-wite to Assise of Arms and 'distraint of knighthood', the idea of a centrally imposed gradation of duties offset, without destroying, the division of England into nobles and serfs. Secondly, they enjoyed an increasing share in the assembly and use of their own forces. In matters of defence, the local communities of Anglo-Saxon times were autonomous—or, at the very least, the king's local representatives were not tied by central control. As both communications and self-government developed, this autonomy developed into local consultation on defence measures, perhaps most strikingly manifested in the northern Marches. Thirdly, as the communities gained a say in the national politics through the medium of representation, they sought to reduce their military obligation to the barest minimum, while evading any active share in the discussion of peace and war which might seem to commit them to a more extensive duty. Therefore it has seemed fitting, in view of the way in which both aristocratic and popular service developed, to conclude our study with a chapter devoted to the element of consultation in the planning of war and the organization of armies.

I

THE FYRD

THE character of English medieval armies was fore-shadowed, and in at least some degree moulded, by the military organization of the Anglo-Saxons. Though Maitland's statement that 'no matter with which we have to deal is darker than the English army on the eve of its defeat' must be echoed by all who have sought to reconstruct the conditions of military service before 1066, the subject cannot be evaded in any survey of medieval obligation. Nor, in view of the fundamental conflicts between the views of specialists who have studied the subject, can any simple summary be attempted. In this chapter, therefore, the roles of king, nobles, and peasants will be re-examined, with a view to dis-covering in particular whether the division of the army into mercenaries, nobles, and local militia was already in being, and in what way.

Before endeavouring to resurvey the evidence, certain general political and social considerations which may illumi-nate, and be illumined by, the study of the armies demand attention.

I

First, we may note that the geography of the country pro-vided limits within which any political or military decisions must needs be made. As an incompletely unified island, wherein even Roman centralization was incapable of reduc-ing the Cambrian tribal areas, Britain presented the Anglo-Saxon occupants with both problems and opportunities. As an island, it enjoyed long periods of relative isolation which served to discourage all but minimal defensive readi-ness and technical progress; though the widely separated wars of defence from overseas attack did, in fact, lead to sudden leaps into more advanced stages of armament, tactics, and military administration. Within the island, divided by forest, marsh, and mountain, as well as by the fact of piecemeal settlement from widely scattered points of entry, the tasks of unifying the Anglo-Saxon parts and of achieving internal social advance and improvement were bound at times to conflict with the military and political urge to complete the conquest of the British fringes; a distinct swing of the pendulum between external expansion and internal unification is to be seen over the period as a whole. Moreover, sharply contrasting forms of service may have arisen from the divergence between local or regional forms of association, military as well as civil, with their attendant custom, and the 'national' laws, forms, and assessments imposed from above.

Overlaying the developments arising in this way was the natural trend from the military ideals appropriate to invaders towards a more pacific outlook, a cycle repeated again after 1066. To those whom it affected, military service tended to appear as an interference with normal pursuits rather than as a natural way of life; moreover, unification of the country under a distant monarch tended to lead to a divergence of outlook as between royal bodyguard and ordinary conscripts, the latter feeling national service as an alien imposition rather than a customary duty.

The social practice and ideals of the Anglo-Saxons were capable of varied developments. The original loose groupings of military freemen or lesser nobility around great military lords in fluctuating associations for war or defence could lead in settled conditions either to the consolidation of a military despotism, or to a gradual conversion of military into political privileges and liberties. However, until social historians can agree whether a free peasantry was growing or declining in this period, any generalizations about military lordship and peasant freedom must be very tentative. In any case, it may be agreed that the traditions were at hand for the creation of a skeleton royal army drafted from the leading warriors of particular provinces and led by provincial officers, while large numbers of warriors could be raised for local defence and for the upkeep of forts and communications.

The development of central government likewise could affect the evolution of the fyrd in different ways. Initially, the governments of strong kings worked to make more effective the military obligation of the subjects. Evidence of this can be seen in such measures as the tribal hidage or the rotation system under Alfred, in the reassessment implicit in the burghal hidage under either Alfred or Edward, and in the reservation of military service in the land books. Eventually, however, the creation of strong institutions of government, together with a buoyant economy, tended towards a combination of taxation and mercenaries, and the conversion of military into fiscal duties. This tendency, resisted for centuries by the magnates, already showed itself in the eleventh century, and was aided and abetted by the accession of the 'foreign' dynasty of Denmark.

In the social ideals of the age we might well expect a conflict between the fierce militarism of the pagan religion and the peaceful ideals of the Church, but this did not happen. As with Constantine and Clovis, so with Oswy and Alfred, the Church found in the defence of justice and of the faith ample reason for canonizing warfare. Further, the curious marriage of Christian and pagan faith in *Beowulf* anticipated the eventual emergence of a Christian knighthood, a status perhaps first achieved in this era. Nevertheless, it is not unreasonable to assume that the teachings of the Church, combined with the geographical isolation of Britain and the increasing addiction of the inhabitants to peaceful arts, accelerated decline in military readiness between periods of emergency.

In the following pages an attempt will be made to examine the nature and development of the Anglo-Saxon army in its various branches, beginning with the men and measures closest to the king, and moving outwards and downwards. It will be necessary to abandon a chronological in favour of an analytical approach, a move for which we may invoke the authority of Maitland's classical technique of proceeding from the better to the less well known.

II

For fifty years, from the accession of Cnut to the battle of Hastings, the huscarls were the most effective element in the English army. The strength of these warriors, who fought on

foot with axe and sword and shield wall, but who rode to
battle and in pursuit after battle, was demonstrated most
decisively at Stamford Bridge, and in the march thither and
back to Hastings. At Hastings they came very close to over-
throwing the numerically superior and much fresher mailed
cavalry of Normandy.

They appear to have been a royal creation, probably
Cnut's.[1] For inspiration he had three sources, the primacy
among which has long been a matter of dispute. First, there
was the precedent of the Germanic and Anglo-Saxon *comitatus*, the warriors gathered round the chief.[2] Second, and
more direct, was the professional army of Jomsvikings,
settled in a military community on the Danish royal estates
at Jomsburg, who are known to have come to England with
Sweyn after the destruction of their base. That Cnut's
Lex Castrensis owed much to the laws of Jomsburg seems
accepted; but the physical continuity of the Jomsvikings
must certainly have been shattered by the successive defeats in
Pomerania and in England.[3] A third source, favoured by
Larson, was the Norse court, where a royal bodyguard of
bearsarks was of long standing.[4]

The received view, based on Steenstrup and Larson (the
former favouring a Jomsburg, the latter a court, origin), must
be qualified by an insistence on the importance of Anglo-
Saxon precedent. The huscarls added a much needed in-
fusion of discipline into the badly mauled king's thegns of
Æthelred's fyrd. But they fitted into the traditional picture
quite well. They were rarely distinguished from the thegns

---

[1] L. M. Larson, *The King's Household in England before the Norman Conquest*
(Wisconsin, 1904), pp. 152–71; cf. Johannes C. H. R. Steenstrup, *Danelag
Normannerne*, iv (Copenhagen, 1882), pp. 127–54; P. Vinogradoff, *English Society
in the Eleventh Century* (Oxford, 1908), pp. 15–22; T. J. Oleson, *The Witenagemot
in the Reign of Edward the Confessor* (Toronto, 1955), pp. 160–9.

[2] E. A. Freeman, *The Norman Conquest* (3rd ed., London, 1877), i. 445. Freeman's view, which in this respect is eminently logical, is mistakenly criticized by
Steenstrup and Larson. Note the precedent of Alfred's devotion of part of his
revenues to the maintenance of soldiers and thegns at his court; D. Whitelock,
Beginnings of English Society (Pelican Books, Harmondsworth, 1952), p. 66.

[3] Cf. G. F. Ward, 'Jomsburg Brethren in England', *Scandinavian Studies*, xxviii
(1956), 135–41. Miss Ward's reliance on later sources and on such authorities as
Augustin Thierry does not command confidence; she assigns an exaggerated role to
the Jomsvikings at almost every point.

[4] Larson, pp. 157–8.

in Latin charters, both being known as *ministri*.[1] Neither
the Laws nor the *Anglo-Saxon Chronicles* made a distinction
between them.[2] Moreover, they were known to the Norse
writers by an English name; they were *þingamenn* of the
þingamannalið, terms derived from the OE. *þegnung* (service),
which was almost certainly also the root of 'thegn'.[3] It is
highly improbable that the Norse would have given a name
of English derivation to an institution which they recognized
as derived from their own country.

In their relationship to the king as personal vassals and
immediate entourage, the huscarls went back to an older
Anglo-Saxon tradition, which in turn derived from common
Teutonic customs as first witnessed in Tacitus.[4] The huscarls
were not entirely an exotic implantation, but a graft of a
more primitive and sturdier plant on to a later growth. The
element of contract and of corporate organization, which
gives the huscarls their claim to novelty, links them to the
stipendiarii of the Anglo-Norman household, while the territorializing process fits them into the normal line of progress
from *comitatus* to feudal levy.[5] Evidence of contract appears
most strongly in later Scandinavian documents, above all in
the *Lex Castrensis*. However, it occurs also in English records
in the *Chronicles*' account of the trial of Swegn, in the corporate witness of documents, and in twelfth-century references to them as *stipendiarii*.[6] Domesday Book evidence
suggests that their maintenance for forty days at the rate of
twopence a day was one way in which certain boroughs could

[1] Freeman, i. 758–9. The special title *praefectus palatinus*, a clear archaism, is to
be compared with *A.S. Chronicle* 'C', 1041: they show that the huscarl, like the
thegn, was a general servant available for special office.

[2] *Two Saxon Chronicles Parallel*, ed. C. Plummer (Oxford, 1892), Glossary, s.v.
huscarl; Freeman, i. 755.

[3] Larson, p. 154, n. 24, is oddly hesitant on this link. On *ministri*, see F. M.
Stenton, *The First Century of English Feudalism* (Oxford, 1932), p. 119.

[4] P. Cornelius Tacitus, *Germania* (ed. Anderson and Furneaux), chaps. 6, 14,
15, 25.

[5] On the Anglo-Normans, see below, chapter two; for the territorializing process,
see F. M. Stenton, op. cit., pp. 119–21.

[6] *A.S. Chron.* 'C.', 1049, and T. J. Oleson, *The Witenagemot*, pp. 103–4; on the
witness of a will, cf. J. M. Kemble, *Codex Diplomaticus Aevi Saxonici* (London,
English Historical Society, 1839–48) [henceforward *C.D.*], iv. 290, and Freeman,
i. 759; on the references to *stipendiarii*, see Florence of Worcester, *Chronicon* (E.H.S.,
1898), i. 204, and William of Malmesbury, *Gesta Regum* (R.S.), i. 282; cf. Larson,
pp. 163–4.

discharge their five-hide duty.[1] Some of the Domesday Book entries also refer to 'butsecarls', and these may possibly be distinguished from huscarls; since the latter were originally boatmen, it may well be that the lithsmen and butsecarls of the *Chronicles* and Domesday Book were those of the original force who continued to be purely mercenaries.[2] Whether on sea or land, these mercenaries were important enough to play a decisive role in the crises of 1035–6, 1052, and 1066.[3] Even this specifically royal force did not escape the inroads of provincial power, for some at least of the great earls formed their own groups of huscarls. Nevertheless, it may be regarded, in general, as a great addition to the royal and national army.[4]

The battles of Stamford Bridge and Hastings have sometimes been described as though the forces at Harold's command were exclusively huscarls. Certainly there is every reason for believing that the huscarls provided the nucleus of the mounted contingent who rode north and south with the king. But there is no good evidence that the thegns, whom we know to have been principally mounted troops, were not an equally important part of these forces, or that they were distinguished from the huscarls in battle.[5]

III

The thegns who shared the honours at Hastings with the huscarls constituted the main support of the eleventh-century

---

[1] Domesday Book (Rec. Comm. ed.), i. 75a; Vinogradoff, p. 20 and nn. The boroughs were Dorchester, Wareham, Shaftesbury, and Bridport. Each five hides had to find ½ mark *ad opus Huscarlum*. Malmesbury, by a similar arrangement, could supply twenty shillings to maintain the king's butsecarls. It is at least probable that the limitation of these plans to Dorset and Wiltshire was as much due to the selectivity of the recorders as to actual variation of custom.

[2] Freeman, i. 444–5. Larson's attempted distinction between lithsmen and butsecarls seems motivated by a wish to discredit the dismissal of 1051; *King's Household*, p. 169. Cf. *A.S. Chron.*, 1046; T. J. Oleson leans to an interpretation of butsecarls as garrison troops; *Witenagemot*, p. 169.

[3] Steenstrup, iii. 414; Vinogradoff, p. 21; Plummer, *Two Saxon Chronicles*, ii. 239–40; *A.S. Chron.* 'E', 1035, 1036; *A.S. Chron.* 'C', 1052; Florence of Worcester, i. 9.

[4] Cf. Stenton, *English Feudalism*, p. 120, for huscarls of Earls Leofwine and Aelfgar.

[5] The only account to emphasize the *stipendiarii* in the Hastings force is William of Malmesbury's *Gesta Regum*, i. 282 ('nam, praeter stipendiarios et mercenarios milites, paucos admodum ex provincialibus habuit').

monarchy. Historians seem agreed on their derivation, via *gesiths*, from the ancient *comitatus*; their reception of land grants and transformation into landlords; their division into king's, earls', bishops', and others' thegns; their predominantly mounted service; and the equivalence of their duty with that owed by five-hide units of land.[1] What historians do not agree about is the nature of the obligation of thegns and of their responsibility for their vassals, and the effectiveness of royal control. As the latter question offers perhaps the least complicated way to the heart of these problems, it will be studied first.

The king's command of the army was by no means uniform.[2] In the first place, there was the division of the army into royal, provincial, and county forces. This division was linked to the question of obligation. The national, or royal, force has been considered by some to have been composed exclusively of nobles, thegns serving by reason of personal allegiance, and on horseback, while peasant levies, barely deserving the name of warriors, made up the local forces.[3] The less radical view of R. H. Hodgkin would rather distinguish the royal, ealdormen's, and shire thegns' followings, the last including ceorls.[4]

Royal control naturally tended to be weaker where the army was not assembled by the king's summons and where the monarch himself did not attend. From the *Chronicles* we learn much of these distinctions. Three kinds of force appear in these accounts—the royally led, the royally summoned or dispatched, and the local. Three entries of A.D. 825 well illustrate this:[5]

---

[1] A few influential works are listed in order of publication; W. Stubbs, *Constitutional History of England* (Oxford, 1874), i. 149–57, 189–94; F. W. Maitland, *Domesday Book and Beyond* (Cambridge, 1897), pp. 156–66; H. M. Chadwick, *Origin of the English Nation* (Cambridge, 1907), pp. 158–62; P. Vinogradoff, *English Society* (1908), pp. 25–32, 79–87, 403–7; W. A. Morris, *Constitutional History of England Before 1216* (New York, 1930), pp. 37–40, 65–67; F. M. Stenton, *The First Century of English Feudalism* (Oxford, 1932), ch. iv.

[2] See H. M. Cam, *Francia and England* (London, 1912), pp. 142–3 and 149–50, for some of the following references.

[3] H. M. Chadwick, *Origin*, pp. 158–62.

[4] R. H. Hodgkin, *History of the Anglo-Saxons* (3rd ed., Oxford, 1953), ii. 590–8.

[5] The texts employed in the following references to the *Anglo-Saxon Chronicle* are those of C. Plummer, D. Whitelock (in *English Historical Documents*, vol. i), and D. Douglas (ibid., vol. ii). Corrected dates are given unless otherwise stated.

'In this year the Britons fought the men of Devon at Galford.'
'In that same year king Egbert fought king Beornwulf at Ellen-
dun.'
'He then sent his son Æthelwulf from the army (*fierde*), together
with Ealhstan his bishop and Wulfheard his ealdorman, to Kent with
a large force (*werede*).'

In these entries the term *fierde* seems to have had a definite
connotation as the 'royal army'.

These three types of force continue to appear without controversial emphasis until Æthelred's reign.[1] For the local—
county or burh—forces neither royal summons nor leadership seems to have been necessary. On the other hand, these
forces must be distinguished from the provincial divisions of
the royal fyrd—those of Wessex, Mercia, Kent, or East
Anglia—which appear to have descended from the armies of
the old kingdoms and for which royal leadership was normally required.[2] From the reign of Alfred at least, the unification of England involved a distinction—by no means hard
and fast—between the royal army of the whole nation and
the provincial armies which formed its subdivisions or fought
as separate 'groupings'. It was the provincial armies rather
than the county forces which engaged on fort construction
under Alfred, Edward, and the Lady Æthelflæd.[3] Burh defence, on the other hand, was a 'non-royal', local business.
Thus in 914 the 'men' of the nearest burhs joined those of
Herefordshire and Gloucestershire in local defence, while
the royal army built two new burhs in Buckinghamshire.

In the reign of Æthelred the Unready (978–1016) this
system ran into crisis, and the royal presence and leadership
was put at a premium. This appears from both the *Chronicles*
and from the laws. From the *Chronicles* we learn that the king

[1] The 'fyrd' is led by the king in *A.S. Chron.*, 655, 825, 829, 830, 836, 838, 851,
853, 867, 870, 871, 877, 878, 893, 900, 903, 912, 914, 915, 917, 918, 919, 924, 934,
937, 948, and sent under deputies in 684, 825, 885, 896, 910, 911, 914, 919. Less
clear entries appear in 868, 895. County or burh forces appear in 789, 802, 825, 840,
845, 851, 853, 860, 871, 885, 893, 913 (*þa land leode*), 914, 917. In 893, 894, 895
the two kinds of force are clearly distinguished.

[2] In 910 we have *firde ægðer of West Seaxum ge of Mercium*; in 917 *West Sexne
fierde* contrasted with the *micel folc* gathered from the burhs; in 919 *het oþre fierd eac
of Miercna peode*. The term *heer* or *here* was used principally, but by no means exclusively, of the Danish forces; see *Two Saxon Chronicles, Parallel*, vol. i, Glossary.

[3] *A.S. Chron.*, 912–20.

was either not present or not mentioned far more frequently than in any previous reign; only in 1000, 1009, and 1013 was he mentioned as leading an army. And the *Chronicles* were bitterly conscious of the defects of leadership this entailed.[1] The term 'fyrd' came to be applied to the 'county' forces in 1001 and 1003, though the distinction between local forces (Brihthnoth's Essex men, the Hampshire men at Athelinga Dene, or the *fyrde of Defenisces folces* at Penhoe) and the national or provincial armies under royal representatives was not finally abandoned.[2] By 1010 the Chronicler was driven to relate that no leader could be found to gather an army together, and that one county would not even help the next. The king's failure was clearly the core of the problem, as had previously been hinted in 999, when the Kentish fyrd broke 'because they did not have the support which they should have had'. In 1016, after the Atheling Edmund had gathered the fyrd, the Chronicler writes 'they were not satisfied unless the king were there, and they had there the burhware of London' ('þa ne on hagode him buton se cyng þære wære, hi hæfdon þære burh ware fultum of Lundene') and the army dissolved. Later, the king was sent for in London to come and join the force, but again he let them down. The transformation on Edmund's succession was astonishing.

This concern about royal leadership is reflected in the laws, and in a significant way.[3] While V Æthelred 28 (cf. VI Æthelred 35) was doubtless but an enactment of custom, its emphasis on royal leadership at this time (1008) suggests the concern of the witan at the ill effects of Æthelred's defections.[4] This law stated that the penalty of desertion from the fyrd if the king was in personal command was loss of life or property (wergild), whereas otherwise it was 120 shillings.[5]

---

[1] Cf. *A.S. Chron.*, 992, 993, 998, 999, 1000, 1001, 1003, 1006, 1010, 1015, and 1016.

[2] In 1066 Edwin and Morcar gathered a *mycel werod*, while Harold assembled his *fyrde*; *A.S. Chron.* 'C'.

[3] See on this subject, H. M. Cam, *Francia and England*, pp. 142–3.

[4] F. Liebermann, *Die Gesetze der Angelsachsen* (Halle, 1903), i. 244, 256. Cf. also the translated editions by F. L. Attenborough and A. J. Robertson, which have been used freely in what follows.

[5] This was the old *fyrdwite* of Ine 51 (on ceorl's service, see below). It was also the fine for failure to turn out on police duty, III Edmund 2.

This rule emphasizes the urgency with which the king's presence was required; it is a measure of the weight such personal leadership carried. The Domesday Book entries which set forth the custom concerning royal armies stress the king's presence as part of the custom in four cases out of eight,[1] and in two others a royal summons is implied. Thus, the famous Worcestershire custom begins 'When the king goes against the enemy'.[2] Similar phrases occur in the entries for the boroughs of Oxford, Warwick, and Malmesbury.[3] The Berkshire entry implies royal summons and direction ('if the king sent the army anywhere'), while that for Calnodeshou wapentake, Lincolnshire, reads, 'if there was need for a royal expedition'.[4] In other cases, obligation for local defence was recorded as distinct from service with the national, or royal, army.[5]

The penalty for failure to respond to the king's summons remained heavy at the end of the Anglo-Saxon period. In two statements of custom it was forfeiture,[6] but from others it would appear to have been convertible into a fine of 100 shillings.[7] A shrieval summons, on the other hand, could be flouted for only forty shillings.[8] In Cnut's reign the penalty of death for desertion in the field had been added.[9]

It would thus appear that military obligation varied with leadership. There was a threefold obligation, in order of decreasing weight:

1. Personal service with the king, on being summoned by him;

2. Supply of service to the king, or personal service without the king, but in his army;

---

[1] Worcestershire, Oxford, Warwick, and Malmesbury. In the case of Oxford, for example, the burgesses either went with the king or paid him twenty pounds.

[2] Domesday Book, i. 172 [henceforward Dd.].

[3] Ibid. i. 154a, 238a, 64b.

[4] Ibid. i. 375b. Cf. *servitium regis* at Wallingford (ibid. i. p. 56a).

[5] e.g. at Lewes, for coast defence, but at royal command (Dd. i. 26); Chester, for wall work (ibid. i. 262b); Shrewsbury, for a local Welsh campaign (ibid. i. 252).

[6] Dd. i. 56b (Berkshire), 172 (Worcestershire).

[7] Ibid. i. 154b (Oxfordshire), 238a (Warwick).

[8] Ibid. i. 252 (Shrewsbury); cf. ibid. i. 262b (Chester). Vinogradoff, *English Society*, p. 111, seems to misunderstand this differential. The explanation of the Chester fine as forty *Norman* as opposed to *Mercian* shillings, on the other hand (D. Whitelock, *English Society*, p. 76), makes the Oxfordshire and Warwick evidence extraordinary.   [9] II Cnut 77.

3. Service with burh, shire, or other local force under a local leader.

A second approach to the problem of royal control can be made through a study of the leaders of national and local forces. These were at first the ealdormen, acting either as local commanders, or in the field army either as subordinates to, or deputies of, the king. They served as deputies at the beginning and at the end of the period (684–1016) for which we have evidence of their military operations.[1] In 684 'Ecgferth sent the army (here) against the Scots and Briht his ealdorman with it'. In 825 Ealdorman Wulfheard shared command of a part of the fyrd with the king's son and bishop. In Æthelred's reign the ealdorman and king's son frequently shared the task of leading the royal army (992, 993, 1003, 1015, 1016). These officials are often known to us because they figured among the dead. Such was the case in 827, when five ealdormen fell with the king of Mercia, and in 836, when two fell in the army of Egbert of Wessex. In 851 an ealdorman fought along with the king in the navy. Little is said of the units which these subordinates commanded. In 903 the Kentishmen formed part of the royal army, and were commanded by two ealdormen, a king's thegn, and an abbot. Kent, of course, was an old kingdom, a provincial as well as a county unit. We cannot then be certain from the role of the ealdorman that the royal fyrd was made up of county units, though this was probably the case. The ealdormen served as commanders of local county forces as well as in the capacity of subordinates in the royal army.[2] They appeared as the former in 802, 840 (bis), 851, 853, 860, 871 (probably), 878,[3] 893, 991, 999, and 1004. In several instances (e.g. 845) the bishop is mentioned along with the ealdorman. In 893 the force was drawn from the burhs.

The role of both county and of ealdorman was superseded when, in the reign of Edward the Confessor, the earls of great provinces more than took over the duties of the

---

1 This and the following are based on C. Plummer's edition of the Chronicles.

2 In what follows, it is to be remembered that the local commanders were, indirectly, royal deputies.

3 In Æthelweard, not in the Chronicle; see Monumenta Historica Britannica (1848), p. 515.

ealdormen. The provincial unit, already active, now became dominant. Each earl seems to have had his own fyrd and to have decided whether to summon it or not—such was the case in 1051, when Godwin, of course, acted independently, and Earls Leofric and Siward only called out their fyrds when they decided they were needed.

The independence of the earls did not mean that they could withstand the royal will. The events of 1051–2 show that it was as a national leader but not as a provincial rebel that Godwin could combat the king. Moreover, if Florence of Worcester's version of the reign, which may in this respect be derived from another version of the *Chronicles* now lost, be accepted, the independence of the earls' actions must be qualified. For on almost every occasion he adds some such term as 'by the king's command' to the account. This is to be seen in the case of Siward's expedition into Scotland (1054), in the terms of Harold's authority in 1055, in Harold and Tostig's expedition into Wales (1063), and in Harold's actions at Oxford and Northampton in 1065.[1] But occasionally the earls appear to have acted as simple successors to ealdormen, as did Earl Ralph in 1055. In 1066 the Earls Edwin and Morcar first fulfilled this traditional role of local commanders, and then acted as deputies of the king in command of part of the national host. It was still only the king's personal family who could be absolutely counted on. Whether as loyal deputies, or on their own initiative, within their own earldoms or outside them—in Wales, Scotland, or elsewhere in England—the earls of 1042–66 dominated the fyrd, in a way that the ealdormen had never done, unless the infamous Ælfric in the reign of Æthelred can be regarded as a fore-runner.

Beside the ealdorman and earl stood the bishop.[2] At least twice (in 1049 as local commander, in 1051 as deputy of the king) he acted independently of them. Occasionally another official took a leading role—the high reeve, and in 1056 the

[1] Florence of Worcester, *Chronicon* (E.H.S.), pp. 212, 213, 221, 223. On 1065, see T. J. Oleson, *The Witenagemot*, p. 29, n. 7; on Florence of Worcester's sources, see Plummer, *Two Chronicles*, ii. lxxxiii–lxxxvi, cxxv.

[2] In 815, 825, 836, 845, 871, 992, 1001, 1016, 1056; in 903 an abbot was among those Kentishmen slain because they lingered behind in East Anglia; *A.S. Chron*. 'A'; Plummer, ii. 124.

sheriff. Thus as early as 789 the *ge refa* rode out to meet the first Norse boats to reach England. According to Æthelweard he was a local commander (*exactor regis . . . morans in oppido . . . Dorceastre*). In 1001 the principal leaders who fell at 'Athelinga dene' were two king's high reeves. The queen's reeve at Exeter was blamed for the loss of that city in 1003. In 1056 Ælfnoth the sheriff fell with Bishop Leofgar (the moustached) while campaigning in Wales.

Does the use of local officials in army commands imply that local forces should not be separated too rigorously from national ones? *A priori*, we should expect that the men whom the ealdorman, earl, or high reeve commanded in local defence would not be too different from those he led in the army of the king, or in that of an earl, into Scotland or Wales or to some distant part of England. Indeed, it may be argued that the performance of local police duty ascended by stages to that of military service. In Alfred's laws the appeal for armed support went first to the ealdormen, then to the king, while defensive fighting on behalf of a lord or of one's kin was allowed.[1] By Athelstan's time the mounted man was in special demand: he was one of the 'seniors' who must ride on penalty of *oferhyrnesse* against those insubordinate to the court.[2] In the case of powerful groups, the king himself would join the local reeve and ride against them with a strong force, while neighbouring reeves joined the chase.[3] Here, in the organization against thieves, lay the basis of the army: a local force was easily transformed into a royal one,[4] the king's reeve becoming a subordinate officer if the king himself took command.

A third approach to the problem is through the question of place of service. Were local forces limited in this respect more severely than was the royal fyrd? Did the same force at times operate locally, at other times coalesce with other forces and operate over a larger area? Everything points to the absence of geographical limits to the royal fyrd's operations.

---

[1] After exhausting self-help; Alfred 42, cc. 1, 3, 5, 6. Cf. II Æthelred 56.
[2] II Athelstan 20; cf. VI Athelstan 4, 5, and II Cnut 25, cc. 2, 29.
[3] VI Athelstan 8.
[4] Cf. III Edmund 2, where the fine for disobeying a 'police' summons was 120s. II Æthelred 5, 2 suggests that the distinction between a private and public war was capable of objective measurement.

In Domesday Book service was to be 'everywhere' (Dd. i. 56), 'by land or by sea' (Dd. i. 100, 230, 238). In the *Chronicles*, the fyrd continually served outside the home county or by sea.[1] The fyrds of the old 'nations', later provinces or earldoms, also served widely outside their own borders, as when the Wessex fyrd went to the aid of Mercia in 853 and 868, or when the Northumbrian fyrd went to Scotland in 1054.[2]

Although 'national' armies seem to have been composed of county groups, the duty of a county to defend itself or its neighbours was not exhausted by such service. Time and again, a county or burh defended itself or associated with its neighbours in self defence. On seven occasions individual counties fought against the Danes or (802) against each other. In 853 Kent and Surrey and in 860 Hampshire and Berkshire fought together, and it is evident from the entry of 1010 that this was normal practice. When, in 1004, 'all East Anglia fought together', the wording leaves us in doubt whether we have a provincial fyrd or an association of counties. At the very depth of Anglo-Saxon fortunes, the Chronicler lists among the causes of failure that 'in the end no shire would even help the next' ('Ne furðon nan scir nolde oðre gelæstan æt nyxten'). This duty of helping the next shire was clearly one of the basic obligations of the period.

The national and provincial fyrds, then, could serve outside the country, and outside the province. To serve in the fyrds, units of county and burh troops had, of course, to serve outside their respective counties and burhs. For local defence, as we have seen, the counties and burhs often banded together, while the minimal duty was to assist the next neighbour. But the county or burh did not serve *by itself* outside its immediate neighbourhood. The place of service seems to confirm the distinction between local and national obligations, lending some credence to the concept of a thegnly fyrd and a peasant county militia.

If the royal force was liable to serve over great distances this was a good reason why it should be a mounted force. In

---

[1] In 829, 830, 840, 853, 868, 875, 878, 885, 893, 903, 914, 917, 919, 934, 992, 999, 1000, 1001, 1003, 1016, 1051, 1054, 1056, 1063, and 1066. Cf. II Cnut 77, 78.
[2] In Florence of Worcester's account, 'by the king's command'.

fact, the chronicles frequently describe it or its provincial counterparts as riding to battle, whereas the local (i.e. county) forces never merited this description.[1] The problem arises whether in this case the personnel of the two types of force must not have been radically different. On the one hand, the thegns, who were normally equipped with horses, must have provided the principal element of the royal force,[2] and the ceorls are never met with in military action in the *Chronicles*.[3] On the other hand, in 991 the ceorl Dunhere shared the front of the stage with the thegns of the dead Brihtnoth in the *Song of Maldon*, and thegns provided the leadership of local forces.[4] Without predicating two entirely separate forces, it may be suggested that the non-noble element provided the bulk of communal defence levies, but only an auxiliary and fringe group for the national fyrd.

The analysis of the royal force has so far been conducted as a simple matter of deciding on what occasions a royal summons was required, and what differences there were between royal fyrd and local levies. A further question which arises is whether the king's summons which is mentioned in the *Chronicles* only in connexion with the royal fyrd or special forces assembled from burhs and provinces was in any way qualified by the necessity for consent. Stubbs's dictum that 'to summon the fyrd he [the king] must have the consent of the witan' does not bear examination.[5] As Stubbs himself realized, the evidence for such consultation is centred almost entirely in Æthelred II's reign.[6] In that reign, too, strategy was discussed by the witan. It was a time, as we have seen,

---

[1] The king's force 'rode' in 755, 877, 878, 893, 895, 900, 937, 1016, 1063, 1066. Provincial forces 'rode' in 903, 1054 (Florence of Worcester), and 1055. For the 'county' forces, cf. 800, 823, 837, 845, 851, 853, 860, 991, 1001, 1003. On many other occasions the uninformative *faran* was used.

[2] That thegns were normally in possession of horses appears most clearly from their heriots (II Cnut 71).

[3] In 892 ceorls were stationed in a half-constructed fort, and may have been workmen; *A.S. Chron.* 'A', 893 (Plummer, i. 84); cf. Chadwick, *Origin*, p. 100.

[4] M. Ashdown, *English and Norse Documents Relating to the Reign of Ethelred the Unready* (Cambridge, 1930), pp. 22–37. As Chadwick observes, this is the only detailed account of the fyrd.

[5] *Const. Hist.* i. 149.

[6] Ibid. i. 147. Cf. F. Liebermann, *The National Assembly*, c. 58; Kemble, *The Saxons in England* (London, 1876), ii. 224–5; *A.S. Chron.*, 992, 999, 1009, 1010.

when the king was failing in his duty, and leadership fell to the ealdormen and, eventually, to Edmund Atheling. One of the principal functions of the witan, and one which persisted into Edward the Confessor's reign, seems to have been to lend support to unpopular decisions, such as the dismissal of troops or buying off the enemy.[1] Consultation, then, was an extraordinary, not a customary, act.

If the king was restricted it was not so much by the duty of obtaining consent as by the existence of such customary rules as are witnessed in Domesday statements and occasionally in the *Chronicles*,[2] and by the existence of other claims, alongside his, to military loyalty. For neither thegn nor peasant owed service exclusively to the king. From as early as Alfred the ties of lordship included duties of mutual defence;[3] forfeiture was owed to the lord by deserters and protection was owed to the loyal man by his lord.[4] That kingship benefited most from these duties, one cannot doubt; but the tie was wider than that, and lordship must be reckoned as a factor which limited as well as strengthened the control of the king.

IV

The second major area of uncertainty about Anglo-Saxon military service is the nature of the obligation by which men served. Was there any universal assessment, or was service based on a series of individual contracts? How closely was service related to land and to the laws of tenure? That the basic military duty was personal rather than tenurial seems to be accepted by all historians. The literary descent of the *comites* of Tacitus, through *Beowulf*'s *eorls*, to the thegns of Brihtnoth is impeccable.[5] The personal oath of loyalty is to

---

[1] *A.S. Chron.*, 1009, 1049–50 ('E', 1047; 'C' 1049, 1050); cf. T. J. Oleson, *The Witenagemot*, p. 97. It should be noted that only one of these accounts ('E') associates the witan with the dismissal, and that one hesitatingly.

[2] There is occasionally a reference to limited duration of service in the *Chronicles*.

[3] Alfred, 42, cl. 5; cf. H. M. Chadwick, *Origins*, pp. 157–8.

[4] II Cnut 77, 78.

[5] Tacitus, *Germania*, ch. 6, 15, &c.; *Beowulf*, ed. Fr. Klaeber (Boston, 1950), l. 1228 (e.g.); 'Song of Maldon' in M. Ashdown, *English and Norse Documents*, l. 205. Many other terms were employed to describe the noble warrior retainers: notably *beorn* in both poems.

be seen in the laws, but cannot be confined to any one group of the population.[1]

A wide divergence of opinion appears as soon as one raises the question of the relationship of land tenure to military service. The divergences refer, above all, to two problems: the origins and the terms of land tenure. With the former we are least concerned. It is simply a question of whether a fully fledged seignorial system existed from the beginning, or whether it developed as a result of impoverishment of free peasants and consequent commendation.[2] But the champions of an early lordship have not suggested that military service was one of the lords' tenurial rights. On the other hand, military service lies at the heart of the second problem. Here the lines are drawn between those who, like Maitland and, more recently, Miss M. Hollings, believe that Anglo-Saxon land tenures had evolved to a point closely resembling post-conquest feudalism, and Stenton who insists on the personal nature of military lordship both in relation to king and to tenants.[3] Stubbs's position lay somewhere between these two viewpoints; Vinogradoff supported Maitland, but neither did justice to J. H. Round's essays on Norman feudalism.[4]

That the possession of book land increased the military duties of an Anglo-Saxon does not admit of doubt. The principle is stated in the *Rectitudines singularum personarum*: 'thegn's law is that he is worthy of book-right and that he shall do three things for his land (*ðreo ðinc of his lande do*): going in the king's army (*fyrd færeld*), burh repair and bridge work.'[5] The charters or 'books' which conveyed such land almost invariably reserved the three services (*trimoda*

[1] III Edmund 1; 5 Athelstan 35. For a useful discussion on non-territorial allegiance, cf. J. E. A. Jolliffe, *Constitutional History of Medieval England* (London, 1937), pp. 51, 79–80, 106–7.

[2] The literature is enormous: the leading early protagonist of an original lordship (which tends to be 'Romanist'), F. Seebohm, has been supported by C. Stephenson and more recently by T. H. Aston and (indirectly) H. P. R. Finberg. However, the 'established' view is that of F. M. Stenton and D. Whitelock.

[3] F. W. Maitland, *Domesday Book and Beyond* (Cambridge, 1897), pp. 156–66 (henceforward *D.B.B.*); M. Hollings, 'The Survival of the Five-Hide Unit in the Western Midlands', *English Historical Review*, lxiii (1948), 467–73, 482–3; F. M. Stenton, *English Feudalism*, pp. 115–35, esp. pp. 118–20 and notes.

[4] W. Stubbs, *Constitutional History*, i. 149–57, 189–94; P. Vinogradoff, *English Society*, pp. 25–32, 79–87, 403–7.

[5] F. Liebermann, *Gesetze*, i. 444.

necessitas) when granting privileges.[1] *Fyrdfæreld* or *expeditio* is elaborated in Domesday Book as a duty of a *miles* from each five hides of land, each hide contributing 4 shillings for two months' expenses.[2]

There are two principal ways of interpreting this evidence. On the one hand, the thegn may be regarded as responsible for the service of free peasants on his estates, at a rate (in 1066 at any rate) of one warrior for five hides, in sharp distinction from his personal duty as a thegn. On the other hand, the service of the books may be regarded as essentially thegn service; the five-hide rule being merely an extension of the rule that the holder of an estate assessed at five hides *to utware* was thegnly.[3]

It certainly seems unwarranted to make a complete break between peasant service assessed on hides and personal noble service. What the five-hide rule of Domesday Book, together with the rule in the code of 'Of People's Ranks and Laws', indicates is that the duties and privileges of the warrior class inhered in land rather than individuals. The rule is that a given quantity of land must support a warrior; and conversely, that an individual in possession of that land is to fulfil the obligations and enjoy the privileges of thegn-hood. This view makes the *miles* of Domesday Book custumal closer to the thegn than to Stenton's 'armed peasant'. However, the existence of a fighting *ceorl* reflected in the *Song of Maldon* does not go unsupported in the texts. It is clear from the 'North People's Law', c. 10, for example, that a *ceorl* might have the arms and armour of a warrior ('helm, coat of mail, and gold-ornamented sword') without acquiring thegnly wergild, if he did not have five hides of land owing national service (for the king's *utware*).

The basic principle of Anglo-Saxon military obligation, it would seem, was that of 'thegnly' service assessed on land, discharged by the lords of large estates in person, and by

---

[1] W. H. Stevenson, 'Trinoda Necessitas', *E.H.R.* xxix (1914), 689–703; F. M. Stenton, *Latin Charters of the Anglo-Saxon Period* (Oxford, 1955), pp. 57–58.

[2] In the celebrated Berkshire custom, Dd. i. 56; also in Stubbs, *Select Charters* (9th ed.), p. 107. There is nothing about sub-tenants, as seems to be suggested in M. Hollings, 'The Survival of the Five Hide Unit in the Western Midlands', *E.H.R.* lxiii (1948), 469.

[3] 'North People's Law', c. 9; cf. 'Of People's Ranks and Laws', cc. 2, 3.

co-operative effort of lesser men in cases of small land holdings. That the unit of assessment for *expeditio* under Edward
the Confessor was five hides appears clearly enough from
Domesday Book.[1]

It may be well to ask how universal and how ancient was
the five-hide unit. In 1008 every eight hides had been
assessed 'to helm and byrnie'. A well-known endorsement of
a charter, attributed to A.D. 801, stated that only five men
(*vires*) were to be sent from thirty hides (*manentes*).[2] This
charter does three things. It pushes back to the eighth
century any serious claim that fyrd service ever had a 'one-
hide' basis; it confirms, by its Middlesex location, the belief
that the hidage assessment to military service was widespread in the south; and its use of the term *vires* rather than,
say, *taini*, or *gesithcundi*, suggests that as in 1066 there was
no legally strict limitation on the status of the warriors to be
supplied. We may conclude that the south was assessed to
find a warrior from varying numbers of hides.

This conclusion leaves the evidence for one-hide service
to be disposed of. The chief source is the 'Burghal Hidage',
which dates from either Alfred's or Edward the Elder's
reign.[3] In this document, the duty of burh defence is to be
performed by one man from each hide. Now burh defence
was one of the duties of the *trimoda necessitas*, and it might be
argued that what is true for one must also hold good for the
others. However, the fact that a similar one-hide duty occurs
in connexion with wall building at Chester in 1066, at a
time when the five-hide unit for military assembly seems to
have been universal, points to the more obvious conclusion
that the servicing of the burhs was more heavily assessed

---

[1] The key study is that of J. H. Round, 'Danegeld and the Finance of Domesday',
in *Domesday Studies* (London, 1888), i. 119–20. For borough five-hide assessment,
cf. A. Ballard, *Domesday Boroughs* (Cambridge, 1904), p. 80; Dd. i. 64b, 100a.

[2] The date is that suggested by its most recent editor, in *English Historical
Documents*, i, no. 73; W. Birch, *Cartularium Saxonicum* (London, 1885–99) [hence-
forward *C.S.*], i, no. 201. The phrase *vires quinque tantum* is strikingly echoed in
the Berkshire Domesday, *tantum unus miles*. In the former case *tantum* distinguishes
the less numerous fyrd numbers from those required for the other two public duties;
it is preserved in meaningless isolation in the Berkshire statement.

[3] A. J. Robertson, *Anglo-Saxon Charters* (Cambridge, 1939) [henceforward
A.S.C.], p. 246; *D.B.B.*, pp. 502–6; J. Tait, *The Medieval English Borough* (Manchester, 1936), pp. 15–20; F. M. Stenton, *Anglo-Saxon England*, p. 262.

than was *expeditio*.[1] For the former, one-hide tenants, perhaps most of them 'ceorls', were quite adequate, but for the
latter, when 'riding' was highly desirable, better equipped
soldiers of thegnly type were much to be preferred.[2] Hence,
while the 'Burghal Hidage' may be regarded as new in detail
when it was promulgated, it may well have been based on an
ancient principle. The one-hide assessment is to be seen as
complementary, rather than antecedent, to the five-hide
principle.

Although no other documents link hidage assessment to
military duty as clearly as do those which have been cited,
there is a very clear likelihood that both general hidages and
the particular assessments in the charters were intended for
military as well as fiscal purposes.

The Domesday and county hidages have been shown to be
connected both with each other and with more ancient assessments.[3] The principle was that of royal, or public, service
imposed from above.[4] The county hidation, because of its
association with the military burghal hidage,[5] and the heavier
incidence of duty on the nucleus area of the kingdom,[6] may
well have had a primarily military purpose. It is perhaps
easier to understand this gradation of census if we adapt
Round's arguments for a fiscal assessment in multiples of
hides to the terms of military obligation.[7] Similar considerations make it even more likely that the 'Tribal Hidage' was
related to the performance of military service in the days of
Mercian or Kentish supremacy. It can even be argued that

---

[1] Dd. i. 262b; also in *C.S.*, no. 105. Confusion occurs in some accounts because the
service of burgesses in *expeditio* (assessed at five hides) is confused with county service
in wall repair and defence.

[2] It may be noted that where the assessment to *expeditio* is mentioned, in the above-
mentioned charter, *C.S.*, no. 201, this clearly does not apply to the *instructio pontis*
and *municio arcis*.

[3] F. M. Stenton, *Anglo-Saxon England* [henceforward *A.S.E.*], pp. 636 f., sums
up current scholarly opinion.

[4] Cf. H. R. Loyn, 'The King and the Structure of Society in Late Anglo-Saxon
England', *History*, xlii (1957), 87–100.

[5] Stenton, *A.S.E.*, p. 638.

[6] *D.B.B.*, pp. 461 2; J. H. Round, *Feudal England*, pp. 95–96. The heavily
assessed counties were Sussex, Surrey, Hampshire, Berkshire, Wiltshire, and Middlesex. It is to be expected that troops would be drawn mainly from the loyal nucleus
but less likely that heavier taxation would be imposed thereon.

[7] Ibid., pp. 44–97. The military explanation put forward by O. J. Reichel in
1901 was rejected by Round on *a priori* grounds; *E.H.R.* xvii (1902), 765.

the change in incidence of hidage reflected in part the shift of the military centre of power.[1]

If units of one and five hides were the basic military assessments, the question arises whether these units were in turn grouped, for military purposes, in hundreds. First, it must be noted that the 'hundred' was a regular Germanic grouping—such is the significance of the evidence of Tacitus. It was applied as readily to the military-cum-fiscal hides of the later as to the primitive levies of the earlier period. It is reasonable to assume that the map of England reflects an attempt to impose a highly formal assessment by hundreds of hides on the social groupings produced by geography, family, and exploitation of resources. The more recent this assessment, the closer the identification of hundred hides and hundred districts in 1066.[2]

While the assessment by hidage undoubtedly was useful for the king's *feorm* and for geld as well as for military service, it is clear from the emphasis on the reservation of *trimoda necessitas* that public service was above all military. Geld, almost certainly, was a later addition, to which the existing assessment was adapted.[3] Many descriptions of this service have been collected by W. H. Stevenson. They all indicate that the obligation was of public rather than private interest. It is *communis expeditio, causa publica, saecularis servicium, communis labor, commune servicium, communis, generale incommodum, quod omnibus est generale terris, quod omni plebi commune est, quod omni populo commune est.*[4] It is also *regalis*

---

[1] Cf. F. M. Stenton, *A.S.E.*, pp. 291–4; J. C. Russell, 'The Tribal Hidage', *Traditio*, v. 193–209; H. M. Chadwick, *Anglo-Saxon Institutions* [henceforward *A.S.I.*], pp. 263–8. Though somewhat tendentious, Russell's is the most emphatically 'military' of interpretations to date.

[2] Liebermann, *Gesetze*, s.v. 'Hundred'; J. H. Round, *Feudal England*, pp. 50, 97–98; Maitland, *D.B.B.*, pp. 450 f.; W. Stubbs, *Const. Hist.* i. 97–98; Chadwick, *A.S.I.*, pp. 209 f., 239 f.; J. E. A. Jolliffe, *Pre-Feudal England* (Oxford, 1933), pp. 39–82; H. C. Darby and Tervatt, *Domesday Book Geography of Midland England* (Cambridge, 1955), pp. 12–14, 228–9.

[3] This view of the *feorm* is strengthened by Miss Whitelock's observation that the only surviving statement of 'the amount the king could draw from an estate as his farm' (from 793–6) bears no discernible relation to hidage. *E.H.D.* i, no. 78. See also J. E. Jolliffe, *Pre-Feudal England*, and R. H. C. Davis, *Kalendar of Abbot Samson* (R.H.S. Publications, Camden, vol. 84, London, 1954), pp. xv, 1.

[4] W. H. Stevenson, 'Trinoda Necessitas', *E.H.R.* xxix (1914), 689 n. 3; *C.S.*, 101, 161, 201, 243, 389, 390; *C.D.*, i, ii, CCLII, D, DCCXIX; *A.S.C.*, nos. xii, cxx.

servicium and *regii exactiones*.[1] The military intention is occasionally underlined by the phrase *contra hostes*.[2] It remains to be noted that the charters, like the 'Tribal Hidage', show the existence of a principle of public service at least as far back as Offa's reign.[3]

The assessment of particular estates to public service measured in hides is implicit in these charters. Some state more particularly that the grantee shall discharge his obligation at the rate of so many hides.[4] The public service (*utware*) would seem to have been due on that part of the estate not kept in demesne (i.e. the *utland*); as has been remarked in another connexion, 'the tenants of the lord . . . are also the taxpayers . . . of the king'.[5]

The interpretation of this evidence has been made unnecessarily difficult, it may be suggested, by the false alternatives of feudal versus peasant services. In the case of the famous memorandum of Bishop Oswald of Worcester, the lines seem to have been drawn between service with the 'essence' of feudalism in it and local escort duty.[6] It would seem better, in the light of the preponderance of both a riding fyrd and public assessment, to argue that the *lex equitandi* of the memorandum refers to public dues, in distinction from those dues owed to the Church.[7] The words *et ut* in the memorandum may perhaps suggest a distinction between the riding service on the one hand and the things which are owed to the Church on the other. As a study of the royal dooms indicates, these services involved all manner of public police as well as strictly military duties.[8] Furthermore, the local riding duties are given attention at a later point in the charter. It may

---

[1] *C.S.*, *passim*.

[2] *C.S.* 332, 335, 348, 370; cf. *C.D.* CLXI for *fossam adversum inimicos*.

[3] F. M. Stenton, *The Latin Charters of Anglo-Saxon England* (Oxford, 1955), p. 57.

[4] e.g., *A.S.C.*, nos. cxi, cxii. The former specifies 'at the King's command', and indicates a reduction of assessment; cf. M. Hollings, 'The Survival of the Five Hide Unit', p. 467.

[5] *A.S.C.*, nos. lxxvi, lxxxiv, cix (the very important Tidenham Charter, where *inlandes* are contrasted with *gesettes landes*); T. H. Aston, 'The Origins of the Manor in England', *R.H.S.*, *Transactions*, 5th ser., viii (1958), pp. 65–69.

[6] *D.B.B.*, pp. 303–9; F. M. Stenton, *English Feudalism*, pp. 122–30; M. Hollings (supporting Maitland), 'The Survival of the Five Hide Unit', pp. 453–87.

[7] The key phrase runs 'Ut omnis equitandi lex ab eis impleatur quae ad equites pertinet et ut pleniter persolvant omnia quae ad jus ipsius ecclesiae juste competunt'.

[8] e.g., II Æthelstan 20; III Edgar 7; II Cnut 25.

be concluded that public mounted service was owed by the bishop's tenants; but it can hardly be urged that this was a *servicium debitum* of a feudal nature. It is simply that the assessed service of a given estate was naturally the responsibility of its lord. However great the influence of such assessments on the amount of the post-conquest *servicium debitum*, there remains a wide gap in the principles of obligation involved.[1]

V

It has been suggested in the foregoing analysis that the royal fyrd consisted primarily of mounted huscarls and thegns. Local thegns, under earl and reeve or *ductor*,[2] supplied the command of county forces. But the majority of these forces must have come from the one-hide tenants— 'ceorls'—as in the case of burh duty. It is probable that the national force would be reinforced by local contingents when this was possible—e.g. in the case of a siege, the expectation of combat near to the enemy's camp, as at Hastings, or, above all, in the case of coast defence.

This local service of ceorls is to be contrasted with the *expeditio* of the Domesday custumals, and of the *trimoda necessitas*. It does not appear to have required a specific royal order, though thegns might presumably receive orders to command local levies in coast defence.[3]

It has been suggested earlier that the principal class on whom local service fell was that of one-hide holders, serving in person rather than grouping to support the mounted fyrd warrior for *expeditio* or the royal fyrd. Some support for this comes from the evidence for an early one-hide assessment.[4] The ceorlish man (*cierlisc*) of Ine's law on fyrd-wite was

---

[1] On the influence of the hidage assessment on the amount of the *servicium debitum* in certain regions, see Chapter II. F. Barlow's conclusion, that the fyrd was 'territorial in recruitment, aristocratic in organisation', is acceptable if we substitute 'assessment' for 'recruitment'; *The Feudal Kingdom of England* (London, 1955), p. 49.

[2] The bishop of Hereford's *ductor exercitus*, in F. M. Stenton, *English Feudalism*, p. 127; or the *heretochus* in the *Leges Edwardi Confessoris*; Liebermann, *Gesetze*, i. 656; cf. *A.S. Chron.*, 993, 1003; Plummer, ii. 177.

[3] Cf. the *sæweard* at the king's command in the *Rectitudines*, 1.

[4] P. Vinogradoff, *English Society*, pp. 30 f.; M. Hollings, 'Survival of the Five Hide Unit', pp. 473–6.

possibly in this category.[1] In another law of Ine, the *gesith-cundman*, who pays four times the ceorl's fyrd-wite, is envisaged as having from three to twenty hides; this would give the *ceorl* of the laws a one- to five-hide assessment.[2] If we recall, however, that elsewhere one hide is considered adequate for a *gesith*,[3] it would seem that the one-hide ceorl is not by any means the average humble peasant. Like the ceorl of the 'North People's Law', he was not separated by an impassable gulf from the mounted thegn.

It seems unlikely that much can be learned of any troops below the grade of substantial peasant. Probably lesser men were linked with him in those tithings and hundreds referred to in the police organization which tell us most about the local defence forces. The laws are especially informative on this subject.[4] The military and police leaders are the same ealdormen and reeves, and the units are burh, hundred, and tithing.[5] While mounted men clearly had a certain priority— there were duties which they alone could perform[6]—at other times responsibility fell on 'all willing to follow', 'one or two per tithing', those living near the shire borders, 'all', the 'burhware', or 'twyhynde and twelfhynde'.[7] Is it in this police or militia development rather than the royal fyrd that we have the foundations of the twelfth- and thirteenth-century writs of watch and ward?

It is unfortunate that the *Chronicles'* accounts of the local forces in action do not assist materially in our understanding of their make-up. Most clearly distinct are the *burhware*, who appear as a group from the later years of Alfred's reign.[8] When the county force operates distinctly from the fyrd it is frequently referred to as the folk—*Sumor sæte*, *Will sæta*, *sæton da Centiscan*. The Hampshire dead in 1001 included 'others' presumably below the rank of the reeves and bishop's thegn who earned mention. But when in the eleventh century

---

[1] Ine 51. *Select Charters* (9th ed.), p. 68.
[2] Ine 63.
[3] Hollings, p. 475, n. 4.
[4] F. Liebermann, *Gesetze*, ii, s.vv. 'Heer' and 'Hundred'.
[5] Alfred 42, cl. 3; VI Athelstan 3, 4, 8.
[6] II Athelstan 20; VI Athelstan 4; III Edgar 71; II Cnut 25.
[7] IV Athelstan 3; VI Athelstan 4; I Egar 2; II Æthelred 67; III Edmund 2.
[8] Cf. Plummer, *Two Saxon Chronicles*, Glossary s.vv. *burhware, burhwaru*. On the importance of the tenth-century borough, cf. Chadwick, *A.S.I.*, pp. 219 f.

the terms *folc* and *þeod* came to be applied to the armies with some frequency, both national and local forces qualified for the appellation.[1] One suspects that these terms had a wide or restricted meaning according to convenience, and we have no way of distinguishing the one from the other.[2]

Conclusion

What is the overall picture which emerges from the foregoing discussion of particular problems ? If we are bold, we can summarize the Anglo-Saxon army in a few large generalizations. First, it was from an early date the king's army, both in allegiance and leadership. A strictly royal force of mounted warriors, consisting chiefly of thegns, formed a nucleus around which the followings of earls and royal reeves might congregate. Unmistakably related to the royal force were the defensive forces of shire and borough district, although their natural focus was the borough walls and seacoast rather than the royal standard. From time immemorial the duties of both mounted fyrd and local militia had been assessed in hides, groups of hides supporting a mounted warrior for *expeditio*, individual hides sending militia men to borough wall, sea-coast, or as auxiliaries when battle loomed in the vicinity. The 'maids of all work' were the five-hide thegns, who formed the backbone of the royal host and the leadership of local groupings. Finally, as royal power was challenged by the almost vice-regal position of the eleventh-century earls, the *élite* force of huscarls was created to add strength to the central force of royal thegns. This structure of service, it may be suggested, contained all the elements of medieval military obligation, and foreshadowed already the main problems which later arose.

[1] *A.S. Chron.*, 1006, 1009, 1010, 1016, 1049, 1051, 1052, 1055.

[2] For examples of highly restricted use of *þeod*, see H. M. Chadwick, *Origin*, pp. 156–7. On the other hand, the *folc* seem to be clearly distinguished from the thegns in the *Chronicles* for 1010.

MILITES, SERVIENTES, BURGENSES[1]

THE Norman Conquest, by its very nature, ushered in a new era in military history. The fact of conquest by a large army of volunteer warriors (military joint-stock holders, as they have been called) led in the first place to a reliance on their future military service in return for the grant of conquered lands. But strong government gave the monarchs a choice between enforcing obligation or converting it into money for the hiring of mercenaries; the organization of the Exchequer and of the county administration in the early twelfth century made possible the partial conversion of feudal service into cash for the pay of the remainder or of mercenaries.

The struggle for military preparedness was acute, as in Anglo-Saxon times, and for the same reasons economic and social development tended to militate against the continued military readiness of the population. Offsetting these powerful forces were the continental ambitions of the Normans and Angevins, supplemented by the fear of renewed invasion and the needs of mobilization against Wales and against feudal rebels. Moreover, with the Crusades, the Church's consecration of warfare was given firmer expression in the Military Orders and in the new concept of Christian knighthood. This concept reinforced the effect of inflation, which, by increasing the cost of horses and arms, reopened in the twelfth century the narrowing gap between Norman knight and English peasant. Hence in the decades before 1154 the English played an ever-declining part in warfare, offset only a little by the rise in importance of the walled towns and their forces.

Probably few arts tend to be so dominated by tradition as warfare. This, rather than any inherent value, probably explains the preference, in military organization, for the full-

---

[1] I am especially indebted to Mr. J. O. Prestwich for criticisms of this chapter.

armed and armoured heavy cavalrymen in the ensuing centuries. However, two different kinds of experience reinforced tradition. On the one hand, a skilful commander could turn a troop of heavy cavalry into a formidable, if irrecoverable, missile with which to break open the enemy's front; so Richard Cœur-de-Lion above all others demonstrated. On the other hand, the willingness of the knights to practise their profession and to make a cult of prowess and loyalty meant that whatever their technical defects they were irreplaceable by mercenaries or commoners. An interesting compromise, which may have owed something to the huscarl tradition and was certainly indebted to the efficient Exchequer system, was the idea of money fiefs or *fiefs-rentes* so illuminatingly discussed by Dr. Bryce Lyon. Closely allied was the system of hiring knights errant or bachelor in far larger numbers than the tenurial *rustici*, while the use of reduced quotas of service to be paid for by the general body of knights retained what was useful and eliminated those not interested in fighting.

In spite of the dominance of the tradition of heavy cavalry, many of the most brilliant victories were won by dismounted troops. The significance of the victories of Tinchebrai and the Standard was that they reinforced the English tradition of dismounted fighting and, therefore, lessened the prestige of the *destrier* and its owner. Hence, in Britain, the foot fighter, whether mounted for transportation or not, retained an honourable role. This meant that most of the military sergeants as well as the great potential of the subjected English remained available for the use of wise or desperate kings. In times of threatened invasion and civil war they could be mustered and organized.[1]

English and other non-knightly troops were used most extensively in the years immediately after the Conquest. It is well to remember that William I came over after years of deadly conflict with the Norman barons; not only was he unlikely to trust himself entirely to his vassals, but he needed

[1] A thorough study of twelfth-century tactics, especially in relation to castles and to the make-up of armies, is much overdue. R. C. Smail, *Crusading Warfare* (Cambridge, 1956), pp. 115 f., offers an excellent model of what might be done. Cf. also J. H. Beeler, 'Castles and Strategy in Norman and Early Angevin England', *Speculum*, xxxi (1956), 581–601.

outside support against them on certain occasions. Hence it was that for some years the native English continued to play an active role, even in overseas warfare. As the barons became tamer the force of this incentive waned. The idea of a general military levy was also promoted by the Church, in the form of the 'Truce of God'; though this instrument was far less used in England than on the Continent.

While political considerations no doubt had great influence on the development of obligation, the influence was not entirely one way. The leading military role of the great tenants-in-chief, especially the Marchers, must be considered along with economic and legal influences in tracing the limits which were set on Angevin despotism. It was at the tourney that these lords could frame political platforms. This aspect of the 'baronage' calls for renewed and detailed examination. Moreover, the question of place and amount of service owed to the king could become a major political issue, especially if aggravated by poor leadership and defeat; and may well have underlain much of the opposition to John.

In the following pages the nature of the military obligation instituted by the Normans, with special reference to the question of continuity from the past, will first receive our attention.

I

The first and most striking result of the Norman Conquest was the superimposing on the existing society of a group of tenants-in-chief and their military followers, who henceforward carried the chief burden of military as well as of political obligation. Whereas the Anglo-Saxon thegn owed a combination of personal and public duty, the Norman knight owed personal service based on tenure; the king's thegn might have had to bring other lesser thegns with him to the army, but less as a tenurial due than as a public duty. A second result was that the English lesser thegns and ceorls who made up the county and borough levies were now, as a class, eliminated. Their new role as freemen, socmen, or villeins remained to be determined. In the third place, the duty of general allegiance to the monarch had now to be worked out afresh in relation to the new feudal society.

It is not proposed here to attempt to add anything to the question of how baronage and military service replaced thegnage. The process has been made clear, and the inevitable disagreements isolated, by the work of Round and Stenton, and in more specialized aspects by Drs. Reid, Chew, and Sanders.[1] The outcome of the Conquest was the creation of the feudal army.[2] This army was assembled through summonses addressed either directly to the king's immediate military tenants-in-chief, or indirectly through the local officials.[3] Those who received direct summonses were eventually to form the parliamentary peerage, but cannot be equated with the baronage.[4] When summoned, directly or otherwise, they were sometimes ordered to appear with their *servicium debitum*. This *servicium debitum* was allotted in round numbers by the Conqueror, and could be made up either from household or from tenants. Its potential appears to have been about 5,000 knights at the time of the Conqueror's settlement. As many financial dues were also based on this service, the king's interest was to keep the assessment in being, and in 1166 and 1212 determined efforts were made to adjust it to the actual number of vassals, who in fact were considerably in excess of the Conqueror's allotment. Conversely, for military purposes, fractions of the full *servicium debitum* were frequently summoned under the Angevins, and this in turn gave place in mid-thirteenth century to a distinction between the military and fiscal *servicium debitum*. Parallel with this development, many military summonses did not require

---

[1] J. H. Round, *Feudal England* (London, 1895); F. M. Stenton, *The First Century of English Feudalism* (Oxford, 1932); R. Reid, 'Barons and Thanage', *E.H.R.* xxxv (1920), 161–99; H. M. Chew, *The English Ecclesiastical Tenants-in-Chief* (Oxford, 1932); I. J. Sanders, *Feudal Military Service in England* (Oxford, 1956).

[2] There is still no good catholic survey of the feudal army in England. In addition to the works cited in the previous footnote, reference should also be made to S. Painter, *Studies in the History of the English Feudal Barony* (Baltimore, 1943); A. L. Poole, *Obligations of Society in the XII and XIII Centuries* (Oxford, 1946); invaluable summaries and independent analysis are to be found in the *Cambridge Mediaeval History*, vol. v, and in the relevant volumes in the Oxford History of England.

[3] The first extant summons is the famous mixed (direct and indirect) one to Æthelwig, *temp.* 1072. Presumably as most early sheriffs were baronial, the earliest summonses were all either direct or mixed.

[4] There may have been an early identity; I. J. Sanders and Miss Chew have demonstrated the distinction between barony and military summons for lay and ecclesiastical tenants-in-chief respectively.

servicium debitum, but called for service either alone, or with a given number of followers, or as powerfully supported as possible.[1]

The feudal army cannot be isolated, though it can be usefully distinguished, from the militia and even the mercenaries. Those holding by sergeanty, which by the thirteenth century was becoming hard to distinguish from free tenure, were naturally often called out with the military tenants. Hence it was but a step to the summons, along with those owing military service, first of the free tenants, and then of the freemen and *jurati*. The dividing-line from mercenaries, also, was not as sharp as might appear at first sight. Much feudal service was discharged by household knights and sergeants, whose numbers might greatly exceed the quota owed.[2] Further, the subtenants might commute with the summoned 'baron' for their service, and the latter might then proffer hired troops at the ensuing muster. Moreover, as the period of service was short and probably varied (though scutage was assessed on the basis of forty days, the most common period), the army may well have been kept in being, as a rule, by the taking into pay of those serving after their customary service was complete. As is suggested below, the large forces of 'twopenny' sergeants found in the Pipe Rolls may well have been peasant conscripts rather than professional soldiers. In short, a distinction must be made in the twelfth as much as in the twentieth century between paid and professional forces. The combination of such diverse forces into an army presented a problem. There were, however, many levels at which the combination might be effected. The baron himself might be responsible for foot service of free tenants along with the production of a knightly quota; more usually, the sheriff and county constable must have had to organize the feudal, communal, and mercenary troops at their disposal—allotting military tenants and royal sergeants, for example, to command the county units to the muster. Finally, the king's marshal and constable would have the

---

[1] On these and related questions, see I. J. Sanders, *Feudal Military Service*, pp. 32 f., 50 f.

[2] Cf. the cases of John FitzGilbert, cited by F. Barlow, *Feudal Kingdom*, p. 253, and John the Marshal, cited by Sir F. M. Powicke, 'The Angevin Administration of Normandy', *E.H.R.* xxii (1907), 42, n. 118.

task of dividing up the available forces according to the exigencies of command, tactics, and morale.

The feudal army owed much to the Anglo-Saxon fyrd; perhaps more than it has been customary of late to acknowledge.[1] In the first place, it was exclusively royal. The initial assessment was an arbitrary act of royal will. The king's leadership and summons remained essential; there was little distinction between the forces owed to the king and those available to the barons. When a gap opened between the assessed *servicium debitum* and the fees created by tenants, the king acted swiftly to close it (the 1166 Inquest). Every fee, and all service, was royal. A force of household knights, endowed with *fiefs-rentes* as time went on, provided continuity with the huscarls.[2] What is more, the king's active leadership was expected not only in the summons but also in the ensuing campaign.[3]

The royal and public nature of feudal service is to be seen not only in the initial assessment, in the summons, and leadership, but also in the persistence of the idea of a general land assessment underlying personal and tenurial obligations; and the source of this idea was clearly Anglo-Saxon. Its expression in hidages and in Domesday Book have been treated at some length in the previous chapter. The persistence of the hidage assessment as a fiscal measure, in the form of Danegeld, is well known. Its influence on feudal tenure was not negligible, though the earlier doctrine of Freeman has been severely—perhaps too severely—handled by Round and his successors. The continuation of the 'five-hide rule' in the guise of knights' fees has been disproved by Round and, more recently, by Miss Chew; Sir Frank Stenton, modifying Round, has shown that inasmuch as there was a 'standard' fee, it was assessed in pounds, not hides.[4] These important

---

[1] The Anglo-Saxon Chronicler identified the feudal host as the fyrd; *A.S. Chron.* (ed. Plummer), pp. 218, 230, 268, &c.

[2] F. M. Powicke, 'Angevin Administration', loc. cit.; B. Lyon, *From Fief to Indenture* (Cambridge, Mass., 1957), p. 187.

[3] Cf. H. M. Chew's summing-up: 'Throughout the period [1168–1340] the constant preoccupation of the Crown was to enforce the doctrine inherent in Anglo-Norman feudalism that all *servicium militare* is *servicium regale*' (*Ecclesiastical Tenants-in-Chief*, p. 35).

[4] J. H. Round, *Feudal England*, pp. 293–5; H. M. Chew, *Ecclesiastical Tenants-in-Chief*, pp. 3–7; F. M. Stenton, *English Feudalism*, pp. 166–8.

conclusions, however, must not be allowed to obscure the fact that as late as 1166 most fees continued to be measured in hides.[1] Further, some of these fees, especially in the west Midlands, were clearly influenced by the late Anglo-Saxon 'five-hide rule'. Thus Roger de Berkeley broke down his seven and a half-hide estate into five and two and a half-hide units. A similar form of return was adopted by the bishop of Salisbury (for Wiltshire lands) and the abbot of Westminster (for Worcestershire estates).[2]

The case of the bishop of Worcester, whose sixty fees, Maitland argues, represented a five-hide per knight assessment on his 300 hide Oswaldslaw lands, is the crucial one.[3] Round and Miss Chew have challenged Maitland's theory on the grounds that the assessment to sixty fees was on far wider estates than the triple hundred, and that the bishop himself contested the assessment.[4] Miss Hollings has introduced new evidence which proves conclusively that a deliberate attempt to equate knight's fees with five-hide units was made in the years following the Conquest.[5] A memorandum in the *Red Book of Worcester*, the principal evidence in the case, states boldly that 'five hides make one knight's fee'. To a remarkable degree, as she shows, this principle was in fact the basis of the assessment. The Worcester estates, in fact, show not that the Anglo-Saxon practice was carried over *en bloc*, but that it persisted stubbornly as a basis of the knight's fee as well as of taxation.[6]

Even after the hidage taxation was abandoned in 1162, this equation continued to be effective in the internal workings of the honours.[7] This was particularly true of the levies made on militarily inactive to support active knights; it was

1 Besides the 1166 *Cartae*, in *The Red Book of the Exchequer* (R.S., 1896), see Stenton's conclusions on the charter evidence, *Eng. Feud.*, p. 164.

2 *Red Book*, i. 188, 237–8, 292.

3 *D.B.B.*, p. 160.

4 *Feudal England*, p. 293; *Ecclesiastical Tenants-in-Chief*, pp. 6–7.

5 M. Hollings, 'The Survival of the Five Hide Unit in the Western Midlands', *E.H.R.* lxiii (1948), 453–87. Miss Hollings's evidence seems to demonstrate more effectively the continuity of the idea of five-hide assessment than the use of this idea in the establishment of the *servicium debitum*.

6 For some other examples, see, for example, R. Stewart-Brown, *County Court Rolls, etc.* (Chetham Soc. 1925), pp. l–lii.

7 Miss Hollings refers to the equation in an extent of 1299, and gives other references, op. cit., p. 457.

here, and not, as Miss Hollings has suggested, in scutage, that the real continuity of Anglo-Saxon custom is to be found. At Ramsey abbey, for example, the active knights were supported by a levy on the hides of the others.[1] In Yorkshire and other northern and eastern parts the carucate had a similar history. As late as Henry III's reign, a Yorkshire plea was concerned with 'the *forinsec* service which belongs to such land where eight carucates of land make one knight's fee'.[2] Moreover, carucages continued to be levied in the thirteenth century, long after the hidages had been abandoned.[3]

The persistence of Anglo-Saxon forms of obligation have been traced in many other features of post-Conquest military service. The two-month period of Domesday reappears in the service, *si werra est*, of the Nettlecombe fee, Somerset; where, however, the reference may have been to *civil* war as opposed to civil peace.[4] That two months was not the normal period for knights is perhaps sufficiently proved by the fact that scutage was assessed on forty days' service, and that the first weighty evidence of actual service is for the latter period.[5] However, it may well have been the term of service owed inside England, in strictly defensive wars. Another reasonable hypothesis might be that Hugh de Ralegh, the recipient of the fee in question, served as a leader of the non-feudal levies, i.e. the foot, who would naturally follow local English custom.[6]

The leadership of the foot, in fact, provided a major link between Norman-feudal and English-communal service, not so much through the agency of knights, as of sergeants.

---

[1] *Ecclesiastical Tenants-in-Chief*, p. 124; F. W. Maitland, *Select Pleas in Manorial Courts* (Selden Society, 1888), i. 53, 56.

[2] *Roll of the Justices in Eyre*, ed. D. M. Stenton (Selden Society, 1937), no. 249. According to A. L. Poole, who lists exceptions to uniform hidage rule, the 10 or 12 carucate fee was common; *Domesday Book to Magna Carta*, 2nd ed. (1955), p. 15. In Leylandshire, in 1385, ten carucates made one knight's fee; *Cal. Charter Rolls 1341–1417*, p. 298.

[3] S. K. Mitchell, *Studies in Taxation in the Reigns of John and Henry III* (New Haven, 1914), pp. 7–8, 32–34, 121–3, 129–30, 148, 351–3.

[4] A. L. Poole, *The Obligations of Society in the XII and XIII Centuries*, pp. 50–51. M. Hollings, 'Five Hide Unit', p. 482. Mr. J. O. Prestwich has drawn my attention to this special meaning of *werra* in the contemporary charters.

[5] *Feudal England*, pp. 270–1.

[6] A. L. Poole, *Obligations*, pp. 38–39, probably exaggerates this role of the knights; that he does a great service in calling attention to it will not be disputed.

These leaders usually held by sergeanty—a term sufficiently wide, to be sure, to be used for any tenure by special service.[1] Tenurial sergeants who were also county foot leaders, as well as those who later merged in the general 'mass' of *libere tenentes*, serve as a warning against too rigidly dividing the old and the new, Norman and Saxon, mounted and foot.

The feudal and the communal levies were also bound together in the administrative system, in which the king's leadership as both lord and *rex* was expressed through the hierarchy of household, county, and borough. The writs of summons for all but the leading barons went through the county officer to both tenants and those bound only by allegiance, to horse and foot.[2] At the muster, the constable and marshal would draw up horse and foot according to whatever tactical grouping might at the time be in favour.[3]

The tie of allegiance, which could easily have become dormant under the impact of feudalism, was deliberately strengthened by the Conqueror and maintained by his successors. The 'Oath of Salisbury', of course, was the instrument employed by William. It may have been taken by the mesne barons rather than the whole body of knights and freemen; but the principle of a common oath of all freemen was certainly established at a later time.[4]

The *liberi homines* were, in fact, the class bound to military service; and they were not confined to *milites* but included Norman baron and English socage tenant. The *Leis Willelmi*, whose value is not doubted by its most recent editors,[5] contained the law, almost as famous as the Oath of Salisbury:

Statuimus etiam ut omnis liber homo foedere et sacramento affirmet, quod infra et extra Angliam Willelmo regi fideles esse volunt, terras et

[1] A. L. Poole, *Obligations*, p. 72; W. A. Morris, *The Mediaeval English Sheriff* (Manchester, 1927), p. 235, n. 251; E. G. Kimball, *Sergeanty Tenure in Medieval England* (Yale, 1936), pp. 69 f.

[2] The writ of 1072 was to the abbot of Evesham as administrator of several counties, for the *servicium debitum*.

[3] See the redistribution of the St. Albans contingent in 1257; Matthew Paris, *Chronica Majora*, vi. 373–4.

[4] F. M. Stenton, *English Feudalism*, pp. 111–13. William of Malmesbury's view that all freemen took the Oath retains its significance for the twelfth century even if it is to be regarded as anachronistic. *Gesta Regum* (R.S.), ii. 317.

[5] *E.H.D.* ii, no. 18. The text used is *Select Charters*, i. 98.

honorem illius omni fidelitate cum eo servare, et ante eum contra inimicos defendere.

For a contemporary definition of *liberi homines* we have that of the *Leges Henrici Primi*—'omnis homo qui voluerit se teneri pro libero sit in plegio'. We may conclude that not only the feudal tenants but also the whole free population were bound by William to serve him in war, both in and out of England. If later kings threw away this priceless inheritance of the royal and public fyrd, the blame cannot be laid at the door of the uninformed foreign conqueror.

The ancient assessment, then, and the national organization had a strong influence on the character of the military feudalism which grew up in England. What of those freemen who, like the knights and sergeants, owed allegiance and military service, but who were not military tenants? They were organized in the frankpledge system, with the hue and cry, just as had been their predecessors in Anglo-Saxon times. The hierarchy of sheriff, bailiff, constable, and sergeant of the peace, who supervised these duties, incidentally kept them in readiness for military emergency;[1] sergeant leaders and standard bearers, and knights occasionally engaged on the same duty, were available to help the sheriff in leading them to war.[2]

How were these men assessed? Land was still assessed in hides, but even in Anglo-Saxon times the hide had become an assessment more for thegns than for ordinary freemen. The continuation of military obligation in terms of hides, at least until the end of the eleventh century, is strongly indicated by the evidence of the 1094 expedition discussed below. It is probable, however, that foot service was owed principally on the personal basis of allegiance until the idea of an assessment on lands and chattels was put into effect in 1181.[3]

[1] See on these, W. A. Morris, *The Frankpledge System* (London, 1910), pp. 72–78; R. Stewart-Brown, *The Sergeants of the Peace in Medieval England and Wales* (Manchester, 1936), *passim*; for possible Anglo-Saxon beginnings, pp. 90 f.; and for the mutual exclusiveness of frankpledge and sergeanties of the peace, chap. viii.

[2] The nature of the large numbers of *servientes* who appear in the twelfth-century pipe-rolls calls for further study. They were too numerous to be sergeanty tenants, and can hardly (except for the Welsh) have been professional troops. That they were in part recruited from the *jurati* seems highly probable. Cf. Kimball, *Sergeanty Tenure*, p. 77.

[3] That the ancient duty of *expeditio* was still, along with its companions of the

Somewhere between the feudal force and the general levies of the shires were the *burgenses*, who played a notable part in Anglo-Saxon as well as in Norman and Angevin wars. Here the Anglo-Saxon concept of public duty based on police organization seems to have been at its most effective. This service seems, moreover, to have been assessed on the community rather than on individuals, nor did it ever become an incident of burgess tenure. Probably, however, all burgesses owed military service in their capacity of freemen. The way in which most of these borough forces were chosen, arranged, and led must probably remain a secret of the internal workings of the boroughs. But while many of the references to their participation in campaigns suggest that they were capable of operating independently, they normally came under shrieval leadership along with the men of vills and the fiefs.[1]

In concluding these introductory remarks, the bearing of the army on the political life of the nation calls for a few comments. Technically, the *jurati* and mercenaries were at opposite poles, representing the nadir of ineffectiveness and the peak of efficiency. Politically, however, they served similar purposes. As long as the only politically active and self-conscious class was the baronage, both were instruments of a powerful monarchy, adjuncts of an effective household. But whereas the mercenary arm was a fitting instrument of expanding and arbitrary power, the communal forces were suitable primarily for a conservative and settled government. The relatively stable powers of the Anglo-Saxon kings were ideal conditions for an army of subjects, bound hand and foot together by custom. Such conservatism was irksome to the new rulers of England, and perhaps one of the most

trimoda necessitas, operative in the years immediately after the Conquest is evident from such charters as those to Battle and to St. Paul's in *Regesta Regum Anglo-Normannorum,* ed. H. W. C. Davis (Oxford, 1913), i, nos. 58, 290; 274; 415; see the charter, also of exemption, to Ramsey abbey in the *Chartulary* (R.S.), p. 202, with which cf. the order for exemption of Ramsey tenants in the Scottish war of 1091–7, ibid., p. 212. By Henry I's time, however, it was certainly an archaism (*Leges Henrici Primi,* x, c. 1).

[1] W. A. Morris, *The Mediaeval English Sheriff* (Manchester, 1913), pp. 58–60; London, as usual, provides a partial exception, but most of the evidence is thirteenth century; cf. W. Page, *London. Its Origin and Early Development* (London, 1923), pp. 135 f., 174, 190, 212 f.

dramatic developments in the centuries after 1066 was the repeated and futile efforts of really powerful rulers to bend the 'communes' into a modern and flexible force. No other king was to achieve so much as did the Conqueror in the years immediately after his victory; but no other king was to have the English people so completely in his grasp. Military obligation, however, affected not only the royal but also the subjects' political experience. As, in feudal matters, the pressure of duty was soon followed by the realization of privilege, so also in the case of the *jurati* the slow pressure of obligation may have contributed to the even slower growth of political consciousness.

II

With these general considerations in mind, an attempt may be made to trace the fortuncs of the non-feudal classes in the armies of the Norman kings. Initially this resolves itself largely into a study of the use made of the English. In the reign of William I the English subjects were still active in arms, capable of forming armies independently of the royal 'Norman' forces; the Kentishmen in 1067; the citizens of various towns: Exeter in 1068 and 1069; York in 1069; Northumbria in 1080.[1] However, the Conqueror was already beginning to reach out to include them in his scheme of English kingship. As early as 1068 William made his first use of English forces, against rebels.[2] The use of the term *provinciales* to describe the forces used in 1069 against Sweyn may have indicated the presence of English troops, though at a later date this implication no longer followed. Probably in that same year William pitted the English against an English counter-invasion.[3] In 1074 the 'general muster' of the people described by Florence of Worcester included the English, two of their leaders—Wulfstan of Worcester and Ethelwold of Evesham—being English, as well as some of

---

[1] Orderic Vitalis, *Historia Ecclesiastica* [henceforward *Hist. Eccles.*], ed. Prévost (Paris, 1838–55), ii. 173, 188, 193; Florence of Worcester, *Chronicon*, ii. 15.
[2] *Hist. Eccles.* ii. 179.
[3] William of Malmesbury, *Historia Regum* (R.S.), iii. 287. *Provinciales* meant 'English' in 1101; see below, p. 42.

their opponents.¹ In 1075 both English and French were used against the rebels.²

Before this, there had occurred one of the most noteworthy uses of the English overseas, to which may be linked a similar occasion five years later. Florence of Worcester attributes William's victory in Maine in 1073 to the English whom he took over with him.³ William of Malmesbury elaborates with the statement that 'though (the English) had been easily overcome (*opprimo*) in their own country, they appeared to be invincible (*invicti*) abroad'.⁴ Orderic implies that foot and horse battalions (*legiones*) were woven together for this victory: were the former William's English forces?⁵ A few years later Orderic describes William leading a large force of Normans and English (*Angli*) against Fulk of Anjou, and in 1080 against Robert in the battle of Gerberoi.⁶

After these active opening years, little more is heard of the English forces until the outbreak of fresh military activity at the very close of William's reign. Then, in 1086–7, came the great flare-up which may have been the cause of Domesday Book and the Oath of Salisbury. The concern of these documents over the obligations of the subjects may well have been in part military. When the Danes threatened invasion in 1085, William was obliged to bring in large numbers of French and Norman mercenaries for defence purposes, the English merely supplying food.⁷ However attractive this may have been to William, we may doubt if the inhabitants found it so. In any case, it suggests that a decline in the English forces had occurred. The great inquest which followed included an inquiry into Anglo-Saxon obligations in terms of county custom, and of the hidage on which it was based, which was, as has been noted, the first and only clear statement of these responsibilities which has survived. That

---

¹ Florence of Worcester, ii. 11 ('congregata magna copia tam Anglorum tam Nortmannorum'); cf. Orderic's reference to the *exercitus Angliae* on this occasion. Cf. Lanfranc, *Epistolae*, xxxiv, in Migne, *P.L.*, vol. 150, col. 533.

² Florence of Worcester, ibid.

³ Ibid., p. 10.

⁴ *Gesta Regum*, ii. 316.

⁵ *Hist. Eccles.* ii. 254; cf. Florence of Worcester and the *A.S. Chron.*, 1094, below, p. 40.

⁶ *Hist. Eccles.* ii. 256, 387; Freeman, *Norman Conquest*, iv. 647, 818.

⁷ Florence of Worcester, ii. 18.

such custom was not recorded for more than two counties and a handful of boroughs indicates how considerably it had begun to fall out of use.

It may also be noted from the above account that to a limited extent mercenaries were alternatives to the 'militia'. Where the one was impossible, for one reason or another, the other had to be used. The role of both was to be auxiliaries (as a rule) and a counterpoise (on occasion) to the feudal levy.

That the general obligation continued to play a role, however subordinate, in English history during the reign of William Rufus is borne out by the reports of two important events and of several lesser ones. The important events took place, first, in the opening years of William's reign, and secondly, in 1094; one was connected with defence and the other with overseas service.

The first of these events is attested by the *Anglo-Saxon Chronicle*, Florence of Worcester, Orderic Vitalis, and William of Malmesbury.[1] In the *Anglo-Saxon Chronicle*, William, faced by a conspiracy of great men, all Frenchmen (*þa riceste Frencisce men . . . ealle Frencisce men*), appealed to the English for help (*sende þa æfter Englisce mannan*), promising good laws; the English responded, 'came to the assistance of the king their lord', took Tonbridge, provided coastal guard against Duke Robert, and on a special summons of all who were *unniðing* along with the French came from town (*porte*) and country and took Rochester.[2] According to Florence of Worcester, the English provided the bulk of the horse and foot army assembled (although William did his best to get Normans) for the siege of Rochester and Pevensey; in a later entry Florence shows the English of Worcester, along with the Welsh and Normans, rallying behind Bishop Wulfstan and the king. Orderic Vitalis tells us that William,

---

[1] *A.S. Chron.*, MS. 'E', in *Two Chronicles Parallel*, i. 222–5; Florence of Worcester, ii. 22–24; Orderic, iii. 271; William of Malmesbury, *Gesta*, ii. 361 f.; E. A. Freeman, *William Rufus*, i. 63–81 (a vastly overblown account, but giving, with full quotation, all the evidence). Unfortunately we do not have Round's comments at this point, for the evidence here is for much wider consultation than in 1090, when the *optimates* gave counsel on war in France (ibid., pp. 221–4; Round, *Feudal England*, pp. 535–8).

[2] The penalty of *niðing* went back to the Anglo-Danish *þingamannalið*. Steenstrup, *Normannerne*, iv. 27.

confronted by the revolt, appealed for help to a great council of prelates, earls, and native English (*Anglos naturales*), whereupon the English flocked to his banner and declaimed on the traditional loyalty of the English (*Anglicenae*) to their kings. William of Malmesbury follows the *Anglo-Saxon Chronicle*—both confirming Orderic's suggestion that an assembly at which the English declared their loyalty was the first stage. Malmesbury's famous account of William's subsequent summons of the English through their leaders to the siege of Rochester, unless they would be called *niðing*, is a typical dramatization of the Chronicler's dry report that he 'ordered that everyone who was *unniðing* should come to him'. While the circumstances show it to have been unusual, it can be reasonably deduced from these parallel accounts that a large, presumably non-feudal, obligation and loyalty remained among the English population, which when neces- sary could turn the political scales. This fact is at least as significant as William's seizure of large treasures, which also figures prominently in these accounts, and which along with his extortions enabled him to become famous as a hirer of mercenaries.[1]

The second important event—that of 1094—is even more far-reaching in its implications. This is recorded in a famous passage expanded by Florence of Worcester from the *Anglo- Saxon Chronicle*.[2] It is the most certain example between 1066 and 1297 of the summons of non-feudal and non-mercenary troops for service across the channel. It fully confirms the evidence of Domesday Book and the *Leis Willelmi* that the Norman kings claimed a customary right to summon their free subjects for service anywhere. In addition, it tells us that the troops had received ten shillings each for their mainten- ance (*ad victum*). This money (*feoh* in the *Anglo-Saxon Chronicle*) is clearly to be identified with the Domesday account of money supplied from each hide to the soldier serving for five hides.[3] We note that the summons was in a moment of great urgency, in the last-ditch defence of the

---

[1] J. O. Prestwich, op. cit., pp. 26–28.

[2] *Select Charters*, p. 109; *E.H.D.* ii. 171.

[3] Above, p. 18. There were variations on the same principle in different parts of the country. In Durnford, Wiltshire, where the ten-shilling payment is confirmed, two men paid five shillings each to support a thegn; Dd. i. 67d.

ducal lands of Normandy, though not of the realm. It is safe to surmise, first, that the dire emergency was put forward as justification and, secondly, that the Conquest alone could have made possible the use of such a plea on behalf of territories which did not constitute the realm to which the conscripts belonged. A comparison of the accounts in the *Chronicle* and in Florence suggests the identification of 'foot-men' and 'English' (*pedorum*—Florence; *Engliscra*—*A.S. Chron.*). While there is no conclusive evidence for confining the English to a foot role and the Normans to one of cavalry, these chronicle entries, with the support of a few others, indicate that the distinctive, though not the only, role of the English was that of foot soldiers.

The less important references to English and foot service in William Rufus's reign serve to support the views suggested by the events of 1088 and 1094. They occurred during the Welsh and Scottish wars and the defence against Magnus of Norway. In the Scottish wars Duncan in 1093 gained his kingdom with the help of English (*Engliscra*) and French but afterwards renounced their use.[1] In the autumn of 1097 the leadership of Edgar Atheling perhaps suggests an English complexion to the army; an impression reinforced by the coincidence of the Chronicler's entry with a remarkable reference to the exaction of *trimoda necessitas*.[2] The Welsh expedition earlier in 1097 was composed of horse and foot.[3] Something more tangible is recorded of the plans for defence against Magnus. Orderic's account tells how the people of the coast raised the alarm, how *armati* assembled from various parts of Mercia, followed by the summons of both French and English (*Francos et Anglos*) by the great Midland Marcher earls of Chester and Shrewsbury.[4] The total impression is that the normal use of the English militia at the turn of the century must have been defensive and supplemental to other forces. The king himself might demand

---

[1] *A.S. Chron.* 'E', in *Two Chronicles*, i. 228; Florence of Worcester, ii. 32.
[2] *A.S. Chron.* 'E', i. 234; cf. ii. 285.
[3] Florence of Worcester, ii. 40–41.
[4] *Hist. Eccles.* iv. 30–31. The sentence to the effect that Hugh, earl of Shrewsbury, arrived first with his *coeti*, then waited for his *auxiliarios contubernales*, is not easy to interpret. They may have been the English foot, though *contubernales* suggests a small household group.

more; but the local commanders—earls and sheriffs—could count on the mass of free English principally for defence purposes.

While giving due weight, therefore, to William II's reputation as a *militum mercator et solidator* and not forgetting that this was the great age of feudal warfare (unfortunately against the king almost as much as on his side), the stress of the Chronicler in his brief character sketch of Rufus is not to be overlooked: 'he was always harassing this nation with military service and with unjust taxes.'[1]

As the chroniclers remarked, Henry I's was a reign of strong government and internal peace. After the opening flurry of activity, there was little scope for the use of the English militia. In 1101, when Robert of Normandy challenged Henry, there occurred one of the most famous incidents of English military support for the king against the feudal nobility. According to Florence of Worcester many of the 'English' nobles went over to Robert, but the bishops, *milites gregarii*, and the English, remained loyal.[2] William of Malmesbury elaborates this tale in the well-known account of Henry's personal instruction of the 'English' (also called *provinciales* or 'county men') in the art of combating cavalry.[3]

In 1102 Robert of Belesme and Montgomery revolted. It is possible that the English played a leading role in Henry's action this time also. According to Orderic, Henry called out the *exercitum Angliae*, and later *totius Angliae legiones*.[4] There followed a remarkable 'debate'.[5] The barons (*consules et primores*) debated among themselves on the danger of making Henry too strong: better to negotiate a peace than to overthrow his enemies. On hearing this counsel, there was a shout of warning protest by the *tria millia pagensium militum* (knights of the countryside—presumably the *gregarii* of Florence); they warned Henry against adopting the soft measures advocated by the lords. Now, without giving any

---

[1] '. . . he æfre þas leode mid here y mid ungylde tyrwigende wæs.' The translation is that adopted by Douglas and Greenaway, *E.H.D.* ii. 175. Garmonsway's translation of *here* as 'depredations' seems unwarranted.
[2] Florence of Worcester, ii. 49.
[3] *S.C.*, p. 113.
[4] *Hist. Eccles.* iv. 170, 172.
[5] Ibid. iv. 174.

credence to Orderic's stylized figures and drama, much can be learned from them. We note that he states 'over sixty thousand foot' were in the expedition to take Shrewsbury after the fall of Bridgnorth.[1] Now, if the 'three thousand' country knights stand for the military tenants, the 'sixty thousand' foot must have been the Englishmen of vill and borough who backed them up. This unconfirmed account of Orderic, a distant Anglophile, can hardly be accepted as a description of what actually happened, even if shorn of its ridiculous numbers. But no more can it be dismissed as mere fancy. Surely it is an imaginative dramatization of what to Orderic were the significant factors in the revolt and its suppression. If so, they are consistent with Florence of Worcester's account of 1101.

Did the foot of the communities serve overseas in Henry I's reign? The question arises because three of Henry I's continental battles—Tinchebrai (1106), Brentville (1119), and Bourgterude (1124)—showed that dismounted troops were still a vital part of the English tactical tradition.[2] However, it seems probable that these were dismounted cavalry rather than 'English' foot.[3] Although their *stipendia* are referred to in 1124, Henry's forces were also, however, called *pagenses* and *gregarii* by the enemy.[4] While not ruling out that English foot took part in these battles, the probability would seem to be that these armies of Henry were composed of mercenaries and feudal levies.

Stephen's accession ended the long internal peace, but it would seem that mercenaries rather than conscripts played the leading auxiliary role in the ensuing wars.[5] The freemen of the counties were victims rather than combatants, and the desuetude noted in Henry I's reign probably went on with little abatement. One or two exceptions may be noted

---

[1] Ibid. iv. 176.
[2] Ibid. iv. 229, 456–8; Henry of Huntingdon, *Historia Anglorum* (R.S.), pp. 241–2. This tradition was continued through the battles of the Standard and of Lincoln. It signified the incompleteness of the triumph of 'chivalry' in England, a fact which helps to explain the later achievement of successful 'knight–peasant' co-operation in the field.
[3] For Tinchebrai, see *E.H.D.* ii. 304; H. W. C. Davis, in *E.H.R.* xxiv. 729 f. and xxv. 295–6.
[4] *Hist. Eccles.* iv. 456–8.
[5] J. O. Prestwich, op. cit., pp. 37–40.

however, sufficient, with the police function of tithing and frankpledge, to keep the folk army alive.

The battle of the Standard (1138) is one of the best recorded conflicts of the century. The Scots invaded Yorkshire and under their energetic archbishop the Yorkshiremen fought back. The question is—who made up the Yorkshire force? However impromptu, it must have been feudal, mercenary, or 'militia', or some combination of them. Richard of Hexham gives the most circumstantial account.[1] The archbishop (as agent of God and king as well as their lord) spoke to an assembly of barons, and promised that the parish priests with their parishioners would lend aid. Later this was done, for at the muster the lords of Yorkshire, Nottinghamshire, and Derbyshire were joined by the parish levies. Ailred of Rievaulx's *Relatio* confirms this levy by parishes—a levy of *omnes qui possent ad bella procedere*.[2] Other writers refer to the *provinciales*, who, as has been seen, were on occasion thought of as 'English'.[3] Although Huntingdon also writes of the *populus Anglorum* and *Angli*, the former term is used of the men who replied to a speech which began 'Proceres Angliae clarissimi Normannigenae', so can hardly be claimed as evidence for lower-class participation; the latter term, however, may have included the militia, for it is used in distinction from the Normans: *tota . . . gens Normannorum et Anglorum*. In the description of the battle itself, Richard of Hexham describes how the choicest men-at-arms formed a front mixed with archers (*sagittarii*), other dismounted men with the barons being grouped round the standard. The mounted troops (*equestris cohors*) were stationed farther back, out of sound of the Scots, while the rest of the host (including pre-

---

[1] Richard of Hexham, *Historia de gestis Stephani et de bello de Standardo*, in *Chronicles of the Reign of Stephen, Henry II, and Richard I.* (R.S.), iii. 159–62.

[2] Ailred of Rievaulx, *Relatio de Standardo*, ibid. iii. 181–9; the levy of parishes appears as early as 1094 in France for the siege of Bréval by the king of France and duke of Normandy (Orderic Vitalis, *Hist. Eccles.* iii. 415). Parish military readiness is enjoined by the archbishop of Rouen in 1096 (ibid. iii. 471) and these levies are again mentioned in 1104–8 and 1119 (ibid. iv. 285, 364). Cf. M. Prou, 'De la nature du service militaire dû par des roturiers au XIme siècle', *Revue Historique*, xliv (1890), 313–32.

[3] William of Newburgh, *Historia Rerum Anglicarum* in *Chronicles of the Reign of Stephen, &c.* (R.S.), i. 34; Henry of Huntingdon, *Historia*, pp. 262–3. The feudal forces were described rather carefully as the *proceres boreales*, armed with helmet, coat of chain mail, and leg armour.

sumably the foot) formed a protective wall.[1] According to
John of Worcester and Ailred of Rievaulx the archers played
a notable role. But the impression left by all contemporary
writers is that the victory of the Standard shows the main
strength of England in 1138, even for local defensive purposes, to have been feudal; though the general levy of freemen, especially the archers, had a useful auxiliary role, and
also bolstered the weak baronial morale.

The other major engagement of the reign was the battle of
Lincoln, 1141. Its chief value for us is in showing the citizens
of Lincoln standing 'beside' the royal force. While no role
was assigned to foot levies in the array described by Henry
of Huntingdon—the traditional one of two lines of horse and
one of dismounted men-at-arms—their presence was indicated in the references put in Gloucester's mouth to the
'citizens of Lincoln who stand next to their city' and in that
of Baldwin of Fitz-Gilbert to the royal superiority in foot.[2]
The townsmen of Lincoln were given an assisting, but not
significant, role in the battle by Orderic Vitalis, being notable
chiefly for their severe losses.[3] In both Orderic's account and
that of Gervase of Canterbury, who otherwise follows Henry
of Huntington,[4] the earl of Chester's foot troops from
Cheshire played an important part. According to Orderic,
Chester and his knights dismounted in order to give encouragement to the 'spirited foot'. However, the battle of
Lincoln clearly shows a combination of feudal and mercenary
troops to be the dominant feature of the day.

Taking the reign as a whole, by far the most prominent
militia were the citizens and burgesses; the Lincoln men
fought not only in 1141 but also in 1147, when they triumph-
antly repelled the earl of Chester. The citizens of London,
thanks largely to the protecting walls and strategic position
of their city, played a decisive role on more than one occasion.

---

[1] *Historia*, pp. 162–3; cf. Henry of Huntingdon, *Historia*, pp. 263–4, Ailred,
Relatio, pp. 196–7, and John of Worcester, *Continuatio*, in *Chronicon Flor. Wig.*
(E.H.S.), ii. 111–12. The foot formed a protective wall.

[2] Henry of Huntingdon, *Historia*, pp. 268–74.

[3] *Hist. Eccles.* v. 129; so also William of Malmesbury, *Historia Novella*, ed.
K. Potter (Nelson's Mediaeval Texts), p. 49. To which, of course, must be added the
exploit of the citizen who provided Stephen with his Danish axe; Symeon of Durham, *Historia Regum* (R.S.), ii. 308.

[4] *Hist. Eccles.*, v. 217; Gervase of Canterbury, *Chronica* (R.S.), p. 113.

But their role was more than defensive. Henry of Huntingdon notes that it was the arrival of the Londoners (*exercitus
Lundoniensis*) which compelled Maud and Robert to raise the
siege of the bishop of Winchester's castle after the battle
of Lincoln.[1] In 1145 the same writer refers to the conscription of a *terribilem et numerosum exercitum* of Londoners,
with whom Stephen easily captured Earl Robert's castle at
Faringdon.[2]

Among other cities which supplied troops to one side or
the other, we may note Bristol, which rallied to the side of
Earl Robert in 1144, and Gloucester, marching against
Hereford, 'armis militaribus instructa, equestri et pedestri
exercitus innumerabili suffulta'.[3] On two other occasions, in
Stephen's reign, the militia appear to have served. In 1136
Stephen's army of 'horse and foot' was described by a later
writer as one of 'English and Flemings'; it is just possible
that the English were here the footmen of the shires.[4] In
1139 there is reference to 'those obliged to guard the sea-
coasts', a duty associated with the local freemen rather than
the nobles.[5]

It would thus seem, from the poverty of references in
Stephen's reign, that the 'common people' of England were
losing their role in the game of war. Anarchic feudal troops
and emotionally unattached Flemings and Welsh were tear-
ing the country apart. Taking the long view of the period
between 1066 and 1154, one can see that the basic Anglo-
Saxon pattern of a powerful royal army and local levies of
much less value had been strongly developed. The former
had, until the last few years, been greatly increased in scope
and effectiveness; but the division between the professional
and noble warriors had deepened. The local levies, after im-

---

[1] Henry of Huntingdon, *Historia*, p. 275; cf. William of Newburgh, *Historia*,
p. 42.

[2] Henry of Huntingdon, p. 278; cf. William of Newburgh, p. 48. The rest of
the force was *sua militia* (Newburgh) or *vires coacti* (Huntingdon)—a combination
of terms suggesting fairly clearly the feudal levy.

[3] *Gesta Stephani*, ed. K. Potter (London, 1955), p. 114 ('. . . et incompositum
Bristoensium vulgus'); John of Worcester, *Continuatio*, p. 119.

[4] Ibid., p. 96; Gervase of Canterbury, p. 95. It must be conceded, however, that
the probability is that the Flemings were the foot. However, they were not always so,
as a reference of 1138 by the same author informs us, ibid., p. 105.

[5] John of Worcester, *Continuatio*, p. 117.

portant contributions to the new dynasty in times of crisis, had latterly lost any real significance. It remained to be seen whether the young king from the new dynasty of Plantagenet would strive to turn these trends to his own advantage or seek to exploit again those loyalties which the earlier Norman rulers had found so useful.

III

THE RECONSTRUCTION OF
MILITIA DUTY

I

WITH the accession of Henry II in 1154 a marked change came over every phase of English life. On the one hand, England emerged as the citadel of an aggressive dynastic policy—the invulnerable defence post to which the king could retire in order to spring back at his enemies; on the other hand, Henry II himself was in many ways more thoroughly European than most of either his predecessors or his successors. Yet England received the benefit of the rule of a succession of able justiciars, chancellors, and treasurers. In administration and law Henry was as enterprising as in dynastic matters, and more successful. In military measures there was a further development in the use of mercenaries, together with a more limited and better defined feudal service of men and money. All this was made possible by his magnificent inheritance of the English Exchequer. In abandoning the chief hidage tax—the Danegeld—the way was cleared for the adoption of new assessments on property not only for new taxes but also for general military obligation and for the knight's fee. Nothing demonstrates more clearly than the reorganization of their duties in the famous assize of 1181 that the service of the people as subjects was still an indispensable part of the military resources. It may well have become more useful than before when the revolt of his sons threatened to deprive him of control of the source of his mercenary captains in the Low Countries, as well as of much of his feudal and financial resources. The form of that reorganization suggests what other sources bear out, that the general obligation was showing a tendency to become even more auxiliary to feudal arrangements than it had been. Without the growing integration of Norman and English, this development could hardly have occurred.

In Henry's reign, also, 'knighthood' as a status and way of

life seems to have been deliberately fostered, especially by the young King Henry, who 'made chivalry live again. . . . He was her standard bearer.'[1] This association of crown and chivalry was to lead to distraint of knighthood after the sad lapse under John.

Although, on his accession, Henry II sought to repudiate the mercenaries, who were blamed for the miseries of the past,[2] his reign was nevertheless to witness the use of paid troops, especially foot, on a scale not perhaps matched again in intensity until the Hundred Years War.[3] The reason for this is in part revealed by his policy in the Toulouse campaign of 1159. In a well-known passage, Robert de Torigny (de la Monte) writes that Henry relied on his chief barons and a great host of mercenaries, levying scutage on the knight's fee, in order not to burden 'agrarios milites nec . . . burgensium nec rusticorum multitudinem'.[4]

The Plantagenet policy of asserting vigorously rights outside the kingdom resulted in several Welsh expeditions. The first, in 1157, was characterized by the new device of using a fraction of the feudal host (one-third), no doubt for the same motive, expressed by Robert Torigny, of sparing the rural knights, burgesses, and free men.[5] In Wales the problem was more one of the kind of troops needed than of distance. Henry's first two expeditions had failed to come to grips with the mobile Welsh (1157, 1163). He therefore needed light-armed foot in large numbers. To obtain these, in 1164 he entered into consultation with his leading lay and clerical barons in the closing session of that same Council of Northampton at which Becket was discomfited.[6] From this

---

[1] *Hist. de Guillaume le Marechal* (Paris, 1891–1901), pp. 37, 111 f., qq. in Powicke, 'Angevin Administration', p. 40.   [2] William of Newburgh, *Historia*, p. 101.

[3] J. Boussard, 'Les mercenaires au XIIᵉ siècle: Henry II Plantagenet et les origines de l'armée de métier', *Bibliothèque de l'École des Chartes*, cvi. 2 (1947), 189–224, must suffice until a study based on a more thorough examination of the Pipe rolls becomes available.

[4] Robert de Torigny, *Chronica*, in *Chronicles of the Reign of Stephen*, etc. (R.S.), iv. 202; cf. the similar view in *Dialogues de Scaccario*, ed. C. Johnson (London, 1950), p. 111.

[5] Ibid., p. 193. It may be noted here that this army seemed to Robert to be 'very great' in that Henry levied one out of three knights. Is the implication that an even smaller fraction had been usual?

[6] William Fitz Stephen, 'Vita S. Thomae', in *Materials for the Life of S. Thomas Becket* (R.S.), iii. 70.

discussion came a promise of aid, in the form of footmen, from leading individuals. In the event, most supplied various sums shown by J. H. Round to be made up of six months' pay at a penny a day for *servientes (de promissione servientium)*.[1] Some of this money went towards foreign mercenaries (*coterelli*),[2] but there is no reason to believe that foot levies were excluded. In fact, William of Newburgh's description of the army as 'tam ex regno quam ex transmarinis provinciis exercitu adunato',[3] suggests a mixed rather than an exclusively mercenary force. The evidence is too slight to justify firm conclusions, but it does suggest that in the Council there had been an attempt to constitute an invading army of infantry on the basis of baronial grants.

Against invasion or domestic threats one expects local levies to play a major role. Such may have been the case in the measures of 1167 against the count of Boulogne, though the description of the defending force as *Anglicana militia* probably referred in the first place to feudal levies.[4] A few years later, in the face of Becket's challenge, Henry sought to bind his subjects closer to him. The value of the militia for police purposes was recognized in the 1169 oath binding knights and free tenants, as well as all those over fifteen years old, to support him and obey his orders by, among other things, arresting newcomers without royal passports.[5] When fealty was sworn to the young King Henry in the same year, *franci tenentes* as well as barons swore it.[6] These details suggest the possibility that the defensive value of the freemen was receiving enhanced recognition and the ground prepared for their reorganization as *jurati*.[7]

[1] J. H. Round, *Feudal England*, p. 283; *Pipe Roll 11 Henry II* (Pipe Roll Society), pp. 19, 37, 74, 81, &c.

[2] J. H. Ramsay, *The Angevin Empire*, p. 74 n., referring to *Pipe Roll 11 Henry II*, p. 31, which is a payment of £137. 9s. 8d. for coterels' uniforms.

[3] William of Newburgh, *Historia*, i. 145.

[4] Gervase of Canterbury, *Chronica*, p. 203.

[5] Ibid., p. 215.

[6] *Gesta Henrici* (R.S.), ii, p. 6. From these mentions in 1170, and many others, it appears permissible to argue that the 'free tenants' of England were the knights, sergeants, socage tenants, and freeholders, who made up the large class liable to military service.

[7] See also the military activity of the townsmen on Becket's return in 1170; Gervase of Canterbury, p. 222.

Three years later real civil war convulsed England along with Henry's continental dominions. It was a war fought in the first place by mercenaries; but these were strongly backed by county forces, which may well have included both feudal and communal troops, as in the case of the *multitudo Lincolniensium*, or the *excercitus* and *provinciales* of Yorkshire.[1] There are equally insubstantial but suggestive references to 'the men of England' and the 'English' in Fantosme.[2] In Fantosme's poem the 'English' seem to be auxiliaries to the feudal forces, as also in Newburgh's story concerning the Yorkshire muster of 1174. Having assembled at Newcastle to resist King William of Scotland, the *proceres* proceeded to formulate their successful plan of counter-offensive without waiting for the foot forces (*pedestres copias*) because of the urgency of the situation.[3] The revolt also brought the burgess forces into action; so that, as in Stephen's wars, they seem to be the most notable troops on the king's side beside the mercenary and feudal troops.[4] Londoners again outshone the others, but several towns won mention from twelfth-century writers. The men (*habitati*) of Dunwich defended their important sea-port against the rebel earls of Leicester and Norfolk in 1173. And Jordan Fantosme refers to the loyalty of the Dunwich burghers, who 'right and valiant knights, issued forth to their defences, each knowing his job: some to use bows (*arc traire*), others to throw spears (*lancier*), and the women to bring up stones'.[5] Again, the *burgenses* and *milites* of Northampton fought the forces of the earl of Leicester in 1174, 200 of them being taken prisoner.[6] Equally in vain, the *burgenses* of Nottingham resisted the earl of Ferrers.[7] The Londoners appear in Jordan Fantosme as one of the king's 'stays and shields'. After inquiring after his chief feudal supporters, the king is made to ask Richard of Ilchester:

[1] Ralph de Diceto, *Imagines Historarum*, ii. 379; *Gesta Henrici*, pp. 65–68, *et passim*.
[2] Jordan Fantosme, *Chronique*, in *Chronicles of the Reign of Stephen*, etc., iii, ll. 983, 994.
[3] Fantosme, l. 1096; William of Newburgh, *Historia*, p. 183.
[4] The town levies outshone the rural militia on the Continent in this period also; F. M. Powicke, *The Loss of Normandy* (Manchester, 1913), p. 312.
[5] Fantosme, ll. 871–2.
[6] *Gesta Henrici*, p. 68.   [7] Ibid., p. 69.

'How are the brave men of my city of London acting?'
'They are the most loyal people of all your kingdom
'There is no one in the town who is of age
'To bear arms who is not well armed.'[1]

Were any of the feudal and communal levies paid? This
is a treacherous subject, as there is no sure way of collating
Pipe roll evidence and evidence of obligation in this century.
Certainly the mercenaries were numerous enough ('a vast
host', 'twenty thousand', write various chroniclers) to account
for the thousands of pounds allowed to the sheriffs of Lancashire and Yorkshire for the wages of troops.[2] The reference
to the recipients as 'knights and sergeants' rather than
soldarii, *stipendiarii*, or *coterelli* at least leaves open the possibility that the local men were sometimes paid too,[3] like
the groups of knights, *servientes*, watchmen, and others who
were paid for their services almost every year.

In the year following the civil war orders went out from
both ecclesiastical and lay councils curtailing the right to
bear arms.[4] The former, in which a canon of the Council of
Meaux was repeated against clergy bearing arms, dealt a
blow at the practice, commoner on the Continent than in
England, of obtaining foot levies through bishops and parish
priests. Checked in that direction, the monarchy might be
expected to turn more vigorously towards other means of
raising such mean, but necessary, troops. The decree of the
Council of Woodstock against the carrying of bows, arrows,
and pointed knives east of the River Severn is interesting in
two respects. It suggests that the bow and arrow was already
considered more dangerous than the Saxon spear (was the
stronger Gwentish bow spreading eastwards?); and it also
suggests that, only six years before 'the Assize of Arms', the
government was still more concerned with the danger to the
peace from too many rather than too few weapons in the hands
of the people.

The bow-armed Welsh troops were already by 1175 beginning to play a vital role in English military history. That

---

[1] Fantosme, ll. 1608–11.   [2] *Pipe Roll 21 Henry II* (P.R. Society), pp. 4, 164.
[3] Cf. *Pipe Roll 21 Henry II*, p. 4, 'in liberatione Militum et servientium quos
habuit secum in servicio Regis', with *Pipe Roll 20 Henry II*, p. 5, 'in liberatione C et
XVIII Militum solidariorum . . .'.
[4] *Gesta Henrici*, pp. 87, 93; Mansi, *Collectio*, vol. 22, p. 150 (cf. vol. 14, p. 827).

eccentric genius Gerald of Wales has left us the indispensable account of how this happened, along with his plea for
the use of light-armed foot rather than cumbersome cavalry
in the mountain warfare of Ireland and Wales.[1]

The account by Gerald of Wales of the conquest of Ireland is, of course, one of the twelfth-century classics. As the
English learned no small amount of the art of war from the
Welsh, and as Gerald's observations on many subjects are
precociously modern in their detachment from contemporary
shibboleths, we may well pay careful attention to what he has
to say. The conquest was, of course, effected by Welsh
marcher lords, largely, it would appear, using local conscripts
and volunteers. Gerald records the numbers of those serving in each expedition, and almost alone, among medieval
chroniclers, he writes sense even on this subject.[2] It is true
that there is something a little formal in his account, rather
like the mechanical application of a recipe; but this failing,
if allowed for, does not destroy the value of his comments.
From the story emerges a picture of expeditionary forces
made up of a small core of knights and other *loricati* (horsed
men-at-arms, in later parlance) who were probably the
leaders of small groups of mounted and foot archers (*arcarii*
or *satellites equestres* and *sagittarii pedestres*). The latter groups
usually outnumbered the *loricati* by five to ten times.[3] Recruitment was probably by a mixture of feudal duty, contract, and conscription. The references to 'chosen' foot seems
to suggest the use of the last device at least for the levy of infantry.[4] Other chroniclers write of 'contracted' *armati* and
of desertions from John's force in 1185 for lack of wages.[5]
The feudal element is, of course, vouched for by the Pipe
roll scutages. The general import of these accounts seems

---

[1] Giraldus Cambrensis, *Expugnatio Hibernica* (R.S.), pp. 394–7; *Itinerarium
Cambriae* (R.S.), p. 54. G. H. Orpen, *Ireland under the Normans* (Oxford, 1911–19),
vols. i and ii, provides a standard account; cf. his estimate of Giraldus, ibid. i. 8.

[2] *Expugnatio*, pp. 230–380, and *passim*.

[3] The ratio varied between 1:3 (Reimund's force, 1173, and the Cogans, 1177)
and 1:14 (de Curcy's force, 1177). The lower ratio was always due to the exclusion
of the foot archers from the followers' total.

[4] *Expugnatio*, pp. 230, 312.

[5] William of Newburgh, *Historia*, pp. 167, 169; *Gesta Henrici*, p. 339. William
writes of Richard de Clare's force: 'armatorum juvenum plurima validaque manu
contracta in terra juris sui'; this in contrast with Henry II's *ingens militia*.

clear. We can perhaps distinguish, though we cannot isolate from each other, the feudal, contractual, and conscripted troops. The various sources of supply were tapped to produce small, well-led forces in which for the first time the archer played a major part, and in which mounted archers— a variant on the typical mounted lancer, not a forerunner of mounted infantry—appeared for the first time on a substantial scale. These early mounted archers probably discharged their bows from the saddle, an impossibility for the true mounted long-bowmen of Hundred Years War fame. Gerald's sharp comments on the unsuitability of the Norman knight, the greater aptitude of the English, and the supreme usefulness of the light Welsh foot, if discounted for racial boastfulness and a hypercritical attitude to authority, indicate the lines along which military thinking had begun to run: although it was much later before such ideas became orthodox doctrine.

Before these Irish wars were over, Henry had issued the famous Assizes of Arms for Anjou and England which marked a turning-point in the history of military obligation.[1] They were a turning-point in regard to assessment of military obligation, in that they substituted a rental or chattel for a hidage census. The old hidage and carucage had been obsolete by the time of the Conquest; though it had survived as a basis for taxation, the feudal or mercenary contract had displaced it as a means of raising armies. In 1166, however, the first general tax based on possessions rather than hides had prepared the way for 1181.[2] Moreover, knights' fees had come to be regarded as normally consisting of land units worth ten, fifteen, or twenty librates.[3] The change thus affected allowed a greater flexibility and range in the duties required.

This change in assessment made possible the revival of ancient obligations. An unresolved question is whether

---

[1] *Gesta Henrici*, pp. 269–70, 278–80. Gervase of Canterbury supplies important evidence that the writ revitalized dormant duties when he writes scathingly that by it 'rustici imperiti, rangis et fossaribus assueti, armis militaribus gloriarentur inviti'.

[2] Stubbs, *Const. Hist.* i. 627; A. L. Poole, *Domesday Book to Magna Carta* (Oxford, 1951), p. 419; S. K. Mitchell, *Studies in Taxation*, p. 6.

[3] F. M. Stenton, *English Feudalism*, pp. 166–8.

Anglo-Saxon or Frankish national service was the more influential of these. On the one hand, Stubbs has shown the direct influence of Carolingian capitularies on the clauses of the Assize.[1] Moreover, the European order was issued several months ahead of the English one. On the other hand, the Anjou order was specific about knightly arms and prescribed both horses and bows. In this, and in its lack of reference to free status, it was half a century in advance of the English writ, which remained closer to the Anglo-Saxon tradition in all these matters.[2] In sum, both Franks and Anglo-Saxons contributed to the ideas in the new scheme.

There was no distinction in the Assize between feudal and non-feudal obligation. In legislating for the armour of knights, two Anglo-Saxon traditions were followed. In the first place the lord was made responsible for his followers' weapons, as had been the case in Cnut's laws and in the distant days of the *Germania*. Secondly, there was no reference in the English Assize to the obligation to have a horse, a feature reminiscent of the law on weapons in the 'North People's Law'. The general principle that so much 'thriving' meant so much added responsibility had respectable Anglo-Saxon precedents. A further step was taken toward considering the knight's fee as a unit in the national assessment, and the way prepared for the distraint of twenty librate tenants to take up knightly arms. In the meantime, the obligation of the knight, on the basis of his general fealty but not homage, was to be the same as regards weapons as that of the *liber homo* or *laicus* with sixteen marks *in catallo vel redditu*.

The Assize distinguished, in a manner reminiscent of Anglo-Saxon usage, between the 'well-established' freemen and the general levy. The former were the 'sixteen and ten mark men' who wore chain armour of some sort and were assessed by the law-worthy men of borough and *visnetum*. The latter wore the quilted (leather) gambeson. We can equate the former with the *libere tenentes* so often summoned

---

[1] Stubbs, *Const. Hist.* i. 633, n. 3.

[2] J. Boussard, *Le Gouvernement d'Henri II Plantagenet* (Paris, 1956), advocates a qualified acceptance of an English origin. The French tradition of public military duty is set forth in M. Prou, 'De la nature du service militaire'.

with knights to military service in the following fifty years; the latter, we may surmise, were essentially local forces more valuable for hue and cry than for military duty. Nevertheless, as later writs of defence were to indicate, there must have been still other armed men: villeins, bowmen, and axemen, who did not warrant mention in the 1181 law. In this respect, as in others, the traditional view of the Assize of Arms as a revival of the fyrd seems amply justified.

The function of the Assize was undoubtedly to consolidate the realm while Henry embarked on the final struggle with Philip Augustus and his own sons. The discharge of the duties thus incurred has left no record, and there was little likelihood of the *jurati* seeing service outside the realm. The foot referred to in accounts of his campaigns in Galloway (1186) and in France (1187) were almost certainly those Welsh and Flemings who were his mainstay in his declining years.[1] On the other hand, there is evidence for the call-up of county forces against Rorand fitz Uhtred in 1186;[2] and in 1189, after the breakdown of negotiations in June, the justiciar was sent to England to call out for overseas service all the knights of England 'even though feeble and poor'.[3] The latter order represents the first of a series of attempts by Henry and his sons to reintroduce English troops into France on a large scale, though it must have become clear by then that the majority of the feudal knights were no more suitable for these campaigns than were the *jurati*.

In concluding this review of Henry II's reign, it may be suggested that while the continued weakness of both feudal and communal forces was ensured by his dependence on mercenaries, the foundations of more efficient use of the former had been laid by the Inquest of 1166 and the Assize of 1181.

II

From the point of view of military obligation, Richard I's colourful exploits abroad are far less significant than the

---

[1] William of Newburgh, *Historia*, p. 237; Gervase of Canterbury, *Chronica*, p. 370. On the Welsh and Flemings, William of Newburgh, *Historia*, pp. 276–7; Gervase of Canterbury, *Chronica*, pp. 347, 433; *Gesta Henrici*, pp. 355–6. Cf. *Pipe Rolls 25–35 Henry II, passim*.   [2] *Gesta Henrici*, p. 348 (*omnes provincias*).
[3] Gervase of Canterbury, *Chronica*, p. 447.

civil struggles of those who stayed at home. The principal drama, as in the previous régime, lay in the contest between feudal and mercenary service. The events of 1191 and 1193 are instructive in this regard. In 1191 William Longchamp, unable to trust the military nobility in his contest with John, turned to local or overseas mercenaries.[1] Two years later the roles were reversed; now John was forced to call in *catervi improborum* against the *optimates* loyal to Richard.[2] Yet on both occasions there are hints of other than feudal and mercenary service. John appealed to his men and 'the men of others' to muster with him.[3] The chancellor ordered *custodes littoris* to keep Archbishop Geoffrey of York out of the country;[4] while he in turn was hemmed in the Tower by the Londoners.[5] In 1193 the evidence grows stronger.

John in this year relied heavily on French and, as in 1191, on Welsh troops. Gervase of Canterbury tells how, in reply to this, a general oath of fealty was exacted throughout England; how not only the military nobility but also the *ignobiles* and *rustici* were summoned to arms; and how John's stronghold at Windsor was besieged by a great number of horse and foot. One difficult problem presents itself at this point. This is the significance of Pipe roll entries regarding the wages of *servientes*. In 1193 there are two important entries of this kind—the pay of 500 foot *servientes* at Bristol for seven weeks and of another 500 at Windsor for forty days.[6] Now as the Welsh were on John's side in that year, it may be argued that Queen Eleanor was unusually dependent on feudal and communal levies. It is hard to resist the view that we have here an instance of foot levies being paid for forty days' service. If so, this was the first time that the *jurati* were employed at royal wages. As such, it constituted a powerful precedent for the future. In any case, the deepening divisions in the realm ensured that the militia would increase in importance.

These last references serve to remind us that, in times of

---

[1] William of Newburgh, *Historia*, pp. 335, 338.
[2] Ibid., p. 390.
[3] Richard of Devizes, *De rebus gestis Ricardi I*, in *Chronicles of the Reign of Stephen*, &c., iii. 409.
[4] Ibid., p. 411.   [5] Ibid., p. 414.
[6] *Pipe Roll 5 Richard I*, p. 148. The limited period of service strengthens this view.

civil disturbance and foreign threat, a loyal and militarily competent local population was indispensable. The technique of Longchamp—the use of local strong-arm squads to over-awe the counties—was just not effective.[1] The general oath of 1195 was a logical sequel of this experience. The oath is well known. Primarily a police measure which resulted in many arrests, the oath is perhaps most important for the provision that local knights were to 'take' it in all counties and for the setting of the age limit of fifteen years incorporated in the later Assize of Arms.[2] As Miss Cam has shown, this measure constituted the *posse comitatus* in a more defined way. Its general significance, of course, lies in the bridge it provided between the measures of 1181 and those of 1205.

With John's reign we are no longer so completely dependent on chroniclers or the chance preservation of documents; the great age of record begins. Contemporaries noted that to hold down the country John relied on mercenaries paid from the fruits of pillage, and that he used his feudal rights to convert military obligation into extortionate fines and scutages or to force consent to aids. Yet he abated no jot of his predecessors' claims to the liegance of all free subjects, as was shown in the oath of 1209.[3] And, of course, in the moments of supreme crisis—in early 1205 as the remnants of his forces reeled back from France, and in 1213 when Philip II waited poised for invasion—the universal levy was called out.[4]

The measure of 1205 carried the organization of the *jurati* a big step forward, so that from then on the burgesses were organized under constables of boroughs and cities, the *rustici* under constables of hundreds and groups of vills, and all supervised for many decades by constables of counties. Moreover, this was the first document on which the obliga-

---

1 William of Newburgh, *Historia*, pp. 334–5 ('. . . sub praetextu publicae provisionis . . . oberrantes armatas immanium barbarorum catervas').
2 *Select Charters*, pp. 257–8 (from Hoveden); the idea of an oath from all fifteen year olds and up had been anticipated by Henry II in 1169. It arose undoubtedly from two facts; it was the age at which a page was initiated into the squirearchy, and it was the age of majority for most free tenants.
3 *Annals of Waverley in Annales Monastici* (R.S.), ii. 262.
4 Gervase of Canterbury, *Chronica*, ii. 96–97; *Rotuli Litterarum Patentium* (London: Rec. Comm., 1835), i. 55; *Chronica Majora*, ii. 538–9, 549; *Continuatio Chronici Willelmi de Novoburgo*, in *Chronicles of the Reign of Stephen*, etc., ii. 514.

tion to arms was firmly linked to the general oath of fealty. The age limit was set at twelve years. On the following 3 April the first extant order of the *jurati* to muster was issued, when all were ordered to hasten with arms to meet the enemy if he landed, on penalty of forfeiture or (for the landless) a payment of fourpence a year:[1] the first evidence we have of the penalties imposed for neglect of service, other than feudal, since Domesday Book. To explain the sense of emergency which occasioned this measure we must remember the extreme tension which drove John to call out his feudal force and then sail in distraction up and down the Channel, at his wits' end how to get in a blow at his wily French opponent.[2] It is also important that, unlike the 1181 Assize of Arms, the measure claimed to have the full consent of the *proceres* of the realm.

The developments of 1212–13 are less interesting from the point of view of organization, but even more striking from that of obligation. In 1212 the towns were called on to make ready over 800 horse troops for overseas service, and all sergeanty tenants-in-chief were called out for a North Welsh campaign.[3] Now, threatened once more by an attack from Philip Augustus, John issued an extraordinary summons. The writ is given by Roger Wendover.[4] All sheriffs were ordered under penalty of imprisonment to call out 'all earls, barons, knights and all free men and *servientes*, whoever they are or from whomsoever they hold, provided they ought to or are capable of bearing arms and who have done homage or liegance to us' to muster at Dover with arms ready to defend 'caput nostrum et capita sua et terram Angliae'. The next clause linked the measure even more distinctly, via the famous summons to the English of William Rufus, to the tradition of the fyrd: 'and that none who can bear arms should stay behind, under penalty of the name of culvertage and of life servitude'. These men were to serve under their lords, and, if landless, were to be supported by

---

[1] *Select Charters*, pp. 276–7, from *Rot. Litt. Pat.* i. 55a. The Waverley annalist wrote that both horse and foot assembled at Portsmouth, thus raising the question whether some of the *jurati* were not possibly being drafted for overseas service (*Ann. Waverl.* ii. 256).   [2] R. Coggeshall, *Chronicon Anglicanum* (R.S.), p. 154.
[3] *Rotuli Litterarum Clausarum* (London: Rec. Comm., 1833), i. 130–1.
[4] In M. Paris, *Chronica Majora*, ii. 538–9.

wages from the king. Finally, the sheriff was to bring a roll of delinquents with him. William of Newburgh's continuator and Wendover's own account show that the principal function of these troops was to defend the coasts.[1] In the former's words: 'Under penalty of the name of culvertage there were assembled all earls, barons, knights and "rustics" ... who were deployed around the sea-coasts.' Wendover tells how victuals ran out after a few days and the unarmed mob was dismissed, only the knights, *servientes*, and 'freemen, along with the crossbowmen and archers', being retained. Once again, we note the contrast between the reasonably effective fighting free men and the mere peasant conscript. The former, now strengthened by the Assize of Arms, had become a worthy fighting auxiliary to feudal knights and sergeants.

When John had left in 1214, Peter des Roches ordered out the coast levies on his behalf, in what is perhaps the first writ of selective service to have survived. This was directed to the sheriff of Norfolk for the levy of a hundred men of Dunwich to be chosen to guard the coast. Expenses were to be allowed at the Exchequer.[2]

Thus, in 1205 and 1213–14 the defensive potentialities of the *jurati* were more fully realized than ever before. The fugitive references to the oath of free men and to coast defence in the past century may have reflected similar measures whose survival did not become possible until the days of chancery enrolments. But there is also a substantial change from a more general obligation to one restricted by rules similar to those common in sergeanty tenures.

The struggle for the Charters added little. The wealthier Londoners, at least, appear to have supported the barons and the baronial forces included both *servientes* and *pedites*.[3] The significance of the struggle is that although John had the country full of mercenaries and royal castles, he was completely helpless; there was no possibility of appeal against

[1] *Continuatio*, p. 514.
[2] *Rot. Litt. Claus.* i. 211 (cf. A. H. Noyes, *Military Obligation*, p. 15). Feudal 'selection' had shown the way, but that of the *jurati* was to outlast it. In the same year John summoned a reduced force from his knights. P.R.O. C. 47. 5/11, from I. J. Sanders, *Feudal Military Service*, pp. 59, 108. Selected numbers of non-military woodcutters and ditchers had been called out the previous year; *Rot. Litt. Claus.* i. 131.   [3] *Chron. Majora*, ii. 585 f.

the great rebels to either the feudal or communal levies, as there had been in 1087, 1101, and 1173. The taunt of *nithing* or *culvertage* was not available to rebels; but it was equally impossible for an unpopular king to resort to it, or to more sophisticated pleas, in his hour of great need.

The Charter itself sought to restrict military obligation to the amount incident on tenure (cl. 16) and to ban mercenaries. These two clauses are of great significance for our subject; the limitation of feudal service, especially overseas, had probably long been a baronial objective and had recently become a national issue.[1] The general character of the restriction in the sixteenth clause, if compared with the more vigorous demands of the Northerners in the 'Unknown Charter', was probably something of a royal victory; alternatively, we may possibly detect the wise influence of William Marshal.[2] The clause against mercenaries could only lead the monarchy to develop other non-baronial forces, amongst which the militia must be included; money-fiefs and militia in fact, developed in response to very much the same challenges.

The period 1066–1216, we may conclude, was marked by a series of developments which began by distorting, but ended by reaffirming, the pattern of Anglo-Saxon obligation. Although the introduction of the military honour and fief profoundly affected every feature of warfare and society, the Anglo-Saxon tradition of public assessment and communal service did not die out. On the one hand, it survived in its contribution to the nature of the English feudal host and to the terms of subinfeudation. On the other hand, the English continued to do service as a distinct group for at least half a century after the Conquest. Indeed, a recent writer has suggested, perhaps established, that the fyrd as a 'five-hide two-month' army lasted into mid-twelfth century and dictated some of the terms of feudal service.[3] The principle of a public census for military affairs was certainly brought very low by 1154, and it took the genius of Henry II

---

[1] J. H. Round, *Feudal England*, pp. 528–35; F. M. Powicke, *The Loss of Normandy* (Manchester, 1911), pp. 314 f.; I. J. Sanders, *Feudal Military Service*, pp. 52–60.

[2] Cf. S. Painter, *The Reign of King John*, pp. 304 f. On the attribution of the 'Unknown Charter', see A. L. Poole, *Domesday Book to Magna Carta*, pp. 471–2 and n. The view here adopted, approximately that of Round, is, of course, controversial.

[3] Warren C. Hollister, 'The Significance of Scutage Rates in Eleventh- and

and the disasters of John's reign to reintroduce militia service on the basis of rental assessment made 'popular' in taxation matters. Another Anglo-Saxon legacy which was given fresh life in the years before Magna Charta was that of royal mercenaries. This force, about which comparatively little is yet known, constituted the ever-present germ of the modern professional army. Its threat to privilege and liberty led to the setback which it suffered at the end of John's reign and in the ensuing decades.

NOTE. LOCAL ORGANIZATION

THE form of militia service in the two great 'liberties' of Cheshire and London are better known than that of other localities, probably because of their very uniqueness. The utmost caution must be used, therefore, in arguing from them. The basic Cheshire evidence is the so-called Great Charter of Cheshire, and like the account of London service dates from 1215.

The Cheshire Charter defined the duties of free subtenants as follows: '[they] shall have coats of mail or hauberks and defend their *fees* by their bodies, even if they are not knights'.[1] As one might expect of the arrangements on the great Palatine fief, this was more like the *arrière-ban* than the *fyrd*. It was, nevertheless, a contribution to the definition of militia in England; and Cheshire, like Durham, was to be rather more active than other counties both in defensive service and in prickliness about rights in supplying it.

The London evidence shows that the aldermen of the wards were expected to act as militia arrayers. They were to assemble all men over fifteen, and to levy a defence tax on their rents and chattels, as well as to conduct a muster of arms. The sub-units were parishes. While the ward–parish organization may have been ancient, the likelihood is that the details were worked out in consequence of the 1181 and 1205 decrees.[2]

Twelfth-Century England', *E.H.R.* Oct. 1960, 577–88; 'The Annual Term of Military Service in Medieval England', *Medievalia et Humanistica*, xiii (1960), 40–47; 'The Five-Hide Unit and the Old English Military Obligation', *Speculum*, xxxvi (1961), 61–74; 'The Norman Conquest and the Genesis of English Feudalism', *A.H.R.* lxvi (1961), 641–63. Unfortunately Dr. Hollister's articles appeared after I had completed my work on these chapters, but I find that his conclusions do not conflict too grievously with mine.

1 J. Tait, *The Register of the Abbey of St. Werburgh, Chester* (Chetham Society, N.S. 79), p. 105; 'Knight Service in Cheshire', *E.H.R.* lvii (1942), 437 f.

2 W. Page, *London*, p. 212; M. Bateson, 'London Municipal Collection of the Time of John', *E.H.R.* xvii (1902), 727–8. The mayoral summons by common bell is described by Wendover in Matthew Paris, *Chronica Majora*, iii. 224.

IV

KNIGHT SERVICE AND KNIGHTHOOD
UNDER HENRY III

Henry III inherited a curtailed feudal army, a reorganized militia, and a recently expanded force
of household and castle mercenaries. The peak of
practical chivalry had been achieved in the person of William
Marshal, and the development of archery was bringing the
non-noble foot-soldier into the forefront.[1] A warlike monarch, who was a successful knight and leader, might have
obtained the support of the nation. As it was, the tendency
of the barons to insularity and opposition to royal ventures
was increased by their lack of confidence in Henry's leadership; and, in spite of the attempt to mount wars in France,
Wales, Scotland, and even far-away Sicily, the reign ended
with the rise of a native Welsh Empire, the acceptance
(thanks to the generosity of Saint Louis) of the *status quo ante*
in France, and civil war at home. In this and the following chapter a summary of Henry's general policy regarding
the army will be followed by more thorough studies of his
measures regarding knighthood and the *jurati*.

The king's weaknesses were magnified by baronial atti-
tudes stemming from the loss of Normandy and from the
enhanced sense of privilege arising from the struggle for
the Charters and the Charters themselves. Yet, in the light of
the buoyant and expanding economy, the level of fiscal and
military effort was far from oppressive. The demands of the
baronage sprang from a determination to increase their
privileges rather than any real suffering. Although the king
and his ministers countered by such measures as the development of the household military establishment and distraint of
knighthood, there is little doubt that active military participation by lords and peasants alike reached a low ebb during the

[1] See S. Painter, *William Marshal* (Baltimore, 1933).

reign. This decline of interest in warfare, particularly over-seas, was offset by fines for failure to serve and by orders for distraint of knighthood issued on the eve of campaigns. However, in the prevailing atmosphere of opposition and defeat, it was only too easy to let what was intended as an encouragement to military preparedness degenerate into a means of raising money.

In spite of the depressed state of military activity under Henry III, important changes in weapons and warfare took place. The increased definitions of obligations regarding the possession of weapons, the keeping of the peace, and the assumption of knighthood naturally affected warfare. It is even possible that a step was taken in the evolution of the long-bow as a weapon of the peasant militia. The elaboration of armour continued, foreshadowing the fantasies of late medieval knighthood and its ultimate eclipse. At the centre, the corps of household knights and sergeants presaged the emergence of contractual troops as the most important element in the army, while the use of special commissioners was developed in the organization and leadership of second-line defence or auxiliary troops.

The wars of Henry III fall into three main groups: over-seas, British, and civil. The overseas campaigns were prestige matters, led by the king in person, reflecting the state of politics in the support they elicited at home, and quite fruit-less. The main campaigns were in 1225 (mostly fee-holders), 1230, 1242/3, and 1253/4. Within Britain armies were sent against Wales in 1223, 1228, 1231, 1241, 1245, 1253, and 1257, and against Scotland in 1244 and 1255. Most of the expeditions to France and outer Britain were small in number and poorly led, serving mainly as political irritants at home. Armies were involved in civil wars on many occasions, but we may note especially those of 1224, 1233, and 1264/5.

The permanent nucleus of all these armies, though by no means the largest or most powerful corps, was provided by the household.[1] This branch of the army consisted of about 100 'king's knights', with an inner core of about thirty

---

[1] For the views in this paragraph I am indebted to the unpublished thesis of R. F. Walker, 'The Welsh Wars of King Henry III' (Oxford, 1953). On *fiefs-rentes* for subjects overseas, cf. Bryce Lyon, *From Fief to Indenture*, pp. 208-9.

regular householders; supplementing the knights were a similar number of mounted household sergeants and a still larger group of foot sergeants and archers. The force was probably dispersed in garrisons for much of the time, but it also provided a headquarters staff, an advance force, leaders for conscripted troops, and a small corps to be brigaded with feudal contingents.

The role of feudalism in the armies of Henry III has been greatly clarified by the studies of Drs. H. M. Chew and I. J. Sanders.[1] At least a partial reconstruction of feudal service can be made from lists of individuals summoned, muster rolls or proffer lists, and, for ecclesiastical tenants-in-chief and barons, accounts of arrangements between lord and tenant. Perhaps the most obvious feature of the writs of summons which set armies in motion was their wide variety. However, three principal forms of summons can be distinguished: the 'traditional' order for service with *servicium debitum*, writs going directly to the chief barons and via the sheriffs to the lesser tenants-in-chief; secondly, there were orders for service with stated quotas; finally, there were summons which either made no stipulation about following or used some very indefinite phrase. *Servicium debitum*, though the best known, was by no means the only, or even the commonest, requirement.[2] Writs requiring *servicium debitum* were issued for service in Wales in May 1223, June 1231, May 1245 (in the *forma vicecomitum* or sheriffs' writs), July 1257, March 1258, May 1263, and (deceptively) March 1264; for Scotland in 1244 (sheriffs' writs) and January 1258; for France in March 1242 (sheriffs' writs). Armies including *servicium debitum* were called out for dealing with internal enemies in July 1217, in March 1260, and in March 1264. The two earliest writs, those of 1217 and 1223, were unusual in that the first coupled the *servicium debitum* with the service of the *jurati*, while the second joined to the *servicium debitum* of military tenants that of tenants by sergeanty. In 1257 the exemplary writ to William de Forz (count of Aumale) ordered service

[1] H. M. Chew, *Ecclesiastical Tenants-in-Chief*; I. J. Sanders, *Feudal Military Service*; Sir F. M. Powicke, *The Thirteenth Century* (Oxford, 1953).

[2] *Report on the Dignity of a Peer* (London, 1829), iii. 3–36. The many other writs on the Close rolls do not alter the general picture; cf., for example, R. F. Treharne, 'The Battle of Northampton', *Northamptonshire Past and Present*, ii (1955), pp. 21–22.

cum . . . servicio debito, but the annex of names of those to whom similar writs were to be addressed was marked *se quarto, se solo,* &c. This would suggest that the acceptance of reduced proffers at the muster was now formally recognized.[1] We also know from other evidence that greatly reduced service was obtained at the musters of 1223 and 1245,[2] so that, while details remained to be adjusted—and were to continue to fluctuate throughout the short life of feudal service—the practice of accepting service reduced by a ratio varying from one-half to one-twelfth dates at least from the twenties.[3]

Summonses of the second type, for reduced numbers, were issued not only in 1257, but also in 1218, 1229 and 1230 (for Brittany), and 1234.[4] For 1229 a muster roll of October is the chief evidence, though the existence of a summons for reduced service can probably be deduced from the order to the earl of Chester. Broadly speaking, there was no great divergence between the reduced quotas summoned in this way and those supplied in response to a feudal summons.

The third and largest group of writs called neither for *servicium debitum* nor for a stated quota, but either simply for service or for a certain kind of service. A military writ to sheriffs in April 1218 called on tenants to serve 'ita paratis . . . quod eis [immo] grates sciamus et quod pro defectu eorum non oporteat nos ad feoda sua recurrere'; in July the words used were 'sic honorem suum et sui indempnitatis diligunt nullatenus obmittant'.[5] For Wales in 1223 the sheriffs were to call on ecclesiastical tenants-in-chief to send *milites suos,* and the others to serve 'ita parati . . . quod eis grates scire debeamus' (the threat being dropped), while the individual barons were summoned *cum gente vestra ita parati,*

---

[1] Although I. J. Sanders notes the identity of much of the service with that in Edward I's time (*Feudal Military Service,* pp. 64, 155 f.), he appears unwilling to accept the permanence of the changes under Henry III.

[2] S. K. Mitchell, *Studies in Taxation, passim;* I. J. Sanders, op. cit.

[3] In Dr. Sanders's table, the variations after 1223 are slight except in two cases where the quota was halved: Marmion and Warenne.

[4] I. J. Sanders, *Feudal Military Service,* pp. 60 f., 108 f.; *Dignity of a Peer,* iii. 5–7.

[5] On balance, it seems unlikely that service of rear-vassals was intended in these writs; it was those who owed the king service who were to be called out; but cf. I. J. Sanders, *Feudal Military Service,* p. 110.

&c. The individual summonses to Gascony in June 1242 did not, like the shrieval summons, ask for *servicium debitum*, but elaborated the 1223 formula in a rather wheedling way, no doubt because of the opposition in the great council. Similar orders, more or less florid, were issued to individuals for the Welsh wars of 1228 and 1245 (important because of the survival of a muster roll for this year) and the Scottish wars of 1244 and 1255. Amongst writs of importance in setting precedents for the future were the demands for service *cum toto posse* (Scotland 1255) and the order of 1252 asking for a helping hand in the defence of Gascony. The implication of the scutage rolls and protections is that in response to these varied orders only small retinues accompanied the lords.[1]

The numbers serving and the conditions of feudal service under Henry III have yet to be thoroughly explored. Some things we do know, and others can be guessed at. In the first place, the ratio of church to lay tenants may normally have been about one to three, if the reduced ecclesiastical *servicium debitum* of 132½ fees in Edward I's time may be compared with a lay service varying from 300 to 500 knights.[2] However, both sets of figures could vary considerably with circumstances—the Church supplying 194 out of 470 knights in 1218 and none in 1230.

For how long, and on what conditions, did the barons, with their small retinues, stay in the field? It would seem that in the later years of the reign they were successful in extending to their reduced service such 'conditions' as the forty days' limit, in much the same way as they were able to make the new quota the basis of commutation.[3] The king's part in this process is aptly described by Miss Chew as one of reluctant acquiescence. This development of baronial traditions into fixed rights appears to have been a general characteristic of Henry's reign: it is to be found at work, though not completed, in such matters as the demand for the king's personal presence in the host and for consent to the

[1] S. K. Mitchell, *Studies, passim.*
[2] I. J. Sanders, *Feudal Military Service*, p. 109; H. M. Chew, *Ecclesiastical Tenants-in-Chief*, pp. 32–33; R. F. Walker, *Welsh Wars, passim.*
[3] H. M. Chew, ibid., pp. 95–96 nn. and 53–58; F. M. Powicke, *The Thirteenth Century*, pp. 33–36.

undertaking of major expeditions.[1] The early writs of summons for 1217, 1221, May 1223, 1231, and 1234 said
nothing of the king's personal presence; a fact which, in the
first few cases at least, may be attributable to the youth of the
king. All other orders stressed that service was to be *cum
corpore nostro* or *nobiscum*, except for those of July 1257
(Wales) and January 1258 (Scotland). Thus all the overseas
summons noted the king's personal presence. It also became
customary to mention the cause of the expedition and the
fact of consent by the barons and/or the council.[2]

It is against this background that the policy of Henry regarding knighthood and the arming of the *jurati* must be
studied. Knighthood had by now been transformed into a
special status; the mark of this status was the conferring of
distinctive equipment (*arma militaria*) at a special ceremony
(*adoubement*). Men so marked were paid double wages in
war, their service was worth twice that of another man-at-
arms at a proffer, and they were frequently required in orders
for juries, commissions of all kinds, and eventually for duties
of representation. It was almost certainly their high prestige
as warriors, above all other considerations, which inspired
royal intervention to expand their numbers.[3]

Possibly the most striking testimony to the influence of the
new cult of knighthood in Henry III's reign is the Latin *Song of
Lewes*, written as it is from a hostile viewpoint. The king had
the flower of the realm's *milicie* on his side, but like the hosts
of Philistines, they were not true to those ideals of knighthood,
which had been symbolized in the ceremony of knighting.[4]

---

[1] Cf. H. M. Chew's suggestive remarks, ibid., pp. 98–100.

[2] Cf. below, Chapter XII.

[3] See my 'Distraint of Knighthood and Military Obligation under Henry III',
Speculum, xxv (1950), 475–70. On the same subject, cf. F. M. Nichols, 'On Feudal
and Obligatory Knighthood', *Archaeologia*, xxiv (1863), 189–244. For knighthood
in general, G. G. Coulton's article in *Encyclopaedia Britannica* (11th edition), s.v.
'Knighthood', is probably the best introduction. See also E. F. Jacob, 'The Begin-
nings of Medieval Chivalry', in E. Prestage, *Chivalry* (London, 1928), pp. 37–
55; N. Denholm-Young, 'The Tournament in the Thirteenth Century', *Studies in
Medieval History Presented to F. M. Powicke* (Oxford, 1948); H. Delbrück,
Geschichte der Kriegskunst (Berlin, 1923), iii, book 3, chaps. 1 and 2; and F. M.
Powicke, *Loss of Normandy*, pp. 443–5. Less scholarly, but useful, is W. C. Meller,
A Knight's Life in the Days of Chivalry (London, 1924).

[4] *Song of Lewes*, ll. 93 f., 167 f.; cf. ll. 245 f.; on the veracity of the first assertion,
however, cf. R. F. Treharne, 'The Battle of Northampton', pp. 18–19.

The arms of a knight differed in quality and elaboration rather than in fundamentals from those of the *serviens* or *valettus*, and the line separating them, though it must have been known to the king's marshal at any given moment, cannot now be precisely drawn. The number of followers, cost of the horse, wearing of pot helm over the basinet, full-sleeved hauberk (*lorica*) with surcoat, knightly belt and sword, leg-guards, and gauntlets all offered points of distinction.[1] Hence Bracton could observe that knighthood's chief distinction lay in being 'chosen' for fighting in defence of country and people.[2] This elaboration of knightly arms probably strengthened the decision to regulate the order by special enactment rather than through the Assize of Arms.

Provision of equipment by the king on the occasion of the knighting of some householder or favoured subject gives some evidence of what was involved in becoming a knight, and at the same time demonstrates the practical interest of the monarchy in increasing the number of knights in the country. Such gifts appear in greatly increased numbers on the Close rolls after 1242, the most important year in the history of distraint of knighthood. In 1158 five pounds had been spent on the arms and equipment for the making of a knight.[3] Ninety years later a robe of silk, two robes of cloth, a cape, couch, and 'other necessaries' were ordered for this purpose.[4] A grant of scarlet robes consisting of tunica, supertunica, pallium, and *capa cum penula de minuta varia* indicates the more lavish scale of some knightings; the scarlet tunic probably going back a long way in princely adornments.[5] The cost of these ceremonies, measured against the paltry fines levied for respite of knighthood, must in the minds of

---

[1] On armour, there is a valuable summary by H. M. Chew, *Ecclesiastical Tenants-in-Chief*, pp. 89–90. The Assize of Arms in 1181 and 1231 included knightly tenants without special distinction; it was concerned with minimal equipment only, however, and not at all with status.

[2] *De Legibus* (ed. Woodbine), ii. 32. Cf. John of Salisbury's 'Knighthood is the armed hand of the state' (quoted by E. F. Jacob, 'Medieval Chivalry', p. 48), and Ralph Niger's dictum that 'chief among those whose proper business it is to carry on war are the knights', quoted by G. B. Flahiff, '*Deus non vult*: A Critic of the Third Crusade', *Mediaeval Studies*, ix (1947), 174.

[3] *Pipe Roll 4 Henry II*, p. 113. The nature of these arms is indicated by an entry in the same year of an identical grant for a *destrier, lorica,* and palfrey.

[4] e.g. *Close Rolls 1247–51*, p. 84.

[5] e.g. ibid., pp. 450–1 (for Geoffrey of Lusignan); cf. the following note.

'rustics' and practical men, have outweighed the appeal of their glamour and prestige.

The ceremony of knighting must have varied very greatly according to time and circumstance, but at the heart of it was the conferring of sword and belt attributed to the Anglo-Saxons by William of Malmesbury.[1] After the Conquest the rise of the cult probably led to a gap between court knightings and mere dubbing. Young heirs to baronies might look forward to an elaborate court ceremonial, possibly in company with one of the royal princes, while others would be knighted in the household of another great man, probably with at least comparable glamour. On such occasions, in Henry III's reign, many must have thought the moment appropriate for the assumption of a coat of arms.[2] Many country dwellers, however, must have first thought of assuming knighthood when they inherited their fiefs rather than when they came of age (unless, in the case of a minority, the two events coincided).[3]

Feudal tenure did not imply knighthood, or vice-versa. A household servant or a foreigner could be made a knight and many feudal tenants would not trouble to take up their order. Did it make any difference to one's feudal dues whether one took up knighthood or not? In spite of A. L. Poole's belief that the lord had an interest in knighthood in order to increase his earnings from relief, scutage, wardship, &c., it has not yet been shown that any such increase did in fact happen. Possibly knighthood made it easier to prove the holding of land by knight service, but has any case ever been adduced of such proof? It is more probable that the military and judicial services of county and nation, not the pockets of the lord, were injured by the neglect of knighthood.[4]

---

[1] William of Malmesbury, *Gesta Regum*, i. 145; Alfred knighted Athelstan before he was of age, with scarlet tunic, jewel-studded belt, and gold-hilted sword. On the primacy of Anglo-Saxon knighthood, cf. Ch. Petit-Dutaillis, *Studies Supplementary to Stubbs* (Manchester, 1908), i. 42–44.

[2] The first extant roll of arms dates from the knighting of the Lord Edward; F. M. Powicke, *The Thirteenth Century*, p. 552; A. Wagner, *A Catalogue of English Medieval Rolls of Arms* (Society of Antiquaries, 1950), p. 3.

[3] F. M. Stenton, *English Feudalism*, p. 34; *E.H.D.* ii. 922–3; for a French example, Robert de Torigny, *Chronica*, p. 258.

[4] A. L. Poole, *Obligations of Society*, p. 4; F. M. Powicke, *The Thirteenth Century*, p. 546.

While the ideals, arms, and formalities of knighthood were all increasing in the twelfth and thirteenth centuries, there is evidence that the numbers taking it up were on the wane. The great decline in the numbers proffered at musters must have contributed to this state of affairs, for the military glory of *adoubement* and coat of arms, war-horse, &c., could have no appeal for the thousands who would never see military service. Hence writs of summons must call out not only earls, barons, and knights, but also 'free tenants and others who owed military service'.[1] Conversely, every attempt had to be made to ensure that those who did serve had maximum equipment, especially where the number serving was limited by problems of sea transport, and to create a reserve of full knights who could be expected to serve as leaders of county foot or to come to court to enter into paid service. The history of these attempts must now be undertaken.

Compulsory knighthood was not absolutely new in the thirteenth century. It is certain that the right to confer knighthood, as enjoyed by both king and lay lords, though not by ecclesiastics (cf. the legislation at Westminster, 1102, against abbots making knights),[2] tended towards the right to compel knighthood. Thus in 1208–10 a tenant of the bishopric of Durham, then in the king's hand, was ordered to become a knight.[3] In Henry III's reign there were twenty-six writs which may be loosely termed 'distraint of knighthood', most of them enrolled on the Close rolls.[4] Not all of these were of equal importance. It will be most helpful to discuss, first, the writs of prime significance—i.e. those of

---

[1] *Dignity of a Peer*, iii. 1–7. A similar adaptation to the situation is indicated in the 'Great Charter of Cheshire', as described in the note to Chapter III, above. The shortage of knights also involved administrative and judicial difficulties; see, for example, *Calendar of Close Rolls 1251–3*, pp. 442–3.

[2] W. C. Meller, *A Knight's Life in the Days of Chivalry* (London, 1924), p. 47; F. M. Nichols,'Obligatory Knighthood', pp. 208–10.

[3] *Book of Fees*, i. 27, cited by A. L. Poole, *Obligations*, p. 35.

[4] See my 'Distraint of Knighthood', Appendix, where nos. (1) and (3) are not in this category. There should be added writs of 18 Jan. 1227 (which is printed in Nichols, p. 203 n. (c) and *Rot. Litt. Claus.* ii. 206); 25 July 1240 (*C.R. 1237–41*, 239–40); 1 Sept. 1243 (*C.R. 1242–7*, p. 70); 21 Mar. 1245 (*C.R. 1242–7*, p. 350); June/July 1245 (ibid., p. 356); 15 July 1256 (P.R.O. C. 47. 1/1 m. 17); 27 Sept. 1268 (*Calendar of Patent Rolls 1266–72*, p. 260).

1224 and 1242—and other orders associated with overseas expeditions; secondly, the less important writs, such as those connected with Welsh and Scottish wars or simply with the raising of funds; and, finally, the limitations placed on the extent of the class affected and the growing concern with the availability of even un-knighted men-at-arms.

The first general distraint of knighthood was that of 16 November 1224.[1] Every layman of full age who held one or more knight's fees was to be made a knight by the Sunday following Easter 1225. Beyond these bare facts, two important conjectures may be made. In the first place, it was probably directed at subtenants as well as at tenants-in-chief. Secondly, it appears to have been issued in order to strengthen an overseas expedition. The first conjecture is supported by a writ of exemption issued at a later date.[2] The second derives from the circumstances associated with its issue. At that time, Henry was planning an invasion of Gascony in force.[3] His whole mind was bent on it; the troublesome interruption of his plans by Fawkes de Breauté's revolt had been overcome the previous August, and Fawkes himself had just gone into exile. The coastguard was organized at the same time, and the fleet must have been ordered to assemble, for it was gathering at the ports in January, when the *jurati ad arma* were also assembled there. These great plans came to very little; the country wanted the Charters confirmed and in return granted a fifteenth, which sufficed to send over a small army. The Confirmation renewed the promise in Magna Carta not to exact more military service than was owed, and this must have been given more point by the very recent order concerning knighthood. In conclusion, then: this first distraint of knighthood was radically wide in application; it was part of the preparations for a big expedition to

---

[1] *Rot. Litt. Claus.* ii. 69b.

[2] Ibid. ii, 25a, cited by F. M. Nichols, 'Obligatory Knighthood', pp. 202–3, note (b). John de Denton, who held land of Robert de Vaux at fee farm but no land by military service, was granted exemption from knighthood.

[3] See my 'Distraint of Knighthood', p. 460, notes; K. Norgate, *The Minority of King Henry III* (London, 1912), pp. 219 21, 244 9, 252; Hugh of Vivonia's letter, *Royal Letters of Henry III*, i. 236–8; *Rot. Litt. Claus.* ii. 10b, 11, 21, 22; *Patent Rolls 1216–25*, pp. 465, 469, 514. The view that this order was connected with the civil war rather than with the Gascon plans runs counter to the probability of the chronology.

Gascony; it may possibly have been a factor in provoking the wide opposition manifested at the Christmas Council which was determined on a solemn enactment against innovations.

The order for knighting associated with the Gascony expedition of 1242 is much more fully documented. The renewal of war brought about the most important single development in the history of distraint of knighthood: the establishment of the twenty librate 'census'.[1] The genesis of this order is interesting. On 25 July 1240 all with a whole knight's fee or less, if they had enough land in either knight's fee or socage to sustain knighthood, were ordered to become knights by 1 November. The names and 'quantity and value' of the lands of those not doing so were to be returned.[2] In July and August 1241 writs were issued in favour of Adam de Blakeburn[3] and Robert de Landplo[4] that they were not to be distrained to become knights, unless they had a whole knight's fee or twenty librates in socage or military tenure. These individual writs prepared the way for the important general writ of 10 December, which extended these qualifications to all. The origin of this twenty-librate 'census' as a higher class of knights fees in the twelfth century has been shown by F. M. Stenton. There is some evidence that it was thought to be a logical successor to the five-hide rule, the rent of one virgate being estimated at one pound.[5]

This writ, with its reissues the following year, was unmistakably part of the measures for the expedition to Gascony.[6] Several important new features demand notice. In the first place, the sheriffs were now for the first time specifically ordered to distrain those liable, i.e. to coerce them if necessary by impounding their chattels. (On 8 February 1242 the

[1] *C.R. 1237–41*, pp. 428, 430, 434, 486; cf. ibid., pp. 348, 482–4.

[2] Ibid., pp. 239–40; there was a precedent for returning the quantity of lands of those concerned in the writ of January 1227.

[3] Ibid., p. 359.

[4] Ibid., p. 362; cf. Nichols, 'Obligatory Knighthood', pp. 205–6.

[5] *English Feudalism*, pp. 164–8; the equation of a virgate with a pound's rent is to be found in the 1256 returns, P.R.O. C. 47. 1/1 m. 16.

[6] See my 'Distraint of Knighthood', pp. 461–2. The connexion with overseas service is accepted by F. M. Powicke, *The Thirteenth Century*, p. 547. F. M. Nichols saw the importance of the writ in setting up a general 'census' of knighthood, 'Obligatory Knighthood', pp. 205–6.

restoration of these to their owners was ordered against security for the taking up of knighthood before Ash Wednesday.)[1] Secondly, and also for the first time, socage tenants were specifically mentioned as being liable. As is clear from the individual exemptions which preceded the general order, the twenty-librate limit constituted a relaxation of liability which made the distraint more acceptable; by the writ of March 1242 holders of whole knight's fees were relieved correspondingly—they were not to incur the obligation unless they held twenty librates in demesne. Thirdly, the form taken by reiteration of the order in 1242 shows two main developments: first, the fact that the poor response so 'amazed' the king is perhaps the first indication that the whole scheme of compulsory knighthood was breaking down, and thus an anticipation at once of the remedial measures of the 1250's and 1260's, and of the conversion of the system into a source of revenue.[2] Secondly, the linking of knighthood to service in Gascony (in the writ of 19 May) demonstrates the military, and especially foreign military, objectives of the measure in these early days.[3] Finally, far from seeking money from fines *ne transfretet* and/or *ne fiat miles*, the king ordered the remission of such fines to those who had paid if they would join him in Gascony.[4]

It would seem that the failure to get an aid from the barons, together with the unreliability of French supporters, had driven the English monarchy into an unprecedented dependence on native troops, which neither the feudal nor household arm could satisfy.[5] A by-product of the new emphasis on knighthood was the beginning of definition and of limitation and an increase in the gifts of robes for knighting.

---

[1] *C.R. 1237–41*, p. 430.

[2] The Close rolls show a sharp increase in individual respites; ibid., pp. 429 f. But see next note.

[3] Ibid., pp. 465, 486.

[4] Ibid., pp. 496–9; cf. *Rôles Gascons*, i. 25.

[5] A consequence of the direct distraint of subtenants was the attempt to compile a roll of their names in preparation for a resumption of the order on Henry's return. *Rôles Gascons*, p. 219; *C.R. 1242–7*, p. 70, from 'Lancashire Lay Subsidies', p. 243, n. 3. The most extensive previous inquiry, that of Jan. 1241, had been into names of those owing knight service, *C.R. 1237–42*, p. 348. On the French allies, F. M. Powicke, *King Henry III and the Lord Edward* (Oxford, 1947), pp. 190 f.

The final overseas expedition of the reign, that of 1253, involved at least two writs for the distraint of the 'knightly' class, and probably an attempt at a third. The first, issued at the same time as other preparations for the assembling of men and ships,[1] was an order for distraint 'by lands and chattels' of all with twenty librates of land or a whole knight's fee worth twenty pounds a year, and not knights, to come to the king at Easter wherever he might be in England (or, for southern counties, to Winchester at Christmas), ready to become knights or pay fines for respite therefrom.[2] The chief innovation (possibly anticipated in 1245) was the order that all should be knighted at the royal court; in addition we may note the definition of distraint (cf. 1237, 1241) and the offer to receive fines in place of knighthood. This offer, now made for the first time, raises the question: were fines now the major concern of the king? To offset any such conclusion, it is to be remembered that there were two important motives for obtaining knights rather than fines. On the one hand, military needs were becoming urgent, for, beyond the requirements of Gascony (for which see the letter from Bordeaux cited by Matthew Paris), were arising tempting visions of Sicily. On the other hand, there was a grave shortage of knights for judicial purposes.[3]

Whatever the king's intentions, it seems clear from the events in the spring of 1253 that a more limited objective was necessary. At the Easter Great Council opposition was strong, and, probably as a result, the scheme was changed from distraint of knighthood to an order to serve militarily. Only tenants-in-chief with thirty librates of land held by military service were to be distrained to serve.[4] This seems to have done little to assuage the opposition.[5] For the time being, an increased volume of fines for respite of knighthood was the most gratifying yield of the writs of distraint, for if

---

[1] Among these preparations may be noted a Great Council of October 1252, when the opposition was outspoken, and a summons of partial service; see Mitchell, *Studies*, p. 253; *Chron. Maj.* v. 324–37; *C.R. 1251–3*, p. 240.

[2] *C.R. 1251–3*, pp. 430–1. My 'Distraint of Knighthood', p. 462.

[3] *Chron. Maj.* v. 378–9; *C.R. 1251–3*, pp. 442–3.

[4] *Chron. Maj.* v. 373–5; *C.R. 1251–3*, pp. 490–1.

[5] See the remarkable distraining writ issued after Henry reached Gascony, stating that many had defied the king's orders. Ibid., p. 502.

neither feudal nor general obligation produced men the burden fell on the treasury.[1]

It is possible that, in the early months of 1254, an attempt was made to enact a third measure which would enforce both knighthood and service on all who enjoyed certain revenues. This attempt arose from Henry's strenuous efforts to assemble a new force from England. One of the more curious aspects of this is that, although an alliance with Castile was a major feature of the diplomatic settlement, it was on the basis of a threatened attack from that quarter that Henry sought to renew his demands on his subjects.[2]

According to the annalist of Tewkesbury, these efforts included the distraint of all ten-librate landholders to become knights and to muster with the magnates on the Sunday after Easter.[3] Although this account cannot be accepted in its entirety, there are several considerations which point to an attempt having been made to renew distraint of knighthood. In the first place, there was a military summons of all the tenants-in-chief with twenty pounds of rents.[4] This followed, or took place at, a meeting of the Council wherein the *universitas* had refused to subscribe to even the half-hearted military aid offered by the great earls and barons.[5] It may be concluded that the king's letter to the regents, who presided over the Council, had suggested a very much wider distraint, and that the actual order issued was a modification of this in the face of opposition. This wider demand survived merely as a rumour picked up by the annalist of Tewkesbury and recalled at a later date by Matthew Paris.

Whether a revolutionary new distraint was attempted in January 1254 or not, the order issued in 1252 continued to

---

[1] Cf. S. K. Mitchell, *Studies*, p. 260.

[2] On the alliance, cf. F. M. Powicke, *Henry III*, pp. 232 f. In a letter of 24 March, the king of Castile was accused of using the treaty negotiations to cover up a treacherous arrangement with Henry's enemies; *C.P.R. 1247–8*, pp. 279–80.

[3] *Annals of Tewkesbury* in *Ann. Monastici*, i, p. 154; cf. my 'Distraint', pp. 462–4. Matthew Paris refers to a distraint of £10 landholders in 1256, *Chron. Maj.* v. 584.

[4] *C.R. 1253–4*, p. 112; cf. the returns in B.M. Cotton MS. Claud. II, fol. 17b, quoted in Vincent, 'Lancashire Lay Subsidies', p. 28.

[5] The sequence of events is important. Henry wanted 'aid', i.e. military or fiscal grants; some great lords offered military service apparently *cum toto posse suo*. The three basic accounts are in *Chron. Maj.* v. 423–5; ibid. vi. 282; and *Royal Letters*, ii. 101–2. The Council, though requested for 13 Jan., met on the 27th, but was delayed till the arrival of Henry's envoys.

be enforced. For the first time the articles of eyre took cognizance of the obligation of knighthood. One read:

De vicecomitibus et aliis ballivis domini regis, qui ceperunt redemptionem de vallettis tenentibus integrum feodum militis, vel viginti libratas terrae ne milites fierent ad mandatum domini regis, cum vicecomites et alii ballivi praeceptum domini regis inde habuerint speciale.[1]

The other read:

De valletis tenentibus integrum feodum militis vel viginti libratas terrae et plenae aetatis existentibus, militibus faciendis.[2]

These eyres may have begun in January 1254; they certainly were going on through the autumn and into the next year.[3] If they began in January, it is very hard to dissociate them from the Tewkesbury annalist's allegation. In any case, they show that the war had stimulated an inquiry into the working of the knighthood obligation, and that fines *ne milites fierent* had recently been exacted, perhaps, as in 1230, in conjunction with fines *ne transfretent*.

There had been one other overseas venture during the reign, the Brittany expedition of 1230. This, too, almost certainly involved a combined distraint of knighthood and summons to overseas service. Whatever the truth of this, it is clear that a large number of military tenants who had sat lightly to their arms obligations were under pressure to take up knighthood and to go overseas with the king. This may well have been the occasion when it was decided to equate two sergeants with one knight at the muster; a decision illuminated by the distinction made, in the post-embarkation issue of the Assize of Arms, between the arms of a knight and those of a sergeant. The fines paid for respite from knighthood and from overseas service were recorded, usually along with scutage payments, in the Pipe roll for that year. These fines varied in form. A typical 'three-in-one' fine was that of

---

[1] *Cart. Monast. S. Petri Glouc.* (R.S.), ii. 276; cf. the variants in *Ann. Burton,* in *Ann. Monast.* i. 331, and Bracton, *Notebook,* fol. 117 (cited Nichols, 'Obligatory Knighthood', p. 206). On these eyres, see H. M. Cam, *Studies,* pp. 88–109. The Burton annalist differs chiefly in the final phrase; instead of 'in spite of the king's order' [of distraint], it reads 'without the king's order' [of exemption].

[2] *Cart. Monast. S. Petri Glouc.,* ii. 278. The Burton annalist's list omits *vel . . . terrae.*

[3] *C.P.R. 1247–58,* pp. 373, 392, &c., in Cam, loc. cit. The January date is from Burton.

Robert de Borham, who paid 'ut quietus sit de transfretatione cum rege hoc vice et ne fiat miles et pro habendo scutagio'. Even more 'omnibus' was the fine of Nicholas of Oxehaye, who paid twenty marks for fine, scutage, respite of knighthood, and relief.[1] It may be concluded that in 1230 a decision to treat full knights as militarily superior to ordinary men-at-arms was made and that in consequence failure to become a knight was considered, along with failure to serve overseas, as a lapse in feudal obligation.

In addition to the orders for knighthood issued in connexion with these four overseas expeditions, there were a great number of less important writs. The measures of 1227, 1232, and 1234 were concerned only with tenants-in-chief, while those of 1232 and 1234 were further limited to those with whole knight's fees.[2] In two of the orders (1227 and 1234) there was a threat of forfeiture (the orders were *sicut tenementa sua diligunt*). That this threat was not idle is suggested by an order of 1232 for the sheriff to take into the king's hands the lands of Roger de Somery.[3] Two other orders, in 1227 and 1237, were concerned with the distraint of the tenants of a particular vassal to take up knighthood. In the former year the vassal was the earl of Aumale, in an order restoring to him his forfeited estates; in the latter year, it was the bishop of Hereford, whose lands were close to the area of the recent Welsh campaign.[4]

Most of the writs issued after the important innovation of 1242 were concerned with the twenty-pound landholders whether tenants-in-chief, military tenants, or not. Some, like those of 1244, 1245, and 1255, were clearly motivated, at least in part, by the Welsh or Scottish campaigns then being planned; an order of May 1262 may have been prompted by defence needs in the north.[5] The order of August 1254 is

---

[1] *Pipe Roll 14 Henry III*, ed. Chalfont Robinson (Princeton, 1927), pp. 52, 86, 131, 135, 136, 139, 172, 196, 230, 304, 309. The taking up of knighthood on the point of departure for, or entry on to, enemy territory was to become traditional, and may have had a long history already. See below, pp. 105, 171 n. 5.

[2] *Rot. Litt. Claus.* ii. 206 (1227); *C.R. 1231–4*, p. 152; *C.R. 1234–7*, p. 156; *Royal Letters*, i. 456; cf. F. M. Nichols, 'Obligatory Knighthood', pp. 203–4.

[3] T. Madox, *History of the Exchequer* (London, 1721), p. 354; C. Moor, *Knights of Edward I* (Harleian Society, no. lxxx), p. vi; cf. *C.R. 1231–4*, p. 247.

[4] *Rot. Litt. Claus.* ii. 172a; *C.R. 1234–7*, p. 575.

[5] *C.R. 1242–7*, pp. 242, 350, 354; *C.R. 1254–6*, p. 135; *C.R. 1261–4*, p. 125; cf.

noteworthy because 'distraint of knighthood' was then associated for the first time with the great ceremonial occasion of the knighting of the king's son; this and similar ends were served by the issue after 1250 of numerous respites of knighthood until the anticipated court knighting.[1]

The obvious profitableness of distraint of knighthood begins to make itself obvious at about the same time; in 1253 the offer of commutation first appeared in the body of the writ, and was repeated in 1256. Even for the latter order, however, we have the highly contemporary opinion of Matthew Paris that the objective of the writ was not purely financial, but in order to strengthen the knighthood of England (*ut Anglia, sicut Italia, militia roboraretur*).[2] Further evidence of the financial motive of the order lies in the greatly increased number of fines for respite or for exemption which appear on the rolls in this decade.

The reformers of 1258 were interested in stopping evasion by the wealthy of knighthood and its concomitant duties, and also in attacking shrieval extortion and royal exploitation. Hence they included such complaints in the articles of the 1258 inquiry and attacked the abuse in the Provisions of Westminster, but rescinded a royal order of June 1260 for compulsory knighthood, probably on the grounds that it was a fiscal measure.[3]

Such few orders as were issued at the end of the reign reflected the collapse of Henry's military ambitions as a result of the baronial revolt; they were sporadic, local, and conservative.[4] At this point one may ask what the orders for knighthood had in fact achieved? Perhaps the most direct source of information lies in the returns of 1256, which show that among the fifteen-pound military landholders only small numbers had failed to take up knighthood—about twenty to

F. M. Nichols, 'Obligatory Knighthood', pp. 206, 211, and R. F. Treharne, *The Baronial Plan of Reform* (Manchester, 1932), p. 282.

[1] *C.R. 1253–4*, p. 154 and *passim*; cf. also *C.R. 1251–3*, pp. 37, 191, 435, 443, 444 f. A writ of 26 Aug. 1251 had added nothing (*C.R. 1247–51*, p. 557).

[2] *C.R. 1254–6*, pp. 293, 418; P.R.O. C. 47. 1/1 m. 17; *Chron. Maj.* v. 589. Matthew, however, was not unaware of the fiscal motive; ibid. v. 560.

[3] R. F. Treharne, *Baronial Plan of Reform*, pp. 109, 171, 174, 237, 246.

[4] *C.R. 1261–4*, p. 125; *C.R. 1264–8*, p. 110; *C.P.R. 1266–72*, p. 260. The continuator of Florence of Worcester thought Henry had decided to rely on household forces; *Cont. Flor. Wigorn.* (E.H.S.), p. 194.

thirty per county; in 1297 there were slightly more esquires among the twenty-librate holders (military or otherwise) than there had been unknighted military tenants in 1256.[1] Moreover, it may be calculated from the two sets of returns that nearly four-fifths of those liable were in fact knights in 1256. Orders for distraint of knighthood may receive some credit for this state of affairs.

As the practice of compulsory knighthood grew old, many questions of procedure and limitation had to be settled by Chancery. The question of who should confer the order of knighthood was disposed of, at least temporarily, in the writ of May 1245 which stated that tenants-in-chief should receive the order from the king, and subtenants from whomsoever they wished. On the other hand, the definition of those who were liable required a large number of particular writs and did not receive any comprehensive treatment until the following reign.

As regards tenures, it has been noted that in 1242 the socage tenants were first included by name; later, however, individual exemptions were issued for lands held by royal sergeanty.[2] Likewise, writs of exemption were secured for land held as dowry of one's wife, and for lands impleaded in the royal courts. A sweeping concession in June or July 1245 exempted lands not held in demesne. Personal status or activity might also secure immunity; orders to this effect were issued with regard, among other things, to clerical status, sickness, minority, and military service.

It must have become evident, by the second half of Henry's reign, that the results of distraint of knighthood were bound to be limited. Fortunately, the government had not abandoned, but had rather developed, the use of the *jurati ad arma* as a source of both foot and mounted troops. Before turning to a consideration of this development, we must note an important innovation in connexion with the Scottish campaign of 1255. In that year, military summonses were served not only on tenants-in-chief, but also on 'other vavassors and

---

[1] P.R.O. C. 47. 1/1 mm. 1–35; for 1297, cf. F. Palgrave, *Parliamentary Writs and Writs of Military Summons* (Record Commission, 1830), i. 285 f.

[2] For this and the following points, cf. *C.R. 1237–42*, pp. 429, 432, 460; *C.R. 1242–7*, p. 356; *C.R. 1251–3*, p. 455; *C.R. 1253–4*, p. 124; *C.R. 1254–6*, p. 433.

knights who do not hold of the king'. The presence of the sheriffs of Yorkshire and Northumberland with Henry in Scotland suggests that they may have taken some of the men thus distrained with them.[1] At any rate, an important and dangerous precedent had been set. From now on the king's interest in the military service of his wealthier subjects was to extend well beyond household and feudal obligation.

[1] *C.R. 1254–6*, pp. 136, 218.

V

HENRY III AND THE *JURATI AD ARMA*

THE reign of Henry III brought changes in the military organization and obligation of the lower classes which were just as definitive as those effected among the feudal and knightly ranks. By the end of the reign a system of recruitment was created which Edward I was able to develop into a first-rate machine, though it must be admitted that here as elsewhere the promise of the reign was greater than its fulfilment.

In obligation the reign brought the definitions which were to outlast the Middle Ages in the terms of the Statute of Winchester; a duty, graded according to rents or chattels, to serve as man-at-arms, mounted spearman, archer, or common foot-soldier. In organization the use of special commissioners to take over the shrieval function of muster was initiated. In pay the 'constitutional' rule was devised of only requiring service outside the county on the condition of pay. As a result, the *piétaille*, who appear to have been falling out of use in most countries, were kept up to date in England; their pride as military men and their consequent political self-consciousness was ensured.

While the assumption of knightly arms was being encouraged in special orders for knighthood, the military equipment of the far more numerous lower classes was being prescribed along with their police duties. The strange feature about the reissues of the Assize of Arms and the (often combined) writs of watch and ward is that they said nothing about military organization. Like distraints of knighthood, they were concerned with the arms, not with the recruitment, of the classes concerned. Moreover, the concentration of these measures on watch and ward, hue and cry, and related matters tended in due course to divorce them from military realities. In the realm of recruitment and command, therefore, special arrangements in the form of commissioners, *custodes*, and leaders had to be made. However, an examination of the development of the arms assizes, along with the somewhat scanty record of infantry service, in Henry's reign shows that in several respects the legislation had important results.

The *jurati* enjoyed a notable secondary role in the civil wars or skirmishes of Henry III's minority. In 1217 men who were not tenants of those owing *servicium debitum* were called out with the feudal levies.[1] Then the *jurati* of neighbouring counties were in 1220 summoned, in a way reminiscent of the fyrd, to serve against Rockingham Castle.[2] Next year they were again out, this time from Westmorland, Yorkshire, and Lancashire to besiege the castles of Cockermouth, Skipsey, and Skipton-in-Craven; their summons so clearly defines their place in the military hierarchy as to deserve quoting: 'To the Sheriff. Summon the earls, barons, knights, free tenants and all who owe service and all *jurati ad arma* etc.'[3] The sheriff's presence and, presumably, command, was enjoined, but leadership of the force lay with certain appointed barons. The wording of this writ shows that the *libere tenentes* were regarded as a separate category between the *jurati* and the *milites*.

The first reissue of the Assize of Arms by Henry III, that of October 1223, followed his first, partial, coming of age, and the launching of his first 'foreign' war, that against Wales in the summer of 1223. It was undoubtedly prompted by the outbreak of revolt.[4] The writ concerning the *jurati* followed on 27 October, and merely ordered the administration of the oath as in the time of John.[5] The writ confirms what had probably been true of John's measure of 1205, that the *jurati* were to carry arms graded according to their

---

[1] Writ of 22 July, in *Dignity of a Peer*, iii. 2.
[2] *Royal Letters*, i. 56.
[3] *Rot. Litt. Claus.* i. 474b.
[4] F. M. Powicke, *Henry III*, pp. 58–59; K. Norgate, *The Minority of Henry III* (London, 1912), p. 197. The high point of the revolt, an attack on the Tower, is not easy to date; it occurred, however, during late October or November. The breakdown of negotiations with France and Louis VIII's declared intention to make good his claim to the English crown provided further reason for defensive measures.
[5] *Rot. Litt. Claus.*, i. 628b; A. B. White, *Self-Government at the King's Command* (Minneapolis, 1933), pp. 93–95.

wealth (goods and chattels)—presumably following the tariff of 1181.

In 1224 the second revolt of Fawkes de Bréauté was suppressed largely with the help of the *posse comitatus*. The sheriff of Devon's letter to the king shows that the ancient distinction between the king's army and the local *posse* was still effective.[1] The *jurati* were to be summoned by the sheriff 'from vill to vill with horn and hue'.[2] The towns appear to have been called out as part of the general feudal summons, in one case (Guildford) owing two *servientes* for twenty days.[3] Moreover, on the demesnes of neighbouring clergy, two men were to serve from each hide—a remarkable, and possibly the last, military use of the ancient form of assessment.[4]

Following the traditional Norman use of 'English' foot, the *jurati* were particularly valuable for coast defence. Hence, when a foreign expedition was being mounted, or when invasion was expected, they came into their own. In 1225 a writ of arms repeated in substance the measure of 1223, in ordering the defence of the Cinque Ports.[5] This measure was part of those preparations for Henry's first overseas venture, following the surrender and exile of Fawkes de Bréauté, which had probably also included the first known general distraint of knighthood. On occasions such as this special officers were appointed to guard the coasts and ports, who appear to have commanded all kinds of troops and even to have had charge of local shipping. These special wardens were forerunners of both commissioners of array and of naval commanders.[6] In the period 1217–30, the coasts of Norfolk,

---

[1] *Royal Letters*, i. 232.

[2] *Rot. Litt. Claus.* i. 632; W. A. Morris, *Medieval Sheriff*, p. 234 n.; for the sheriff of Shropshire, cf. Miss Cam, *Hundred and Hundred Rolls*, p. 190.

[3] *Rot. Litt. Claus.* i. 614–15, referred to in S. K. Mitchell, *Studies*, p. 149. The towns appear to have made 'proffers' of foot; the bailiffs of Bury St. Edmunds being ordered to have their promised fifty footmen ready; P.R.O. Ancient Correspondence, xxxii. 75, quoted by M. Lobel, *The Borough of Bury St. Edmunds* (Oxford, 1935), p. 75.

[4] *Annals of Dunstable*, in *Ann. Monast.* iii. 86; cf. the comment in Ralph Coggeshale (*Chronicon*, p. 206), where the levy is a general one. The writ in *Patent Rolls 1216–25*, pp. 464–5, on the other hand, merely asks for men from the demesnes; cf. Mitchell, *Studies*, loc. cit.

[5] *P.R. 1216–25*, p. 503; cf. ibid. 465, for the appointment of coast wardens.

[6] A. H. Noyes, *Military Obligation* (Columbus, Ohio, 1930), p. 18; F. W. Brooks, *The English Naval Forces 1199–1272* (London, 1933), pp. 168 f.

Suffolk, and Essex seem to have had a semi-permanent warden.[1]

The well-known writs of 30 April and 13 June 1230, although purportedly a repetition of those of John's reign, actually achieved a distinct advance in several ways.[2] The second writ was an elaboration by the regent of the first, which was a hasty royal order issued at the time of embarkation. They bridged the gap between the 1181 Assize, John's and the Minority period measures, and the definitive orders of 1242 and 1285. In the first place, by the writ of 13 June, commissioners were appointed in each shire to swear the population and assess them to arms; in this respect, it was the forerunner of those Commissions of array by which later the *jurati* were to be both arrayed and levied.[3] Secondly, this same writ contained the first 'tariff' of obligation since that of Henry II, with which a comparison is, therefore, worth attempting. It is to be noted, first, that the 1230 measure was much less concerned with the knightly and esquire class, though the provision that whole-fee holders were to have *lorica* (full hauberk) and half-fee holders *haubergellum* (half hauberk) respectively was important. This was the first official act to acknowledge what was to become common form in the muster rolls of the ensuing century; the equating, for feudal obligation, of two relatively lightly armed men-at-arms with one knight. This preoccupation with half fees was reflected in the summons of half- and whole-fee holders to muster at Hereford three years later.[4] Moreover, it gives more significance to the provision that fifteen-mark chattel owners were to have the full *lorica*, or knightly equipment, thereby being classed as whole-fee holders; the half-fee holder was equated with the ten-mark class.

It is in the lower categories, however, that an even more significant change is to be noted. In the 30 April writ the

---

[1] *P.R. 1216–25*, pp. 121, 469, 492; Richard Aiguillon's appointment was during the king's pleasure.

[2] *C.R. 1227–31*, pp. 395, 398–402; *Royal Letters*, i. 371–7. Cf. H. M. Cam, *The Hundred*, p. 189.

[3] Commissioners may have been appointed in 1205, or possibly *custodes pacis* on the lines of 1195. But we are entirely reliant on Gervase of Canterbury's choice of detail, of course, and this included neither tariff of arms nor addressees.

[4] *C.R. 1231–4*, p. 545.

unfree were included in the order for the first time, though
as is well known they had been exempted from taxation on
the arms to which they were sworn in 1225.[1] In the provisions of 3 June, the '*burgenses* and whole community of
freemen' of 1181 were divided into forty-shilling and twenty-
shilling chattel owners, the former to have iron cap, pourpoint (1181, gambeson), and lance of 1181, and the latter
'axe or lance'. These provisions prepared the way for a larger
use of the lower class in island wars in the ensuing decade.

A third feature of the writ was the provision for the
mobilization of the *jurati*. This did not advance on the 1205
writ except in simplicity; one constable for each vill outside
a city or borough, and several, according to size, in the latter,
being appointed to conduct the array. The chief constable-
ship of 1205 was abolished. The county commissioners took
over the job of enrolment, but leadership returned to the
sheriff.

The 1230 reissue of the Assize, with the new provisions
analysed above, had a discernible effect on the ensuing
armies, especially on those in Wales. In 1231 the *jurati* of
the border shires were summoned to a muster which was
cancelled in favour of the first example (other than for coast
defence) of a 'fractional' summons of their number. A third
of them were called out to serve in Wales with the arms to
which they were sworn, with food (*estover*) for forty days. In
some of the counties only axes (*secures*) were to be brought.
A special writ to the sheriff of Gloucester, however, was
based on the new provisions.[2] By this, all men sworn to iron
arms—i.e. to *lorica*, *hauberk*, and *pourpoint*—were to be sent
to the army. These were the arms which had been required,
in 1230, of those with over forty shillings of chattels. All the
men of the county sworn to *minuta arma*, on the other hand,
were to find victuals for forty days for 200 axemen from
their number. These were clearly the twenty-shilling chattel

---

1 *Select Charters*, p. 352.
2 *C.R. 1227–31*, p. 595; *Select Charters*, p. 355. Cf. *Const. Hist.* ii. 297; W. A.
Morris, *Medieval Sheriff*, p. 235; S. K. Mitchell, *Studies*, p. 195. Gloucestershire
was not enrolled as receiving the earlier writ, but this must have been an oversight.
Walker gives evidence for the service of Nottingham and Gloucester foot from the
Pipe roll and Memoranda roll (Pipe roll no. 76, m. 4; K.R.M.R., no. 12, m. 1, in
Welsh Wars, p. 284). [All MS. references are to P.R.O. unless otherwise stated.]

owners obligated to 'axe' and 'spear'. This principle that the inactive should support those who served was of ancient lineage. It was more fully developed in the Assize of Arms of 1253.

A writ of 4 August 1233, issued during the troubles over Richard Marshal, was also based on the 1230 Assize, while at the same time anticipating some features of that of 1242.[1] Although cancelled almost immediately, it is informative on the duties of the *jurati* during civil disturbance. As in 1231, most of the twenty-shilling class were not wanted; only those with *lorica*, *hauberk*, or *pourpoint* (i.e. the 10-mark, 5-mark, and 40-shilling classes) were to muster from certain hundreds at appointed strategic points. If these were unable to arrest passing armed *gentes* as they had been instructed, the rest were to join in a general hue and cry. The prominence of the 'hundred' is interesting in view of its absence from the provisions of 1230; it was, perhaps because of its proved utility, reinstated in 1242. Later in the year all footmen willing to serve were summoned to Hereford.[2]

In 1238 there was an unusual example of the co-operation of household, feudal, and communal forces in a police action covering several counties.[3] A writ to the justice of the forests on 24 August told him to assemble his foresters and verderers, and the sheriffs of Wiltshire, Gloucestershire, and Northamptonshire with the knights and 'liberis hominibus juratis ad arma cum armis suis' for the pursuit of bandits in the forests of Chippenham, Melksham, and Braden. In the meantime, Nicholas de Bolevill was being dispatched with ten of the household sergeants to search for them.

An extremely important writ was issued on 20 May 1242.[4] In the distraint of knighthood of the preceding December the twenty-librate obligation to knighthood had been established. Now, on 20 May, the tariff of *jurati* obligation was drastically revised, the age qualifications (15–60) established,

---

[1] *C.R. 1231–4*, p. 318. There had been a reissue of the Assize of Arms in May 1232 and a measure concerning watch and ward in 1233. The former stressed that the *jurati* were to find their own arms and necessities, while the choice of four watchmen in the latter may have inspired the idea of 'quota' service; ibid., pp. 60, 309–10, 317, 354; F. M. Powicke, *Henry III*, p. 127 and note.

[2] *C.R. 1231–4*, p. 542.   [3] *C.R. 1237–42*, pp. 144–5.

[4] Ibid., pp. 482–3.

and the 1233 police arrangements incorporated. This was the last major change before petrification set in with the Statute of Winchester.

The Assize of 1242 was truly revolutionary—even if only in the sense of recognizing a revolution—in some of its arms clauses. Now, for the first time, the two most important classes in English medieval warfare were officially recognized. The first class was that of mounted men-at-arms, the second that of archers. The former, now that the obligation of knights was receiving separate attention, were the highest group of militia. They were to be drawn from those with fifteen librates or sixty marks of chattels, whereas, by an order issued a few months earlier, the knights came from the twenty-librate group. The change was effected simply by adding horses to the equipment required of this group. That many had horses already may be deduced from the fact that the rudiments of knightly armour had long been prescribed for them;[1] in fact, the order of 1242 may have been designed to prevent a drift from the 'squirearchy', no less disturbing than the drift from knighthood, caused by the shortage and increasing cost of horses. As a result of the Assize of 1242 and its subsequent re-enactments, a reservoir was created from which could be drawn the sergeants of the contracted companies and the leaders of county foot.

Even more revolutionary was the recognition of the bow as the national weapon, and its association with that most important and seriously under-investigated class, the forty-shilling landholders. Whether this was yet the real long-bow may well be doubted. But that it was something on the evolutionary path from the Norman bow to that ultimate medieval weapon is almost certain. That Henry II had in 1180–1 prescribed the bow for his continental subjects but not for the English may seem to argue against attaching any special significance to its introduction into the 1242 order. It is more likely, however, that the measure was related to the growing menace of the weapon, reflected in the clause that forest-dwellers were to have bolts rather than arrows and in a growing volume of references in contemporary

[1] See, for important discussion, J. E. Morris, *Welsh Wars of Edward I*, pp. 50–53; C. Oman, *The Art of War*, i. 367–8.

sources to the use and misuse of bows.[1] Here, then, was the tactical complement to the men-at-arms; the reservoir from which could be drawn the county archers of Edwardian armies and the yeomen of the companies.

Between these two classes were those with rents of five and ten pounds per annum, and below were those with three to ten marks of chattels. The former, with their swords and knives, were not yet organized as the redoubtable skirmishing hobelars and horse archers of the next century. The latter, with their 'gisarmes', were forerunners of the pikemen and halberdiers of centuries to come.

One or two minor developments in the 1242 writ deserve mention. The drastic revision of the chattels assessment, so that chattels worth one mark were now equated with five shillings' rather than one pound's rent, must have corrected a serious weakness in the earlier assizes. In the organization of the *jurati*, also, there were significant minor changes. The cities and towns were put under their regular officials— mayors, reeves, and bailiffs; the hundred constable became a chief constable in place of the county officer of that name, with authority over constables of vills; the vacancy of the county command left the way open for the development of special commissioners of array, *custodes*, and captains. A new sense of the existence of a potential military force was reflected in the clause that no one was to call out the *jurati* unless specially deputed to the keeping of the peace.

Less than a year later there was a general inquiry into the operation of the Assize. We learn from it that the oath prescribed in 1242 had been administered by the sheriff in association with a panel of knights. These same knights were to search out deficiencies in arms, and to report these to the 'archbishop of York [Walter de Gray] and others of our council'.[2]

In 1244 the *jurati* were summoned for service in Wales. A writ of 10 July, cancelled three weeks later, ordered the

---

[1] Cf. the limitation on the use of archers by the monks of Holme Cultram, Cumberland, in 1235, and the inquiry into the possession of bows in 1253; *C.P.R. 1232–47*, p. 93; *C.R. 1251–3*, p. 47. See also, for killings by archery, *C.R. 1237–42*, p. 134. Brigandage by archers was known in Sussex in 1220; F. W. Maitland, *Select Pleas of the Crown* (Selden Society, vol. i, 1887), no. 189.

[2] *C.R. 1242–7*, p. 127.

sheriffs of Somerset and Devon to come in person and to bring all the 'jurati ad arma . . . de quocumque teneant'.[1] The foot of the Northern counties, however, were to be arrayed *cum arcubus et sagittis*, a clear consequence of the provision for bows and arrows in the 1242 Assize. For the 1245 Welsh campaign, on the other hand, the foot was supplied in the form of foot sergeants, summoned along with mounted sergeants, from Worcestershire.[2]

In 1253 the Assize was reissued with significant additions.[3] There were no changes in the scale-of-arms obligation. Hence the interpretation of Matthew Paris of the writ as 'distraint of knighthood' applies equally to 1242, except in so far as the provisions of 1253 were more stringently enforced.[4] In the writ, enforcement was entrusted to the sheriff and a justice with the aid of an assembly of free tenants and juries from vills and boroughs. In addition to stricter enforcement, there were further innovations. In the first place the 'light arms' (bows, arrows, and 'other light arms'—presumably axes and halberds; not *all* arms) of the watch were to be provided at the cost of each vill and kept for its use. This provision is momentous in supplying the first evidence of communal responsibility for arms.[5] Further, the writ introduced the infamous 'Savoyard' custom that the men of the town should give safe conduct to, and make good the losses of, merchants travelling through; though this provision had been anticipated in an order of 1251 enforcing collective liability for losses due to violent robbery when the robbers were not apprehended.[6] This measure seems to have provoked a good deal of resentment on the grounds that new and great changes in the law should not be introduced without the consent of 'the baronage'.[7] Although at one point Matthew Paris, who liberally paraphrases the measure and describes its reception, writes that 'the matter was delayed, or came to

---

[1] *C.R. 1242–7*, pp. 132, 256; *Close Rolls* (Supplementary), i, m. 1d (from Walker, *Welsh Wars*).

[2] *C.R. 1242–7*, p. 360. They were to receive wages from Chester.

[3] *C.R. 1251–3*, pp. 492–3.

[4] *Chron. Maj.* v. 368; *Flores. Hist.* ii. 382 3; *Hist. Angl.* 134–5.

[5] H. M. Cam, 'The Community of the Vill', in *Medieval Studies Presented to Rose Graham* (Oxford, 1952), p. 2, seems to over-estimate the extent of this responsibility.

[6] *C.R. 1247–51*, p. 540.   [7] *Chron. Maj.* v. 369.

nothing', he later describes the opposition of the knights of Shropshire both to 'having and shewing arms' and to the Savoy custom.[1] In general, it may be concluded first, that though the measure was probably ultimately withdrawn or allowed to lapse, it was not until an attempt at enforcement had been made; secondly, that the arms clause may well have been the more serious of the two occasions of protest. It was certainly the beginning of a new attitude to the duties of the local communities which culminated in the great schemes of Edward II's reign.

The use of county archers continued, though there is no evidence of the effect of the 1253 changes. For Wales, in 1257, a small force of archers was called out.[2] The following year archers were again required in the array against Scotland, the northern Marcher lords being ordered to serve with horses and arms and to bring 'a great number of footmen and of archers'.[3]

In spite of the influence of the writs of arms, the frequency and amount of *jurati* service seems to have declined since the opening years of the reign. However, a notable revival occurred in the civil-war period, thanks largely to Montfortian initiative.[4] The first measure was, however, royalist. In 1260 Kent was to provide an escort of archers for the returning king, if needed.[5] In the preparations for war of 1264, Simon planned to use a levy of four or five men from each vill, to be maintained out of special taxes.[6] At Lewes the Londoners supplied a wing of the rebel army, though their performance was lamentable. The coastal duties of the *jurati* are exemplified in writs of great importance arising from the invasion scare of the summer of 1264.

[1] *Chron. Maj.* v. 369 and 410–11. Why Shropshire? Possibly the influence of Richard de Clare is to be detected, while the absence of frankpledge in the region meant that the collective responsibilities enjoined thereby would be less known; R. Stewart-Brown, *The Sergeants of the Peace in Medieval England and Wales* (Manchester, 1936), chap. viii.

[2] *Cal. Lib. R. 1251–60*, p. 388.

[3] *C.R. 1256–9*, p. 292.

[4] Cf. H. M. Cam, *The Hundred and Hundred Rolls*, pp. 190–1 (stressing the role of the *custodes pacis*, e.g. at Northampton); W. A. Morris, *Sheriff*, pp. 236–7; W. Stubbs, *Const. Hist.* ii. 283.

[5] *C.R. 1259–61*, p. 283.

[6] *Foedera* (Rec. Comm.), i. 433; see F. M. Powicke, *Thirteenth Century*, p. 181, n. 3.

Two especially illuminating writs were issued on 8 July and 7 September 1264.[1] They demonstrate quite remarkably how the ordinances and writs of the past century could be utilized in an emergency to produce a new kind of force. On 9 July the whole community of the counties of Norfolk and Suffolk were ordered to be ready with horses and arms and their whole *posse* for defence of their region against foreign invasion. The *jurati* were to be warned to arm by the sheriffs and informed that their service was not to be a precedent. The sheriff was also to choose a levy from each vill based on population, some to be mounted and all to be armed with lances, bows and arrows, cross-bows, and axes. These, needless to say, were the weapons laid down in the latest writs of arms, those of 1242/53 (wherein the 'tariff' as we have seen, included horses, lances, and bows with arrows or bolts) and, in the case of the axe, of the 1230 writ. The forces were to be organized under an officer to be appointed by the justiciar and wardens, or keepers, of key ports;[2] also, it would appear, the bailiffs of the principal coastal towns were to have some authority. The people (commonalty) of Essex were similarly briefed with regard to the defence of Harwich.

The writ of 8 July, directed to the sheriff and whole community of the county, which included the clergy, barons, knights, and free men, of Cambridgeshire, ordered all knights and free tenants to come to London, the readying of all classes for defence, and choosing of the foot to serve along with the mounted troops.[3] The method of choosing the foot was specified: four, six, or eight of the best foot armed with lances, arrows, bows, swords, cross-bows, and axes were to be chosen from each vill (*villata*) with forty days' expenses provided *de communi*; the same was to be done from the counties,[4] and larger numbers were to be raised because of their greater

---

[1] *Foedera*, i. 444; *C.P.R. 1258–66*, pp. 360–1, 367–8.

[2] Cf. the writ of 7 Sept. to the 'keeper' of Orwell.

[3] *Foedera*, i. 444. The *custos pacis* was to assist in the array. The writ is inconsistent and clearly incorrect in its present state.

[4] Is it difficult to understand how forces could be raised from the 'county' as well as from the *villata* within it. Is it possible that the copy of the writ summarizes a longer provision which called for material support from the county as a whole, such as is revealed in the 7 Sept. writs (below)?

size from the *castri et burgi*, whence also horsed men were to be expected. From a writ of the following September, it appears that the *jurati* were, in the main, assigned to guarding the Norfolk coast. While the form of this array was clearly conditioned by the developments of the 1242 and 1253 Assizes of Arms with regard to arms and expenses, there were also echoes of earlier coastguard schemes and arrays for Wales, besides quite new features such as one might expect from Montfort. The spirit is one of radical traditionalism.

The writs of 7 September tell us more about the coast array. They were addressed to the sheriffs of Norfolk, Essex, Suffolk, Cambridgeshire, and Huntingdonshire. In them the 'king' wrote that he hears that the men appointed to coast defence proposed to return home as they had completed their forty days' service. They were to be ordered, on their fealty, to stay—the sheriff choosing some knights of the county to support him in this; however, if any were hampered by the cessation of expenses so far provided 'in common' they were to have money from the common expenses until 15 September. Any who had stayed home or deserted were to be distrained in their lands and goods. In Suffolk not only men of that county but also those of Cambridgeshire and Huntingdonshire (called for the defence of Orwell, &c.) were to be adjured and reassured likewise. The sheriffs of the last two counties were to send expenses 'as in times past'. The sheriff of Wiltshire was given similar instructions about his men at Portsmouth.

The principle embodied in these writs goes back to that of the Domesday custumals, whereby a selected force of the county was supported by the rest. In comparison with the previous summons of this type, that of 1231, the role of knights and boroughs and vills in relation to the county as a whole had become clearer. The methods of selection and the payment of maintenance had improved, both clearly building on the 1253 provision for the arming of four to six men in each vill at the expense of the whole, while the latter pointed towards the obvious, if unpopular, solution of a tax levied locally on the whole community: a sort of new scutage. For the second time forty days' service had been demanded, but it was too long since the first occasion, and the circumstances were too different, for this to have constituted a custom.

If the government could claim that the *jurati* service was normally on this basis, it would have won a great victory over the steadily hardening inertia of the subjects. But the actions of a revolutionary government in time of national emergency were exceptional in the highest degree. The distribution of responsibility between nation, county, and local authority remained a problem for the future.

The following years saw both 'traditional' and more radical use made of the *posse*. It was summoned from neighbouring counties to serve under the sheriffs in the siege of Kenilworth.[1] In the same year the constable of Bristol Castle had been given command over the forces of Bristol and of four hundreds in Somerset and Gloucestershire, the sheriffs of the latter counties being in support.[2] Whether any militia troops were retained to serve under Grey in the uniquely documented garrison of Nottingham Castle may be doubted. That force is significant as a landmark in the use of bowmen in a key role, along with knights and cross-bowmen.[3] Henry, however, did make use of militia archers.

When he wanted a picked force of archers to serve under the earl of Warenne, he made a fateful move. For the first time the county levy was to be paid from leaving the county, and what is more, the period of service was restricted to a month from the London muster. This was to be a precedent of the gravest kind.[4]

A concluding note on the relation of the *jurati* to the other branches of the army and to the civil administration may be worth attempting. Broadly speaking, all were united as royal instruments. Wardrobe and Exchequer shared the task of financing, while Chancery had general administrative responsibility. The sheriff was chiefly responsible for both feudal and non-feudal forces, but was liberally supported by

---

[1] W. Stubbs, *Const. Hist.* ii. 297; *Foedera*, i. 467. The summons was dated 26 Dec. 1265.

[2] H. M. Cam, *Hundred and Hundred Rolls*, p. 190. The local *posses* were frequently readied throughout these years of crisis: e.g. Dorsetshire, Lynn; *C.P.R. 1258–66*, pp. 420, 491; cf. Rishanger, *Chronica* (R.S.), pp. 44–45.

[3] *C.R. 1264–8*, 191.

[4] J. E. Morris, *Welsh Wars*, p. 33.

constables of castles and special wardens or *custodes*. The units in the field, judging by the terms of summons, were intended to be in tens and hundreds;[1] whether these units were commanded by vill and hundred constables and bailiffs except when hundreds operated as units, as in 1267, it is not possible to be certain. However, special commanders drawn from sergeants and knights were almost certainly appointed, as in the great scheme of 1296. Though a fragmentary pay-sheet of Welsh March troops (from the Forest of Dean, Coyty, Llanddarrog, &c.) shows the foot of those parts under mounted constables and *standardarii*, in irregular 'companies' varying from 13 to 180 in number, the muster must normally have provided ample opportunity for the organization of more uniform contingents.[2]

We may conclude, then, that in spite of military ineptitude on the part of the king and a comparative peacefulness in the outlook of the people, certain big strides were taken in the development of military obligation and service. A class of twenty-pound 'knights' and another of two-pound 'archers', as well as a category of fifteen-pound sergeants, mounted for travel, had emerged as the government's concept of how the free and noble should be arrayed. Here, as Morris observed of the army of Edward I, was the 'army reserve' of the future. Less developed as yet was the intermediate five- and ten-pound class, with their potential 'hobelar' and 'mounted archer' fame. At the bottom were the masses of stick-armed villeins fit for little but the hue and cry. The selection of the better troops by commissioners, and their pay by Exchequer and Wardrobe, could provide a force which, given adequate leadership, might most effectively support the household and feudal men-at-arms. All that was needed was a leader to use and develop it, and money—lots of money—to pay for it.

[1] A papal decree on the array of crusaders from vills, burghs, and cities ordered them to be placed in tens under captains; *C.R. 1254–6*, p. 221. The tithing group of the frankpledge system, wherein the oath to keep the peace was sworn, underpinned the whole, and made 'tens' a natural subdivision for defence service. Cf. W. A. Morris, *The Frankpledge System* (London, 1910), pp. 86 f.

[2] C. 47. 21/1. For tenurial constables and standard-bearers, see A. L. Poole, *Obligations of Society*, p. 72, and E. G. Kimball, *Sergeanty Tenure*, pp. 79 f.

VI

EDWARD I: FOUNDATIONS FOR
A NEW ARMY

BY providing popular chivalric leadership, by initiating
the successful co-operation of knights and archers in
battle, and by professionalizing the business of war
through his Wardrobe organization, Edward I effected what
amounted to a revolution in the English army and laid
the foundations for Creçy and Poitiers; a revolution no less
impressive because his father's ministers had provided the
essential ingredients.

The lines along which the Edwardian reorganization was
conducted had already been indicated in the previous
century; yet there was nothing inevitable in the process.
Edward's appreciation of chivalry and of the leadership of
the barons enabled him to win their support in all his earlier
wars, even while engaged in a vigorous recovery of royal
privileges. The transition to a paid feudalism combined with
professional and communal forces was possible because the
country approved of his policies and was willing to vote him
taxes and customs. A buoyant economy, in which increased
demesne farming and wool production figured largely, provided a background and base for his demands very different
from the famine-racked economy of his successor.

The army created by Edward was both the product and
the instrument of this new national self-consciousness. It was
but one of the achievements of a monarchy which had
gained a mature grasp of its powers and principles after the
struggles of the previous years; with it, the rulers of the
following two centuries were able to bid, though in vain, for
a united Britain and then for a union of Britain and France.

It is a commonplace that success abroad and harmonious
progress at home marked Edward's earlier years. The relations of the two branches of politics were manifold. Here we

must emphasize that the successful mobilization of the different classes of the nation behind the royal banner was at least as important a factor in victory as the emergence of new techniques in the assembling and use of the army. The army of Edward I achieved a balance between contractual, feudal, and communal troops which exceeded anything achieved before or after. The most striking development of the reign was the great extension of the use of pay, and, associated with it, the first extant military contracts.[1] This was not, of course, a sudden revolution, but rather the logical climax of a long development going back to the Anglo-Saxon huscarls;[2] at its heart was the fluctuating household force of knights and sergeants, put on a more permanent basis after 1291. Nor was pay and contract to oust obligatory service; for not only was a military nobility, rooted in the land, still needed for purposes of leadership, but also the element of contract was far too weak to obviate the need for an exercise, and even expansion, of feudal and communal duties. A study of the development of this twofold obligation shows that Edward was very far from abandoning it. The writs which expressed his intentions fall into three categories: feudal or quasi-feudal orders; writs organizing or arraying the *jurati ad arma*; and orders for the distraint of knighthood. It is from these expressions of intention that any study of the development and force of the military obligation under Edward I is bound to start.

The tactical developments of the reign required armies made up of men-at-arms and of archers. The close co-ordination of these forces in the field was ensured not only by that overall direction of the household to which Tout has drawn attention, but also by the fact that the principal classes which supplied them—the potential knights and the substantial peasant landholders—were also the backbone of

---

[1] J. E. Morris, *Welsh Wars*, *passim*; T. F. Tout, *Chapters in Administrative History* (Manchester, 1920), ii. 131 f., iv. 100–1, 413–14; N. B. Lewis, 'An Early Indenture of Military Service', *Bulletin of the Institute of Historical Research*, xiii (1935), 85–89; 'The English Forces in Flanders', *Studies in Mediaeval History Presented to F. M. Powicke* (Oxford, 1949), pp. 310–18; B. Lyon, *From Fief to Indenture*, pp. 188–9; the whole subject is surveyed helpfully in Sir F. M. Powicke, *The Thirteenth Century*, pp. 540–59.

[2] The development of contract is briefly surveyed in Chapter IX.

local administration and justice. The twenty-pound landholders who supplied the bulk of the men-at-arms had no
cause to despise their two-pound neighbours who shared in
the common tasks of local politics.[1]

I

Feudal summons

A distinguished student of military feudalism has written
that 'the feudal levy formed the nucleus of every army he
[Edward I] led into Wales or Scotland' and that 'the actual
value represented by the late thirteenth- or fourteenth-century *quota* was certainly not less than that of the full contingent of Norman or Angevin days'.[2] The new quotas were
firmly established by 1272. Perhaps the most striking feature
of the reduction which they represented is that it was dis-
tributed very unevenly; the greater lords secured a very
heavy reduction, the lesser very little. The aim, like that of
Richard in 1196, seemed to be that every tenant-in-chief
should bring a small retinue; this is confirmed by the levy of
very heavy fines for failure to serve. Many of the barons
served in addition as paid leaders of troops of horse which
were much larger than their feudal retinues; while the earls
continued for a while to stand on their dignity, refusing to
turn themselves into mercenaries.

For our purpose a feature of this new system which has
been somewhat obscured by Morris's concentration on the
pay records is of major importance. The armies, however
rewarded, continued to be made up, in the main, of men
obliged to serve by feudal or general duty; the chief supplement came from extensions of existing obligation. Put differently, there were strict limits within which contract could
operate at this time; there was either some other, antecedent,
tie between the parties, or at least the individuals concerned

---

[1] By the Statutes of Westminster II and the law *De illis qui debent poni in Juratis
et Assisis* (1293) only those with forty shillings per annum in rents were to be put
on assizes, juries, or recognitions. *Statutes of the Realm*, i. 89–90, 113; cf. *C.C.R.
1288–96*, p. 381. I am grateful to Mr. E. E. Rose of Toronto University for this
reference.

[2] H. M. Chew, *Ecclesiastical Tenants-in-Chief*, pp. 71, 73. On the new quotas, see
above, p. 65 f., and the references there cited; J. E. Morris, *Welsh Wars*, pp. 43–65,
fails to take into account the developments of Henry III's reign, and offers an unsatisfactory explanation for the reduction.

were bound to serve as a result of some more general duty.[1]
A key writ in this respect was that of 1298, with its postponements of 1299.[2] Here, undefined *bones gentz d'armes* were
summoned to serve at pay. In all probability they were the
feudal tenants-in-chief and rear vassals, those obliged to
knighthood, and the upper classes of the *jurati*. Thus, three
kinds of obligation were probably involved in what has been
called a 'household' force.[3] On other occasions all liable to
knighthood were summoned to serve at wages (e.g. in 1300
and 1301).[4] At other times, noted by Morris, those summoned feudally came into wages, and the feudal carried over
into the paid.[5]

The full or exclusive feudal summons was a rare thing in
Edward's reign, even though the practice of summoning
specific numbers ceased with the decisive victory of the new
servicium debitum.[6] Only in the first two Welsh wars (and in
1282, after protest) were there unadorned feudal summons.
For Gascony in 1294 a long roll of exemptions was attached
to the shrieval summons, personal summons going only to
fighting bannerets and barons.[7] In 1297, as is well known,
only the clergy, women, and minors were summoned with
their *s.d.* On 30 December 1299 the *s.d.* was demanded as
the situation was so serious (*in tam arduo casu*), but in addition
(following the precedent of 1256) the tenants were to bring
as many well-armed horses and men as possible. The order
of 7 November 1302 was for 'horses and arms and full *s.d.*',
but the same writ conveyed a request for a sufficient force of
armati for the realm's common utility. The last call-out of the
reign (5 April 1306) was for *servicium debitum*, but fines were
openly invited, moderation in the levy of these being enjoined.

The same, or similar lists of individuals were more

---

[1] Cf. Morris, op. cit., pp. 70–77.

[2] *Parl. Writs*, i. 317 (1), 322 (19), 324 (23). Unless otherwise stated, all writs cited
in the remainder of this chapter come from this source, and detailed references will
not be given.

[3] T. F. Tout, *Chapters in Administrative History*, ii. 138–9.

[4] Cf. my article, 'The General Obligation to Cavalry Service under Edward I',
Speculum, xxviii (1953), 829–30.

[5] e.g. in 1277; Morris, *Welsh Wars*, pp. 69 f., 120 f. [henceforward *Welsh Wars*].

[6] In November 1298 an individual was called out with twenty *equis coopertis*.
But this was the summons of a troop, not of a quota. For a valuable discussion, see
F. M. Powicke, *The Thirteenth Century*, pp. 554 f.   [7] Cf. *Welsh Wars*, p. 240.

frequently summoned (on fealty) to serve *decenciori et meliori modo quo poteritis, cum . . . decenti apparatu,* or *cum . . . toto posse.* As J. E. Morris has shown, many of these writs were 'affectionate requests' for service at pay, and those addressed were largely bannerets in command of paid troops.[1] The first and last summons of the Welsh war of 1282–3 were of this type.[2] So was the only one for 1287.[3] The Gascony summons of seven previously exempted lords in July 1294 was a request for service *prout statum vestrum decuerit.*

For the Welsh expedition which resulted, the writs of summons were even less feudal. The principal one was a request for personal attendance at a Worcester great council and for the dispatch of their men with barbed horses to the muster at Chester; a few lords were ordered to serve *cum toto posse.* The relief force of the following spring was made up of men-at-arms recruited from the forty-pound class.[4]

For the Scottish campaign of 1296 (Dunbar) those 'who owed service' were called out to serve with horses and arms as fitly as possible.[5] In one special case the order was to send 'some men' similarly arrayed. It is worth noting that unlike most previous uses of this formula the summons this time contained no hint of a request. On the other hand, pay seems to have been forthcoming, although it was not mentioned in the writ.[6] Here again, however, one must reserve judgement on the question of unrecorded unpaid service.

The summons of 1297, of course, contained every element: *servicium debitum* (from female tenants-in-chief and clergy), 'a helping hand with horses and arms' (from greater tenants-in-chief), and the order to twenty-librate landholders.[7] When renewed in the autumn, the summons was in the form of a

[1] *Welsh Wars,* pp. 74–80.

[2] Morris mistakenly calls the latter a 'feudal order'; it did not, indeed, specify wages, but it was even less of an order than the first writ, which contained the verb *mandamus. Welsh Wars,* p. 192.

[3] *decenti praemuniti;* cf. *Welsh Wars,* p. 210, who regards the campaign as marking a stage in feudal cavalry, there being no unpaid service, and the lords grouping for pay under earls and other leaders.

[4] Cf. *Welsh Wars,* pp. 261–2.

[5] B. Cotton, *Historia Anglicana* (R.S.), p. 308.

[6] *Welsh Wars,* pp. 273–4.

[7] The chief study is N. B. Lewis, 'The English Forces in Flanders', which should be read in conjunction with *Welsh Wars,* pp. 274–81.

request for service with horses and arms *personaliter*. It is impossible to calculate how much each kind of obligation contributed, or to balance the whole against the mere incentive of wages, but, as has been suggested in the case of the twenty-librate holders, there is a good case for the summons being something more than a formality.[1] Perhaps the best conclusion is that the order and request to serve increased the advantages of appearing, having one's horse valued, and getting oneself put on the Wardrobe pay roll, even if a few continued to respond without so doing, and even though another small number were now binding themselves by those contracts which made the summons almost a formality.

On several occasions between 1297 and the end of the reign, the shrieval summons of lesser tenants-in-chief was abandoned altogether in favour of the array of knights and *valetti* of the shires by sheriff or arrayer. A more detailed study of these occasions may be postponed for consideration with those distraints of knighthood and commissions of array which were their immediate antecedents.

For Scotland, after the defeat of Stirling Bridge, the summonses requested service with horses and arms *personaliter*, as has been noted. For the Falkirk campaign, service was ordered 'with horses and arms'; while for the winter of 1299, the writ went, 'nous vous prioms e . . . enjoignoms qe . . . soiez . . . as chevaus et armes le plus afforceement qe vous purrez . . .'. On the first of these occasions, the abbots were to send a *comitiva* with horses and arms.[2] The resultant forces of the winter of 1297–8 and of Falkirk were large and paid, but those of the winter of 1299–1300 do seem to have shown some results for Edward's persistent attempts to combine what was left of feudal with the revived national obligation.[3]

For Carlaverock (1300, summer campaign), for the 1303 campaign, and for the final effort of 1306, Edward turned back towards the *servicium debitum*, in his summons to individuals, though not in those to sheriffs.[4] Between times—

---

[1] 'The General Obligation', pp. 826–7. See below, p. 111.

[2] *Welsh Wars*, pp. 285–6; J. Bain, *Calendar of Documents Relating to Scotland*, ii, no. 1044; E. 101. 7/2.

[3] *Welsh Wars*, pp. 285–98; cf. my article, pp. 827–9.

[4] *Parl. Writs*, i. 327 (8), 366 (1), 374 (1); *Rot. Parl.*, ii. 191, 216; *Welsh Wars*, pp. 299–305; cf. *Le Siege de Karlaverock* (ed. N. H. Nicolas, London, 1828), ll. 3–7.

in 1301—the familiar request for service was made. The feudal writs of 1303 and of 1306 both went on to request additional service with as large troops of armed men and horses as possible, in the name of common utility; while the 'request' of 1301 was followed by the distraint of all knights with forty librates to serve in Scotland, of which more must be said when we turn to the service of this class. There are many signs of renewed vigour on the part of the crown towards the end of the reign, manifested not only in the calling out of the *servicium debitum*, but also in the distraint of knighthood, and the new determination to use the knightly class in Scottish warfare. The net effect of the reign, however, was a shift towards 'requested' paid service—though only rarely as yet is there evidence that pay was either contracted for or promised in advance.[1]

The co-ordination of household knights and sergeants, feudal levies, foreign mercenaries, and communal troops was improved as a result of pay, for now the Wardrobe, as principal administrative instrument in the field, was able to supervise the whole.[2] In the great 'books' of the Wardrobe which have survived from the last ten years of the reign, one can trace the payment of robes and fees to the nucleus of household troops; the taking into pay of retinues of lords,[3] of small groups of companions, and of men from shire and town; the valuation of horses, raising of supplies, engagement of auxiliary troops from tentmakers to artillerymen; in fact, the whole business of running the army. Prior to the muster, however, the Chancery and Exchequer took the leading part, the former in issuing summons and protections, the latter in paying arrayers and troops in transit.[4] To co-ordinate the efforts of all it became customary to appoint a 'receiver of moneys', or wartime paymaster.

The development of this organization would have in-

[1] A. E. Prince has suggested that service was contracted verbally; 'The Indenture System under Edward III', in *Essays in Honour of James Tait*, p. 285.

[2] T. F. Tout, *Chapters*, ii. 131–45.

[3] In wartime a large number of lords' retinues were added to the household list; i.e. presumably they received food and lodging as well as pay. This device, reflected [at a later date] in wage scales, hardly seems to justify their description as 'household troops'.

[4] The documents collected by H. Gough, *Scotland in 1298* (London, 1888), are mostly representative of the Exchequer and Chancery class.

creased the power of the king inordinately had there not been
a parallel growth in cohesiveness and regular political activity
on the part of the various 'communities' of the realm and of
the land. Moreover, money and organization could not con-
jure troops out of thin air. The need for a 'recruiting ground'
of armed and trained men outside the household was implicit in the whole system; it is to the distraints of knighthood and allied measures concerned with this problem and
to the use of compulsion over and above feudal levies that we
must now turn.

II

Hardly less significant than the triumph of the paid
retinue over the feudal quota were the moves made by
Edward to increase the available knights and men-at-arms.
These were, in part, what Morris calls the search for 'a good
recruiting ground' or 'reserve force'.[1] On the whole, the
Anglo-Saxon distinction between the horsed troops of the
well established and the foot of the commonalty continued,
and we may conveniently consider them separately. The
obligation to serve as a horse soldier was developed and enforced in three principal ways. First, the obligation to bear
the arms of a knight (*arma militaria*) continued to be imposed
on most tenants with a certain income; secondly, through
the Statute of Winchester, a rather larger class had to have the
arms of a *valettus*, *serviens*, or *scutiferus*; finally, towards the
end of the reign, the 'feudal' summons to sheriffs gave way
to the summons of all those liable to knighthood.

The obligation to knightly arms may have been degenerat-
ing in the last few years of Henry III's reign into a mere
question of status easily escaped by the payment of a
relatively light fine. It does not appear to have been enjoined
later than a local writ of 1268, and the attempts to reform the
practice by the Montfortians may have exhausted what interest there was in the measure. For Edward I, however,
with his military ambition and his interest in knightly tradition fostered by his crusading activities, the concept was far
from moribund.

The gap between knightly arms and those of ordinary

[1] *Welsh Wars*, pp. 72–74.

men-at-arms was now steadily increasing. Heavier and
more complicated armour, and therefore heavier horses, and
the ever-developing practices and rites of chivalry, such as
the assumption of coats of arms, raised a barrier between
the real knight and the ordinary man-at-arms. It has been
estimated that of 3,000 landholders of knightly wealth, there
were 1,500 actual knights and but 500 warriors.[1]

In his first measure concerning knighthood, Edward took
up, where Henry had laid it down, the task of stamping out
abuse. Unlike the articles of eyre of 1254, however, the
inquiries in the 1274 inquest were concerned with the king's
rights rather than the subjects' grievances.[2]

Qui summonuerint aliquos ut fierint milites et pro respectu habendo
ab eis lucra receperint, et quantum et quo tempore. Et si aliqui
magnates vel alii sine precepto Regis aliquos distrinxerint ad arma
suscipienda, et quo tempore.

A comparison with the articles of 1254 shows that the
question of bribery had now taken second place to that of
usurpation. Now, though there is no clear evidence, it is
fairly certain that in the twelfth century knightings by great
magnates were common enough.[3] The right of the lord to
confer knighthood had not disappeared under Henry III; it
had even received official sanction in orders for distraint of
knighthood issued by the king. But Edward was determined
to enforce royal monopoly. In this he was demonstrating, as
in the accompanying *quo warranto* inquiry, the overriding
claims of the crown. That successful prosecution of these
claims was at best short-lived appears from later evidence.
Moreover, such returns as are recorded to this inquiry
suggest that illegal exploitation of orders of distraint by
bailiffs of honours, hundred constables, and sheriffs, rather
than usurpation by lords, was probably the chief offence un-
covered.[4]

The equating of a knight's fee and twenty librates of

---

[1] See F. M. Powicke, *The Thirteenth Century*, pp. 549–52, and the useful references there cited; and N. Denholm-Young, 'Feudal Service in the Thirteenth
Century', *Collected Papers*.

[2] *Foedera*, i. 517 (*ex* Patent rolls). See, for Henry III's inquiry, p. 77.

[3] F. M. Nichols, 'Obligatory Knighthood', pp. 208–9.

[4] *Rotuli Hundredorum* (Rec. Comm.), i. 105, 114, &c.

socage land for the purpose of an aid by the Statute of Westminster I[1] raises the question whether socage land was to
incur the liability to knighthood, a question left in abeyance
by Henry III. The knighthood writs since 1256 had said
nothing about forms of tenure. In 1256 tenants not holding
by knight service had been exempted, but perhaps this may
have been an extraordinary concession in return for the extension of the order to fifteen-librate holders. However, individual exemptions since 1256 had tended to confine the
obligation to military tenants.

The first Welsh war occasioned the first order for distraint
of knighthood in Edward's reign. It was issued on 3 January
1277 and applied to the people of Gloucestershire: all those
with thirty librates or a whole-knight's fee of that value, who
ought to be knights and were not, were to receive knighthood from the king.[2] The purpose of the writ was undoubtedly to 'back up' the local operations under Mortimer, Lacy,
and others.[3] It was not until the war was over that a nation-
wide order went out, that of 26 June 1278, which, according
to Morris, was issued 'probably because of the needs arising'
from the war.[4] These needs were largely financial; but it is
unlikely that military considerations were absent. The writ
made no distinction between military and other tenures, nor
did it require that whole-knight's fees must be worth twenty
pounds to incur distraint. As in 1260, tenants-in-chief alone
were to receive knighthood from the king. Two knights of
each county were to be responsible, with the sheriff, for the
compilation and return of the nominal roll.

The issue of the order, and its vigorous prosecution, revived all those problems which had been quiescent since the
later years of Henry III's reign. Was knighthood to be
a superior class of militia (as Morris supposed) or was it to
be a slight enlargement, or redefinition, of the category of
military tenants? There had been intermittent 'legislation'
on the subject in past years, in the form of special exemptions.
Now the attempt to revive knighthood made a more general

---

[1] Cap. 36; in *Statutes of the Realm*, i. 35.
[2] *C.C.R., 1272–4*, p. 366.
[3] *Welsh Wars*, pp. 120 f.
[4] Ibid., p. 46; *Parl. Writs*, i. 214; cf. F. M. Nichols (giving 1277 as the date),
'Obligatory Knighthood', pp. 214–15.

statement of the law imperative. This took the form of the *Statutum de Militibus*, once erroneously attributed to 1 Edward II.[1] This concession, probably issued at either the Michaelmas or the Christmas assembly, laid down the exemptions and qualifications governing the obligation to knighthood. Total exemption was awarded to those who, as a result of being impleaded or of payment of debts to the Exchequer, had suffered a reduction of their annual revenue to less than twenty pounds. This was simple enough: there was no point in robbing the Exchequer of its dues. Also exempt were those under twenty-one years old (thereby associating the obligation to knighthood with military tenure rather than with the *jurati*),[2] sokemen on the privileged ancient demesne if tallageable, and burgage tenants. The plea of insufficient lands (to be made in Chancery) was to be met by a county inquisition taken by two knights. In two cases the rolls of chancery were to be searched and precedent followed. These were, first, where socage tenants of mesne manors claimed to owe no *forinsec* service (i.e. where the service discharged was entirely 'internal', not contributing to the service owed to the king by the lord); and secondly, where clerks held lay fees which would otherwise owe knight service. These last two clauses suggest very strongly that at least in 1278 the aim of 'obligation of knighthood' was the more efficient discharge of feudal service or its equivalent. The searching of the rolls would establish whether service was really incumbent on the fees in question. A further clause promised that new, aged, and infirm tenants would be fined reasonably, and in fact from 1292 writs customarily stated that, to carry liability to knighthood, land must be held 'in fee and heredity' for at least three years.

How definitive was the 'statute'? In the first place, it does not appear to have been referred to in those inquests and pleas concerning obligation to knighthood which figure first in the Sergeanty files,[3] and later in the Memoranda rolls, until the time of Edward III. Then under the third Edward,

---

[1] *S.R.* i. 229. See my 'General Obligation', pp. 818–19. Actually, F. M. Nichols had already redated the writ to 1278; op. cit., pp. 216–20.

[2] The tenant by knight service came of full age at twenty-one, the socage tenant at fifteen. *H.E.L.* ii. 438. The age limit of the *jurati*, following the rule for socagers, was at first fifteen, but later sixteen.   [3] E. 198.

on at least one occasion, a citizen of London successfully pleaded this 'Ordinance' as exempting him on the grounds of burgage tenure.[1] By this time the *concessio* had achieved status through its inclusion in the *Liber Horn*.[2] However, some of the confusion about liability seems to have been cleared up. There remained the problems of lands held in dower or by special tenures, and these occasionally obtained special licence. Thus, in 1280 'Gavelkind' tenure was declared exempt as the tenement was partible.[3] Sergeanty (if indeed tenure rather than office was involved) did not save king's sergeant Oliver de Ingham in 1281, though it had been accepted as a reason for exemption in Henry III's reign.[4] This was quite in accord with the *concessio*, but on the other hand an inquest declaring John de Garton's lands to be worth less than twenty pounds was not sufficient to exempt him without the king's 'special grace'.[5]

While Tiptoft and Bek were administering the discretionary part of the *concessio* in the spring of 1279[6] an order of enforcement went out on 12 March, whereby commissioners were appointed in each county to enforce the order by means of distraint and assessment of those liable and of their mainpernors. Returns have survived for Hertesmere in Suffolk, which indicate both the thoroughness of the inquest and the possible bearing of the 1278 *concessio*.[7] Thus of one Richard, rector of two churches, it was reported that he held twenty librates but that it was not known if he was in sacred orders or not. It is useful to know that of the seven individuals inquired into, two had taken up knighthood at Christmas, another two in January, an extent was needed of the estates of one who had been found to have twenty librates under a previous sheriff, one was perhaps in holy orders, and one was believed to have respite from the king. At this rate, over 50 per cent. were taking up knighthood in response to the

---

[1] Memoranda roll (K.R.), 16 Edward III, fol. 201.

[2] *Liber Horn*, Corporation of London Records Office, p. 76.

[3] *C.C.R. 1279–88*, p. 35.

[4] Ibid., p. 87. In 1279 he had been one of the commissioners for the enforcement of the distraint.

[5] *C.P.R. 1277–81*, p. 329.

[6] Cf. *Parl. Writs*, i. 218 f., for various respites.

[7] E. 198. 1/7.

order and the remainder were being accounted for. Even if the rest of the country did worse, the impact of the measure is seen to have been greater than previously thought. Furthermore, we know that heavy fines were exacted for respite— as much as five pounds for each year, as compared with the 'half mark into the Wardrobe' familiar in Henry III's reign.[1] Finally, as the case of Richard Brod shows, 'distraint' as used in the writs meant distress of chattels, and was enforced stringently enough to make it worth Richard's while to drive his livestock into the liberty of the Cinque Ports.[2]

The Welsh campaign of 1282–3 is notable for two developments; the 'distraint of war-horses' in 1282 and the summons of twenty-librate holders to a muster in 1283. The first is significant because it indicates that the new vigour with which distraint of knighthood was prosecuted arose from a need for *arma militaria*—especially the 'great horse' of the knight—rather than (as in Henry III's reign) the need for belted knights. In fact (at least for a time) the writs speak less often of *cingulum militare* and more of *arma militaria*. On 26 May each man with thirty librates of land was to have one 'great horse suitable for arms' together with suitable armour (*armaturis*) ready to serve with him in cases of emergency and as often as necessary. The cause and corollary were indicated in the ensuing writ of 22 June, when it was stated that owing to the great shortage of war-horses, and the consequent difficulty in supplying their *servicium debitum*, those who did not have such horses could compound for their service. Thus, by the relief of feudal and the strengthening of non-feudal obligation, a new kind of social contract was emerging.

Even more important was the summons of twenty-librate tenants—whether mesne or in chief—to military assemblies with military equipment, in preparation for the winter campaign.[3] This was the first time since 1256 that the mesne tenants had been called out as a class, and the first time ever that a given rental group had been so called. By it the traditions of 1230, that knighthood involved special obligations of foreign service, and of 1256, that the *libere tenentes* whether

---

[1] *Rot. Fin. 1272–1307*, p. 135; cf. *C.R. 1256–59*, pp. 72, 381.
[2] *Parl. Writs*, i. 217.   [3] Ibid. i. 10.

tenants-in-chief or not were bound to serve at the king's command, were united. As in 1256, the writ was stillborn, except that the four representatives of the counties granted an aid which fell on this class of twenty-pound tenants.[1] In fact, Northampton and York were such unlikely places for a muster, and the troops required so unsuited to the kind of campaign needed (at least, after Llewelyn's death), that it seems probable that the conversion of the obligation into cash had been in mind from the beginning. In any case, it is unlikely that the representatives themselves would have anything to do with a military levy of this kind, and a money subsidy was therefore the only alternative. In conclusion, we may observe that in this writ there was no reference to knighthood in any form. Service or subsidy were the things required.

In 1285 a well-known writ relaxed the obligation to knighthood on all with less than £100 per annum. This was on account of 'free and gratuitous' service given by the community 'in our expeditions in Wales'.[2] Some of the returns to the 1285 writ have survived, making it possible to weigh more accurately the extent of the concession. In Wiltshire seven lay landholders had £100 rents, compared with twenty-five with £40 in 1295 and the twenty-eight summoned in 1301.[3] This represented the utmost relaxation of military vigilance for many a long year.

A 1292 order brought a partial return to the normal level of obligation to knighthood.[4] As there were no military preparations in hand, this probably constituted a reassertion of the tendency, already noted in the later years of Henry III, to treat the measure as an almost exclusively fiscal device. The forty-librate level now established was, with one or two fluctuations, to become the standard until compulsory knighthood was abolished. Specifically, the writ ordered those with forty librates in fee and heredity, with three years' tenure, who ought to be knights and were not, to become knights by Christmas. The order seems to have been largely ignored,

---

[1] Ibid. i. 13 (14); cf. Stubbs, *Const. Hist.* ii. 119–20.

[2] Cf. *Welsh Wars*, p. 76.

[3] E. 198. 3/3, 6; *Parl. Writs*, i. 350. See below, p. 115.

[4] The writ was enrolled on the Parliament roll, a fact which may well help to explain why it became the traditional form; *Rot. Parl.* i. 79 (no. 7).

for eleven months later a general inquest into the lands of those who had failed to obey was ordered (the terminal date being advanced from the previous Christmas to New Year's Day), such lands being taken into the king's hand. The returns to this inquest have survived in a file of 113 membranes.[1] These returns not only contain the fullest extant information on the cavalry 'pool' available to Edward I, but also tell a great deal about the implementation of the writ.

On the latter subject, it is clear that the action of Edward's officials was vigorous. In Somerset and Dorset, for example, ten individuals were returned as not having taken up knighthood. Although seemingly good reasons—minority, absence, and insufficient land—were given, all their lands were taken into the king's hand until ordered otherwise.

The crisis years 1294–7 brought on a resumption of the 1282 type of writ, concerned not with knighthood, but with the distraint of the forty-librate or twenty-librate class to serve as cavalry. The first of these writs was the order of 10 February 1295 for the sheriffs to make inquiry into all with forty librates, knights or others; which done, they were to warn them to be ready with horses and arms 'to go on our service and to stay at our wages at our will' on three weeks' warning.[2] Service at wages was invited from those with less land, but with horses and arms. It is clear from a study of the current developments in Wales and Gascony that the order was prompted by the collapse of the existing feudal-contractual system under the strain of revolt and foreign war. As Morris writes: 'there is no question of compensating fines. The men were wanted.'[3] For some years the wealthier landholders had been obliged to become knights; on two occasions they had been summoned to a muster; now they could be more definitely drawn into the military system. In the last twelve years of Edward's reign they were to play a distinct part in the war-crowded scene.

In January 1296 the earl of Arundel, one of those appointed to lead the Gascon expedition, was ordered to compel

---

    [1] E. 198. 3/5.
    [2] *Parl. Writs*, i. 267; Bartholomew Cotton, *Historia Anglicana* (R.S.), p. 299.
    [3] *Welsh Wars*, pp. 77, 240 f. Evidence of one troop (Grey's) raised from these men is analysed by Morris, pp. 261–2.

those who had not yet provided themselves with horses and arms to do so. The forces thus readied must have strengthened Edward in both France and Scotland. Moreover, there is evidence that men raised in this way, especially on ecclesiastical lands, provided leadership of levies in the elaborate coast-defence schemes of that year.[1]

The climax of Edward's reign came, of course, in 1297. The demands on his military and fiscal resources reached a peak. But resistance to financial exactions and resentment on the part of his leading military subjects, the Marcher earls, constable, and marshal, all ran high.[2] In these circumstances, Edward ordered the muster at London of all with twenty librates with horses and arms, ready to cross overseas with the king's person.[3] As in 1295–6, no mention was made of knighthood; but neither were wages promised. The result, as might have been expected, was a coalition of this class under the already disgruntled earls, the production of the *Monstraunces*, and the winning of pay.[4] Both Cotton and 'Hemingburgh' emphasize the role of the twenty-librate class —who received summonses in lieu of, and comprehended, the lesser tenants-in-chief—at this stage of the proceedings.

The writ of summons was followed by an order for the return of the names of those with twenty librates; returns for thirteen counties survive, containing 713 names. Seventy-six of these received letters of protection.[5] Allowing that 2,000 twenty-pounders had been returned and ordered to serve in all counties (a figure somewhat less than Morris's 2,750 available cavalry), we may safely say that 200 of these figured among the 'protected'. Again, of the 76 protected twenty-pounders from 13 counties, 24 were paid leaders of

[1] Cotton, *Hist. Ang.*, p. 312; *Parl. Writs*, i. 268–75.

[2] Sir J. G. Edwards, '*Confirmatio Cartarum* and Baronial Grievances in 1297', *E.H.R.* viii (1943), 147–69; J. E. Morris, *Welsh Wars*, chap. vi and pp. 274–84.

[3] *Parl. Writs*, i. 281. Already, in November 1296, the Cheshire men with thirty librates had been distrained to knighthood; ibid., p. 280.

[4] Cotton, *Hist. Ang.*, p. 325; 'Hemingburgh', *Chronicon* (E.H.S.), ii. 122–4, now to be consulted as *The Chronicle of Walter of Guisborough*, ed. H. Rothwell (R.H.S., Camden Series, lxxxix, London, 1957), pp. 289 f.; B. Wilkinson, *Constitutional History*, chap. vi.

[5] *Welsh Wars*, p. 81, from *Parl. Writs*, i. 285–94. P.R.O. C. 67/12 (Supp. Pat. Roll 25, 26 Edward I).

troops in or out of the household.[1] This leaves a further 52 twenty-pounders for 13, or approximately 150 from all, counties. Presumably most of these must have figured among the paid retinues. Such computations as this are far from infallible, but they do enable us to reach two conclusions. First, the obligation to service as twenty-pounders was not totally ineffective. Over a hundred cavalry *may* have been added this way. Secondly, these men did not form a separate 'brigade'; they served as followers in unpaid troops, as paid householders, and as paid cavalry outside the household. They were a class of conscripts, not a formation.

What had made it possible to strengthen the cavalry with twenty-librate landholders was the grant of pay recorded by Cotton.[2] That the result fell short of what had been planned is evidenced by the inclusion of the twenty-pound landholders with the earls in the pardon for failure to cross to Flanders, in the *De tallagio non concedendo*. Although this document was probably a draft for the *Confirmatio Cartarum*, the pardon clause was not included in the latter. Instead, separate pardons were issued on 5 November in favour of the earls and 'all others who had neglected the royal summons or request'.[3] The net effect of all this was that Edward had received a sharp lesson in the need to pay any troops levied over and above feudal or other customary dues. The combination of overseas and domestic hostility had made him pause.

Edward, however, did not relax his ambitions, and the last ten years of his reign were expended in a series of very powerful expeditions into Scotland, launched in the teeth of continuing conflict over the charters and their appendixes.[4] In these Scottish wars the levy of a body of cavalry from the wealthy gentry of the counties was an increasing preoccupation.

In 1297 itself, after Stirling Bridge, Edward's regents

---

[1] B.M. Add. MS. 7965; E. 101. 6/19, 28, 36. I am grateful to Dr. N. B. Lewis for the loan of his tables compiled from these sources.

[2] *Hist. Ang.*, p. 327.

[3] *Register of Winchelsey* (Canterbury and York Society, 1925), pp. 207–9.

[4] *Welsh Wars*, chap. viii; J. Bain, *Calendar of Documents Concerning Scotland*, vol. i; H. Rothwell, 'Edward I and the Struggle for the Charters', in *Studies . . . Presented to F. M. Powicke*, pp. 319–32.

called out for service against the Scots the knights and *valetti* of three northern counties, who had already, along with many others, been arrayed for a muster in London. These knights and *valetti* can only have been the bulk of the twenty-pound householders who had stayed at home; this time, they were promised wages in the writs of summons. Taken in conjunction with the 'affectionate request' of a month later, addressed to over a hundred individual lords who were not in Flanders, this amounts to a partial repetition of the May 'scheme'.[1] Thus there remained a useful role for the general obligation at a time dominated by the great contract printed by Bain and the implied contracts of the horse inventories.[2]

The writs of summons for the Falkirk campaign, together with Cotton's comment, suggest that a highly diluted form of the May 1297 plan was being employed. Cotton writes, in a phrase used previously to describe the levy of May 1297, that the king caused to be summoned all those who owed service 'and those who did not'.[3] This must have referred to the third of the three writs addressed to individuals, of which the first was a simple request and the other two *mandamus rogantes*. The third writ was addressed to an unusually large number of individuals (156) in twenty-four counties. Most of them appear to have been the class of twenty-pound tenants-in-chief, but clearly some rear-vassals were included.[4] Perhaps the most serious justification of Cotton's description of the order, however, was the very large number (for a Scottish campaign) drawn from Suffolk, Norfolk, Essex, Kent, and Sussex.[5]

1 'Hemingburgh' antedates the scheme to the time before Stirling Bridge, stating how Edward assigned the whole 'militia' of Yorkshire to the earl of Warenne. The *populi*, or horse and foot of Carlisle who (he says) joined Surrey, on the other hand, were probably the Cumberland forces of the summer whom Clifford (not Percy) commanded; Walter of Guisborough (C.S.), pp. 297, 301; 'Hemingburgh', *Chronicon* (E.H.S.), pp. 131–2, 137; cf. *Parl. Writs*, i. 294 (24).

2 *Calendar*, ii. 1044; E. 101. 7/2; *Welsh Wars*, p. 285.

3 *Hist. Ang.*, p. 343. See my 'General Obligation', p. 828.

4 Of the thirty summoned from the eight counties for which the 1297 returns of twenty-pound landholders are extant, seventeen had been so returned. An example of a rear-vassal included in the summons is Walter de Urtiaco of Somerset (see *Parl. Writs*, i. 335 (19)).

5 e.g. there were thirty-one from Norfolk, but only two from Yorkshire. The northern element, with arms and seals, is usefully analysed by C. H. Hunter Blair, 'Northern Knights at Falkirk', *Archaeologia Aeliana*, 4th series, xxv (1947), 68–114.

The long-delayed follow-up to the Falkirk victory took place in the winter of 1299–1300. The measures leading up to it included the now familiar summons to the *libere tenentes* of the counties, this time in the form of a shrieval order for the summons of 'all good men-at-arms of sufficient wealth to serve at the king's wages'.[1] After several postponements, Edward ordered a muster at York on 12 November 1299.[2] Closely associated with the array of men-at-arms and foot in the counties of Nottinghamshire, Derbyshire, Yorkshire, and Northumberland was the assessment of all these persons to provide one barbed horse for every thirty librates.[3] This measure is remarkable for reintroducing the principle that it was not individuals holding land but rather the land itself which was to be assessed, i.e. lesser holdings were to be 'grouped' to form liable units. In this way the infantry class contributed to the cavalry assessment.

The army which assembled in December was thus the product of a large-scale application of the principles of May 1297, but at pay. It is hard to see, from the evidence of the Wardrobe book, that this was a huge contracted army, as Tout has argued; moreover, the great contract printed by Bain for 1298, and redated by Morris to 1297, cannot be put back to 1299.[4] A return to the principles of 1297 makes sense of the ensuing larger-scale desertions and complaints;[5] in fact, the writ against deserters issued on 14 January was specifically concerned with 'assessed men-at-arms' who had been summoned for 13 December.[6]

The revulsion from this enterprise is seen not only in the *Articuli super cartas* but in the character of the ensuing muster for the siege of Carlaverock. The lords were again

---

[1] In stating that this force was never mustered, Morris appears to overlook the series of postponements noted below (*Welsh Wars*, p. 297).

[2] *Parl. Writs*, i. 322–4.

[3] Ibid. i. 319 (9), 320 (16), 326 (5); *Cal. Chanc. Warrants*, i. 104: a warrant for an order to intercept the assembling troops and postpone the muster until 13 Dec.

[4] T. F. Tout, *Chapters in Administrative History*, ii. 138–9; *Liber Quotidianus Contrarotulatoris Garderobae* (Society of Antiquaries, 1787); cf. *Welsh Wars*, pp. 297–8, and my article 'General Obligation', p. 829.

[5] *Welsh Wars*, 298; *Parl. Writs*, i. 329 (12), 339 (22). On the Durham deserters and their connexion with the *Articuli super cartas*, see C. M. Fraser's article cited below, p. 131.

[6] *Parl. Writs*, i. 339 (22); *C.C.R. 1296–1302*, p. 379.

called out to serve with their *servicium debitum*.[1] Two weeks after these feudal writs, however, the forty-pound land-holders of all countries were 'requested and warned' (in the same language as the 1298–9 assessment to horses) to attend the same midsummer muster,[2] ready to serve at wages on pain of forfeiture. The opposition, now at its height, secured the grant of the *Articuli super cartas* in March, as its price for the grant of a twentieth. However, even before the *Articuli* were published, the array was reordered (on 11 April), the sheriffs being ordered to 'require and induce in all ways that seem best'. It would seem, according to Morris, that some of these men served in the cavalry force of that summer, in troops: e.g. Hugh of St. Philibert, the Oxfordshire arrayer, with five knights and twenty-one *valetti*;[3] others, according to the same source, served as *socii* from the various counties.

In 1301 Edward for the fifth and last time used a variant of the formula first essayed in 1295; a request for service from the feudal earls and barons, and a request for service at wages from 856 forty-pound landholders.[4] A previous writ had ordered the sheriffs to request the service of all the *equites* and *pedites* of the northern Marcher counties without mentioning wages.

This proved to be the last occasion on which Edward tried to get at his wealthier subjects in this particular way. At the end of 1302, it is true, he called for voluntary non-feudal service, appealing to those personally summoned to bring not only the *servicium debitum* (as ordered) but also a sufficient force of armed men for 'the common profit of the realm'. This appeal was, in fact, a return to the earlier tradition of calling for service *cum toto posse* over and above the *s.d.* A month later, in December, the special obligations of the Northern marchers were again evidenced in the offer of the Northumberland knights, sergeants, esquires, and burgesses to serve unpaid for eight days.

In 1306, following the revolt and coronation of Robert

---

[1] *Welsh Wars*, pp. 299–300; J. H. Ramsay, *The Dawn of the Constitution* (Oxford, 1908), p. 472, who states that proffers were made.

[2] *Parl. Writs*, i. 330 (15); J. Bain, *Calendar*, iv, nos. 1778, 1779; *Welsh Wars*, loc. cit.

[3] E. 101. 8/23; *Welsh Wars*, loc. cit.

[4] 'General Obligation', p. 830.

Bruce, Edward roused himself to a final effort. As in 1302–3 the *servicium debitum* was ordered from both individuals and counties, and moderate fines were promised. A fragmentary muster roll shows that at least some feudal service was forthcoming. But the outstanding measure, of course, was the mass knighting which set the expedition off in a chivalric aura as yet unparalleled in England.[1] Perhaps Edward recalled his own knighting at Burgos in 1254, when all with sixty librates had been ordered, and those with less had been invited, to share in the great ceremony. At any rate, an invitation did go out, to the effect that all who were not knights and wished to be should come to London at Whitsuntide to receive the necessary equipment for the ceremony from the Wardrobe, so as to receive *arma militaria* that day. This was not an offer of arms, but of those *necessaria* which it had been the frequent practice of Henry III, and the dwindling one of Edward I, to provide for household and other *valetti* on the occasion of their being knighted. The 'Monk of Westminster' states that this grant applied to such 'as were bound in succession to their fathers to become knights, and had means whereby they could perform the duties of a knight'; even more important, he states that it was 'ad augmentandum ... profectionem suam in Scotiam.'[2] The only writs for the expedition had been for *servicium debitum*, and the 'desertions' of leading military barons were shockingly numerous.[3] But the stout Aymer de Valence was also ordered to call out *the men* of the north.[4] The final impression of the reign is of a return to conservatism, a deliberate revival of both knight service and of knighthood.

The levy of men-at-arms, and occasionally (as in September 1297) of knights, by commissioners of array affords a bridge between the system of compulsory knighthood and the *jurati ad arma*. Such levies began for the war of 1287 in the counties of Wales, the Marches, and Chester. In the Scottish campaigns of 1298–1300 they were raised from northern Eng-

---

[1] H. Johnstone, *Edward of Carnarvon* (Manchester, 1946), pp. 106–7; N. Denholm Young, 'Feudal Society', in *Collected Papers*, pp. 65–66.

[2] *Flores Historiarum* (R.S.), iii. 131; northern candidates could go to Carlisle, *Northern Registers* (R.S.), p. 181.

[3] *Parl. Writs*, i. 378 (24).

[4] Bain, *Cal. Doc. Scot.* ii. 471, 472.

land. An entry in the Memoranda roll for 1298 shows that they served on similar terms to the foot.[1]

Conclusion

Edward left unsolved the question whether the monarchy could replace the largely abandoned feudal recruiting ground with a new form of obligation. The attempt had been made to combine such a shift with a form of hidden taxation, whereby troops levied on the basis of rents would serve at the cost of either themselves or their counties; this had been decisively rejected.

In the meantime, a new form of staffing and of contracting for companies of horse had been evolved. One of the most intriguing problems for a future monarch would inevitably be that of striking a reasonable balance between compulsion and contract in the levy of knights and men-at-arms.

[1] The *Ordinacio solucionis vadiorum equitum* printed by H. Gough, *Falkirk*, pp. 64–66. The *Ordinacio* distinguishes between the 'contracted' horsemen and the *electi*; it is with the latter that we are concerned. The specific ruling involved was that, like chosen *foot*, they were to receive no wages while within their own county borders.

VII

EDWARD I AND COMMISSIONS OF ARRAY

THE revolution by which foot troops came to share the place of honour with cavalry was the work of Edward I. That the English tradition lent itself to these changes should not detract from the importance of the king's innovations. Although the household, as well as foreign crossbowmen, increased in importance in his reign, it was above all from the shires and hundreds and vills that the bowmen of England were drawn. These local communities supplied defence forces and auxiliary field troops, among which the archers came to predominate. The question of the terms of their service was henceforward almost as important as the terms of taxation, though open conflict, except in the guise of compulsion and desertion, was postponed yet a while.

Edward also introduced the systematic use of commissioners of array for the assembling of selected communal troops under his standard. His practices in this regard have been declared 'constitutional' by the watchful Stubbs, while the organization and performance of service has been analysed by J. E. Morris.[1] It has not perhaps been adequately realized that in his over-mastering desire to achieve military victories, Edward took little care to insist on his rights as king to the unpaid service of his subjects. The duty of foreign service at local cost has been exemplified from the previous century and a half. In the distribution of cost between king, community, and individual, Edward paid more attention to the effectuality than to the legality of his measures; but this tipped the balance in favour of the subjects, not of the king. He left it to his successors, from Edward II to the Stuarts, to attempt to recover royal rights so unconcernedly abandoned by himself.

[1] W. Stubbs, *Constitutional History*, ii. 297, 569 (though commissions of array were somehow unconstitutional in themselves, it would appear); J. E. Morris, *Welsh Wars, passim*; cf. also A. H. Noyes, *Military Obligation*, pp. 22–31. I am indebted to Professor A. Z. Freeman of Allegheny College for much help with this chapter.

As with all military matters, the first Welsh war prompted the initial action on the duties of the *jurati*. On 12 July 1277 the sheriffs were enjoined to swear all men to arms for keeping of the peace.[1] An interesting innovation was the appointment (or election) of a 'good man' in full county, who was not liable to go to Wales, to attend to this. The preamble shows that the measure was prompted by fear not of Welsh incursions, but of the opportunity presented to criminal elements by the absence of the royal forces in Wales.

There was no revision of the obligations of the *jurati* until the Statute of Winchester (1285) and, far more seriously, no formal revision was attempted thereafter.[2] Thus the peasants in 1381 could appeal to it in much the same way as Anglo-Norman rebels had appealed to the laws of Edward the Confessor.[3] This permanence of the Statute was particularly unfortunate as it was for the most part a mere revision of the 1242 and 1253 writs of arms, and was manifestly concerned with police duties, not war. Moreover, it was issued at a time of relaxation, midway between Welsh revolts, when the census of knighthood was raised to £100. Such few changes as the enactment of 1285 made in the arms requirements may be briefly noted. For the fifteen-pounds rental class the *lorica* gave place to the hauberk, a term less rigid in specifications.[4] The spear was no longer required from those with five pounds rent. A new group, those with less than twenty marks, were to have swords, knives, and lesser weapons. The bow and arrow received no enhanced recognition. There is no means of telling whether it was indeed the long-bow which the Statute enjoined; perhaps this is natural, as that weapon was probably not yet universally known. It is extremely likely, however, that the long-bow was already widely used, and therefore probably encouraged, among the *jurati*. In fact, it was never to receive legal recognition in the terminology of

1 *C.P.R. 1272–81*, p. 218.

2 *S.R.* i. 96–98; in *S.C.*, pp. 464–9.

3 This interpretation has been questioned, and it has been suggested that Wat Tyler wanted the borough customs of Winchester, one of which was the substitution of mutilation for hanging as the murder penalty, to be made universal.

4 The same obligation was imposed on men with forty marks worth of chattels, as compared with sixty in 1242. There was a similar adjustment in the other rental equivalents. This represented a compromise between 1242 and the 1181 equations of rent and chattel values.

the writs of arms (*arcs, setes* serving for both old and new
types of bow and arrow).[1] It is surprising that the 1253 innovation enjoining the keeping of bows and arrows and other
light arms at the cost of the vill was not repeated.[2] Thus the
one possible contribution of the Statute to the military muster
was dropped.

The Statute's regulation of the view of arms and for
enforcement was more original. The view of arms was now
entrusted to two constables in each hundred, these to be
responsible to the 'justices', who in turn were to present defaulters to the king in parliament.[3] Less than two years later,
commissioners, who were to be men of substance in the
county of their office, were appointed to supervise the working of the Statute and to deal with complaints.[4] In 1293 the
sheriffs were to see that the Statute was proclaimed and
observed; whether this meant that they now became responsible for the work entrusted to the two commissioners in 1287
is not clear.[5]

The reference to the Statute in a clause of the *Articuli super
cartas* shows how far it was regarded as simply a police
measure.[6] This clause enjoined that the Statute should be
kept as strictly as the two great Charters, in order to check
the increase in crime; not, as one might have expected in
view of the steady increase in military obligation at all levels
for the Scottish wars, in order to prevent infringements of
the Statute itself. Three knights with the position of justices
were to be assigned in each county to redress contraventions
of the Charters *and* to ensure the observation of the Statute.[7]
The rules for public reading of the Statute, enjoined in the
Articuli, were elaborated in a writ of 16 June 1306, when the

[1] It was not until Edward III's reign that writs of summons occasionally recognized the distinction.

[2] Although not included in the Statute of Winchester, there is evidence that this
clause remained operative, at least as regards military supply. Below, p. 130.

[3] It may be remarked here that the responsibility of the towns for the compensa-
tion of losses from robbers, &c., was now extended to the *pays*, defined for this purpose as the hundred (clause II).

[4] *C.P.R. 1281–92*, p. 264; *Parl. Writs*, i. 388 (24). A commissioner was replaced
within three weeks because he had insufficient lands in the county to support the
office; ibid. i. 390 (25).

[5] *C.C.R. 1288–96*, p. 330.

[6] *S.R.* i. 140 (clause XVII).

[7] *Parl. Writs*, i. 398–9 (43), for the writs of appointment.

emphasis was again, as in 1277, on the keeping of peace while Edward was out of the country with his army.[1]

When we turn from legislation for the *jurati* to their employment in war, it is primarily with the development of Commissions of Array that we must be concerned. The foundation of this system, like that of indentured retinues, was firmly laid in Edward's Welsh wars, though its beginnings are almost as old as the *jurati* themselves. The supplementing of the sheriff by special arrayers to handle military affairs goes back at least to the chief constables of 1205. From thence it developed in two channels: through special *custodes* in maritime or marcher districts, and through special arrayers or commissioners. As the former were normally commanders more than arrayers, with powers of array only occasionally bestowed, they must take second place to the commissioners of array in any account of the subject. While both had been used in Henry III's reign, the employment of *custodes* had, with the famous defence measures of Simon de Montfort in 1264, been more fully developed.

It was in Edward I's reign that the secret of combining dismounted men-at-arms with archers was first discovered. The importance of the foot levies in English armies, already greater in England than on the Continent, was thereby greatly enhanced. We know from the pay sheets that the organization of the foot in millenaries, centenaries, and vintenaries, their regular pay in the field, their equipment with rough uniforms, and the increasing emphasis on archers were all developed in the Welsh wars of the first decades of Edward's reign.[2] The Wardrobe books of the reign enable us to see how the whole force—household, feudal, contractual, conscripted—was, once in the field, brought under one overall organization.[3]

As Morris has shown, the great majority of those serving, even in the Welsh wars, were Marcher and Welsh foot.[4]

---

[1] *C.C.R. 1302–7*, p. 397. The three writs for the proclamation of the Assize or Statute in 1277, 1287, and 1306 were all prompted by Edward's absence.

[2] *Welsh Wars*, pp. 92–105, gives the best summary of these developments. On the tactical developments, see ibid., pp. 182–3, 255–8. For corrections see F. M. Powicke, *The Thirteenth Century*, chap. ix and the references there cited.

[3] T. F. Tout, *Chapters*, ii. 131.

[4] *Welsh Wars*, pp. 92–99.

Their great contribution was the long-bow, perhaps already adopted or developed separately by the English of Macclesfield and Sherwood, but not yet (it would seem) in general English use.[1] It seems likely that most of the Welsh, at least the levies of Morgan and Gwent, were armed with this weapon. Their terms of service were that they fought unpaid in strictly defensive war—defined as within their county or march—but came into pay immediately on crossing into 'foreign' territory. An exception was that they received pay for certain major local campaigns after three days' service. They served, as a rule, for short periods and in relays.

The English levies were selected from the *jurati* and from the counties near to the scene of action. The extent of these was confined, in the Welsh wars, to the central midlands; but there was a rapid expansion in the Scottish wars. Inevitably, the northern counties played a major role in the supplying of forces for the latter wars, but they seem to have been slow to mature into really reliable auxiliaries; and expeditions were often still dominated by the seasoned troops from Wales (e.g. Falkirk, Flanders).[2] The only time that it was proposed to use English foot from the southern counties (including east midlands) on a large scale was for the (stillborn) French expedition of 1295/6, when many cross-bowmen and archers were to be arrayed.[3] However, the renewal of war in Scotland forced Edward to be content with a much less ambitious force. Occasionally southern counties supplied isolated contingents in Wales or Scotland.[4]

The towns continued to contribute small quotas to the armies. Many such quotas are doubtless hidden with those of the vills in the county levies.[5] Winchester, Bristol, and Gloucester were required to supply fifty or sixty cross-bowmen for a Chester muster, possibly in 1277, to receive pay on arrival.[6] London's main contribution seems to have been to

[1] It was in more general use, however, than Morris thought; in Henry III's reign there are many indications of its spreading popularity.

[2] On Falkirk, see H. Gough, *Falkirk* (1888), and Morris, *Welsh Wars*, pp. 286 f. On Flanders, N. B. Lewis, 'The English Forces in Flanders'.

[3] *Parl. Writs*, i. 270 (15), for writs of 3 Oct. 1295.

[4] See *Welsh Wars*, p. 93.

[5] This comes to light in Edward III's reign, when the ratio of urban to rural levies became a matter of negotiation.

[6] C. 47. 2/2 m. 14.

the coast-defence plans of 1295–6,[1] though in 1287 she had fifty-two foot cross-bowmen at Hereford on 27 July, where they were shortly joined by a smaller contingent from Bristol.[2]

The writs of summons can tell us the terms on which service was required. In conjunction with the pay sheets, they can also tell us about the actual practice regarding pay, duration, and organization. On the subject of arms, however, the writs are strangely silent. Although the Statute of Winchester was issued between the second and third Welsh wars, it added little to the duties of the *jurati*, and was rarely referred to in commissions of array. Nevertheless, its broad categories of foot archers, foot men-at-arms, and horsed men-at-arms were those in demand. It is curious that, for this reign, the phrase, later a commonplace, 'armed according to his estate [*status*]' was not widely used. However, in the great levy of southern county foot for service in France, issued in October 1295, the arrayers were to choose only archers and cross-bowmen. The scheme required such large numbers that if pressed it would surely have been as intolerable to the two-pounds class as that of 1297 was to the twenty-pounds squirearchy. A writ of 1297 merely required that the levies should be 'fencible and vigorous', though the more common formula was 'strong foot' or 'stronger armed men' or 'stronger foot more skilled in arms', &c. None of these phrases, of course, informs us which weapons were required. It is, therefore, mainly from the pay sheets that it is possible to deduce the substitution of archers for spearmen,[3] a development which meant that the two-pound class was in point of fact coming to bear the main burden of service.

There does not appear to have been any continuation of the tradition, which Edward II and III were to seek to revive, of unpaid service for a given period of time. The first recorded offer of pay from the point of leaving one's county had been made in 1257, and was shortly to become normal. This is the more remarkable in view of the tradition since

---

[1] H. T. Riley, *Memorials of London* (London, 1868), pp. 31–33.

[2] E. 101. 4/17 (William Pedewardyn's particulars); cf. Morris, *Welsh Wars*, p. 208. The Bristol men joined at Cowbridge. One list also refers to forty men from Gloucester.

[3] Ibid., p. 160 and *passim*.

Anglo-Saxon times, recently exemplified in 1230 and 1264, of service at the expense of the county. There was, it is true, the Welsh tradition of three days' unpaid service outside one's county.[1] But, service in the field apart, it is clear enough that some expenses did devolve on either the individuals or the local communities. From the writs themselves we learn that wages were at first to be paid from the place of muster or assembly: in 1287 they were to begin at Monmouth, Brecknock, and presumably Lampeter; in 1297, for Welsh troops serving overseas, at White Monastery, Llandaff, Hereford, and Usk, and so on.[2] The pay sheets examined by Morris seem to confirm this picture. In 1287, for example, the foot summoned from Derbyshire and Nottinghamshire, London and Bristol, did not come into pay until they reached Hereford;[3] others began at Dryslwyn and other places in the campaign.[4] There were no special payments for the period of assembly and march to these points, though such payments were made for the return journey.[5] Who bore the cost of these preliminaries? There were four broad possibilities: the men themselves; the counties or lesser communities from which they came; the crown, either by allowing deductions from the sheriffs' accounts or by sending special paymasters; and finally, the arrayers and officials who were in danger of heavy penalties if they did not produce the men at the place appointed. The central government's contribution, it should be pointed out, might take the disguised form of free food and lodging *en route*; pay is not to be regarded as 'take home wages' but as a means of subsistence, the household acting as 'stores' where possible.[6] Moreover, the sheriff might make a special contract for the pay of levies from county to muster, as Roger Springhouse of Shropshire did in May 1283.[7]

---

1 *Welsh Wars*, pp. 165, 204. Cf. ibid., pp. 160 f., 244 f., 301 for other campaigns.

2 *Parl. Writs*, i. 252 (3), 283-4, 294-5.

3 E. 101. 4/17; *Welsh Wars*, p. 208; however, the Derbyshire and Nottinghamshire troops received pay at Hereford for three preceding days—which may have been 'travel' time—on 24 July.

4 Ibid., p. 213.   5 Ibid.

6 In Edward III's reign pay was decreased as troops crossed into enemy country, where they were permitted to forage; A. E. Prince, 'The Army and Navy', in *The English Government at Work*, vol. i (Mediaeval Academy of America: Cambridge, Massachusetts, 1940).

7 J. G. Edwards (ed.), *Littere Wallie*, no. 330.

This burden of the cost to the muster was sufficient for remedial measures to become necessary, and these took the form of sending pay clerks to meet the incoming troops well before they reached the muster. In 1297, as has been noted, the Welsh were to receive pay from *Welsh* muster points, not from Winchelsea or overseas. In October 1297 the arrayers for Scotland in North Wales and Cheshire were informed that wages were being sent, by implication to some point before the Newcastle muster; the same assurance was not, however, given to the north English foot. In 1298 the arrayers of the Welsh, Lancashire, and Cheshire men for the Falkirk campaign were informed that clerks had been assigned to pay wages until the troops arrived at Carlisle; Gough gives the details of these pay arrangements from the Memoranda rolls.[1]

This system was extended to the northern English counties in September 1299 for the ensuing winter muster. Writs of 14 and 17 January 1300 suggest that the demarcation was then between county and muster, the vill or borough supporting the militia to the county border, after which the king's clerk took over.[2] For the Carlaverock campaign, it was first of all proposed that one of the arrayers should collect the troops' wages, after the task of choosing foot was completed; this proved unsatisfactory, and the array was held up until pay clerks were appointed. Similar appointments were made for the summer reinforcements, but no pay was recorded until the troops reached Carlisle.[3] In 1301, though the commissions of array contained no clauses governing pay arrangements, it appears from the terms of the inquiry into collusion and bribery that the troops levied in the Welsh border counties and in Derbyshire, Nottinghamshire, and Yorkshire were paid both by men of the county and by one of the arrayers.

For the winter of 1301–2 some interesting writs of array (mostly cancelled later) indicate that arrangements were still very flexible. In Northumberland one of the arrayers, who

---

[1] H. Gough, *Falkirk*, pp. 56–66; cf. especially the *Ordinacio solucionis vadiorum*. The Cheshire foot, for example, received pay from Chester.

[2] *Parl. Writs*, i. 329 (12); deserters had received pay from both crown and vill *en route* from their counties to Berwick.

[3] E. 101. 8/20; *Welsh Wars*, p. 301.

this time were probably a pay clerk and three colleagues, was to bring pay after the array, as for Carlaverock; in the other northern counties the sheriff was to pay wages out of the shire revenues until the muster. A later writ to the sheriff of Nottinghamshire and Derbyshire distinguished between those with funds and those without. This can only mean that the shire revenues assigned for the purpose only covered a minority (100 of 900) of those originally arrayed. The idea of assigning county revenues to the pay of levies was not new, but this was the first writ of array specifically to do so.[1]

In 1303 the logical system adopted for the Welsh levies of 1297 was extended to those of the north: a place was appointed in each county at which the pay of those levies was to begin (e.g. Northallerton for Yorkshire). To discourage loitering, the amount of pay was confined to the calculated time it would take to march to Roxburgh (e.g. from Yorkshire, five days; from Durham (Gateshead) two days). In 1306, on the other hand, the *custodes pacis* of Berwick and Carlisle were to notify the Chamberlain of Scotland when pay was needed for their foot, and a king's clerk was appointed to receive such funds.[2]

In 1307 writs went out for foot from the northern Marches and from the Clare lands. Only in the latter case was pay to the muster enjoined in the writ. The principles of this muster —that Scottish March service was owed at local expense by northerners, but not by others—was to remain in effect for the next two centuries at least.

So far, a consideration of the arms and pay conditions of the foot levies suggests that the local community played a part in the supply both of arms and of pay or maintenance. Before considering the nature of this part a word needs to be said on the question of organization. The key was, of course, the appointment of special arrayers whose function, as far as the writs tell us, was in Edward's reign to select a given

---

[1] The need for such an arrangement is illustrated by the difficulty of Roger Springhouse, sheriff of Shropshire, in getting allowance at the Exchequer for wages paid in wartime, *Rot. Parl.* ii. 163–4.

[2] Cf. the appointment of 'Receivers of Moneys' in 1297–8; Gough, *Falkirk*, pp. 64 f. The Receiver was to audit the accounts of pay clerks and to pay travel wages to some small troops.

number of the stronger foot from the counties, liberties, or other administrative areas. The Exchequer would appear to have been the central office responsible—in conjunction, of course, with Chancery which issued the writs. Thus a Chancery warrant of 30 April 1300 ordered the Chancery to prepare commissions of array in consultation with the Exchequer.[1] Returns were usually made to the Exchequer, and the Exchequer inquired into irregularities.[2] During the campaign, of course, the Wardrobe became more directly responsible, but the Exchequer had to see to the provision of pay directly at least up to the muster, and indirectly thereafter. This Exchequer function can be most easily studied in the series of extracts from the 1298 Memoranda rolls printed by Gough.[3] The *Receptor denariorum* in Yorkshire and Northumberland is ordered to pay the sum of wages for the Lancashire levies to a pay clerk Peter Dunwich, who is going to Lancashire to join William Dacre in leading those troops from the county town to the muster. Peter is to receive his own pay from London to Lancaster as well, and is to account for the moneys he receives by witness of William. Other writs show the collectors of the ninth being ordered to supply pay clerks with funds, if necessary borrowing what was required. Some of the lesser levies were awarded pay, including travel money, on arrival. A further order stressed that levies should on no account receive wages while serving in their own counties.

The main interest of the organization of the levies lies in the relation of the arrayers to the local officers and communities, as they carried out their duties. This relationship was no doubt made easier by the fact that a substantial percentage of the arrayers, not yet estimated, was drawn from the 'community of the county' rather than from the household. A writ of intendance and aid usually went out to the sheriff, bailiffs, and other officers as well as to the *fideles* of the communities where the arrayer was to do his work. There existed the hierarchy of hundred and vill and borough con-

---

[1] *Cal. Chancery Warrants*, i. 108.

[2] See *Select Pleas of the Exchequer* (Selden Soc., vol. 48, 1931), pp. 194–5.

[3] Gough, *Falkirk*, pp. 56–66 (extracts from K.R. Mem. R., 26 Edward I, mm. 106 d–105 d.

stables set up by the Assizes of Arms, who were the natural
assistants and possible leaders in the array.[1] In 1282 and
1283 the eligible men of the border counties and Marcher
lordships were to be assembled at times and places decided
on between the arrayers, sheriffs, and bailiffs. At such
assemblies the arrayers had to use what mixture of force,
persuasion, and bribery the situation required. Thus in
1294 there was an inquiry into those eligible, and, as is
well known, the Welsh revolted; hence in 1297 one finds
the arrayers strictly ordered to use the utmost tact in per-
suading the assembled men to serve. The function of the
local officials is clarified by the terms of the inquiries into
corruption of July 1300 and of July 1301, wherein the
arrest was ordered (in the words of the latter writ) of
'some bailiffs, ministers, and others of the county who had
chosen foot and had received gifts to let them go home'
and to put in their places others of little or no value; these
officials had changed the names in the lists sent to the
arrayers. As an inquiry of Edward II's reign shows, the
local official would sometimes choose good men at an
assembly before the arrayers, but would substitute poor
ones after the latter had departed.[2] Even such insignificant
officials as the 'hayward' of a village played their part in
the process, as one John Beaucosin of Littleport found to his
profit.[3] Although the lords played an important part, it was
not essentially different from that of other local officials.
Sometimes they had their own following of foot (e.g. at
Pentirick),[4] but they were not systematically used to array
their own foot tenants until Edward II's reign, except in
the case of some of the Welsh Marchers and of Cheshire.[5]
On the other hand, in the inquiry of 1300 the lords were
accused of obstruction by forbidding their tenants, when
chosen, to go on service.

---

[1] *Welsh Wars*, pp. 92–93; behind this 'peace' organization lay the whole system of
frankpledge.

[2] *Cal. Chanc. Warrants*, i. 436.

[3] H. S. Bennett, *Life on an English Manor* (Cambridge, 1937), p. 122.

[4] Ibid.

[5] R. Stewart-Brown, *Calendar of Court, City Court and Eyre Rolls of Chester*
(Chetham Society, N.S., v. 84, 1925), pp. xliii–lix, 109–16; H. S. Hewitt, *Medieval
Cheshire* (Chetham Soc., N.S., v. 88, 1929), pp. 157–8.

It was probably the job of the arrayers to draw up the county muster rolls, wherein the men were grouped in vintenaries and centenaries.[1] Possibly there were two stages, the men of each wapentake (or vill) being first of all grouped roughly into vintenaries and then re-grouped into 'full' vintenaries and centenaries at the county level.[2] It is more than likely that a further element of selection went on when the army moved from the local to the national level.

What of the people themselves? In isolated cases the assembled people of the shire seem to have formed themselves into a negotiating body. Thus in December 1302 the 'barons, knights, *prodes homes*, and all the *communauté*' of Northumberland met with the treasurer and granted the service of all liable between sixteen and sixty with provisions for fifteen days, other costs being borne for eight days in the Marches by the horsemen and within the county by the foot.[3] This brings in the question of the role of the local community in the choice of the levies, which may be studied together with its function in matters of pay and equipment.

As we have seen, arrayers, sheriffs, bailiffs, constables, and quite minor local officials, all had their role in the selection of foot and assemblies were normally called to facilitate the process. It has been suggested, on the basis of evidence in the Court roll of Halesowen (Shropshire), that the men of the village elected those who were to go 'just as the officers of a village were elected'.[4] This evidence, however, is far from conclusive. Mr. Homans writes that the Halesowen roll 'speaks of a number of men "elected" to go to Shrewsbury for the king's array in Wales. A certain Thomas Hill . . . had gone to each of the men elected, and each had paid Hill to go as a substitute . . . Hill had then disappeared.' But there is nothing here to indicate 'election' in any other sense than

---

[1] The only rolls from Edward I's reign of which I am aware are from Yorkshire C. 47. 2/21 mm. 14–16, mm. 26–28. A list of defaulters is in ibid., m. 17.

[2] If this theory is correct, the lists in C. 47. 2/21 mm. 14–16 represent the first stage, and those in mm. 26–28 the second.

[3] *Parl. Writs*, i. 369 (10). From the last year of Edward II's reign (and in view of the rapid growth in the powers of the *populus*, this cannot be taken as a guide to earlier practice) the arrayer was to have the support of a 'sworn council' in each region.

[4] G. C. Homans, *English Villagers of the Thirteenth Century*, pp. 329–30. Even should 'election' by the villagers be accepted in this case, it is to be noted that the array orders had been unusually indeterminate; *Parl. Writs*, i. 266 (2).

that used in the writs to the arrayers—viz. *eslire* or *eligere*, to choose. Nor is other evidence of 'elections' collected by various writers any more satisfactory.[1]

The vill did not elect its military 'representatives', but it had to support them. The initial evidence for this comes from those writs concerning deserters, already cited, which referred to the money taken from the local community as well as from the king by the malfeasants. Further evidence comes from Assize and Plea rolls. Thus in 1295 a Lincolnshire vill paid four shillings towards the expenses of its soldiers.[2] In 1300 one Nicholas de Styvelingfleet was attached in the Exchequer on a plea of trespass. The charge, brought in the king's name, was that as a vintenar he had received various sums (totalling 63s. 6d.) from four vills, for which he was to provide twenty armed foot with expenses, but failed to do so, whereby the king lost twenty men for the period of the war.[3] Nicholas defended himself vigorously, claiming that he received nothing from two of the vills, and that from the others he received money for expenses and for proper arms—viz. sword, bow, and arrows—for six foot, who were to come to him at (North) Allerton, ready 'to set them forth on the king's war'. This they had failed to do, and he had returned the money to the constable of the vill (in one case; in the other, he would do so).[4] Another case was that at Halesowen against one Thomas in le Putte who had received ninepence from the community for his expenses in Wales, but had not gone.[5] We may conclude, then, that the local vill or town frequently found the expenses of the foot until the king's paymaster took over.

That the local communities had some responsibility for the supply of arms is clear from the writs and returns of Henry III's and Edward II's reigns. Under Edward I the one piece of evidence suggesting common responsibility for

---

[1] H. S. Bennett, *English Manor*, pp. 121–2; H. M. Cam, 'The Community of the Vill', p. 2.

[2] W. S. Thompson, *Lincolnshire Assize Roll*, xxiv. 59, quoted in H. M. Cam, 'The Community of the Vill', p. 2, and G. C. Homans, op. cit.

[3] Select Pleas of the Exchequer, *Selden Society*, vol. 48 (1931), pp. 194–5.

[4] The case is also interesting in showing that the Yorkshire foot assembled at Northallerton even before it became, in 1303, a royally appointed muster-point.

[5] Homans, *English Villagers*, p. 330.

the supply of arms comes from Cotton's account of the arrayers at work in Norfolk. They assembled a large number of foot from both cities and vills, had uniforms, knives, and swords bought for them *de communis sentibus* [? *expensis*] of the county (through a levy, or assessment, on all free men?), chose from the mass the most suitable, and marched away with them.[1] According to Cotton, these men returned in four days, though some at least may have served longer, 'Hemingburgh' describing Edmund's and Lincoln's army of January 1296 as containing 'seven hundred *armati* and many of the people [*plebi*]'.[2]

The palatinates, with their privileged position regarding extra-comital service, were usually called on to serve 'saving their liberties'. The great levies of the autumn of 1299 led in the palatinate of Durham not only to large-scale desertions, but to claims of exemption from service beyond the rivers Tyne and Tees. In May 1300 the opposition bound themselves by oath, and grievances were laid before Bishop Bek; these grievances combined with the national opposition in the Lincoln parliament of January 1301, and in February 1303 Edward indemnified the men of Durham for uncustomary military service. But the struggle went on until the end of the reign.[3]

In the foregoing account, no mention has been made of those captaincies and wardenships which materially added to the burden laid on the population. They differed from the Commissions of Array in that they were primarily posts of command, and only secondarily officers of array. Yet on several occasions captains were given the power to array troops, and one writer has even regarded them as forerunners of commissions of array.[4] Such captaincies were familiar features of the Welsh and Scottish Marches, but the wording of the commissions suggest that they were not usually regarded as a satisfactory vehicle for experiments in obligation. Thus the captaincies of Mortimer in the border counties (1276, 1282) gave him authority over the *fideles* and com-

---

[1] *Hist. Ang.*, p. 307.

[2] *Chronicon*, ii. 72.

[3] The above account is taken from C. M. Fraser, 'Edward I and the Regalian Franchise of Durham', *Speculum* (1956), pp. 329–42.

[4] A. H. Noyes, *The Military Obligation in Medieval England*, p. 23.

munities, who were to serve *cum equis et armis* or *cum toto posse*—traditional enough forms. The Scottish border custodians and captains, however, seem to have had wider powers of impressment and recruitment.[1]

By far the most interesting special command was that given to the custodes of coast defence in 1295–6, in a scheme which, as Mr. Denholm Young has pointed out, went back to the well-known Montfortian defence plan of 1264.[2] In August, constables and wardens were appointed in the coastal districts of Norfolk, Suffolk, and Essex with the task of assessing both horse and foot to arms according to past custom. The sheriffs were to distrain those so assessed to serve in defence. In October the whole north was put under the military wardenship of the earl of Warenne and the bishop of Durham, the sheriffs being enjoined to summon two men from each vill to hear their orders. At the same time a more comprehensive scheme was broached for the whole south-east. The coastal counties were divided into groups of hundreds (or into rapes, in the case of Sussex); and the various vills were assessed at so many foot for the defence of the coastal district of the area in which they lay. In addition, mounted troops had to be found to act as 'supervisors', vintenars, and decenars, and wages had to be found. The former were provided from the knights and potential knights, returns of an inquiry into those dwelling in Essex and Sussex being extant. The basis of this obligation was, as one might expect, twenty librates of land.[3] Pay was to be found by levies on the counties, apparently on the basis of knights' fees or their fiscal equivalent. London was treated differently, and in response to a request for help an assembly granted the service of 400 men with barbed horses and 500 foot crossbowmen at the city's expense.

The problem, then, which Edward I bequeathed to his successors was how to levy the right kind of troops without trespassing beyond the narrow limits of the received tradition, and at the least possible cost. So far there was no political

---

[1] *Parl. Writs*, i. 307 f.; ibid. i. 369 (10) is especially interesting as showing the *locum tenens* negotiating for service.

[2] N. Denholm-Young, 'Feudal Society', in *Collected Papers*, p. 61.

[3] See the Sussex return, *Parl. Writs*, i. 275; and compare with Cotton's report of the assessment of ecclesiastics, *Hist. Ang.*, p. 312.

reaction on a national scale to these county levies of foot. In fact, Edward had very largely bought it off in advance, by the generous terms he offered. But with a heavy debt and the northern enemy more active than ever before, it was clear that the young Edward was going to find such practices impossibly costly.

VIII

EDWARD II: EXPERIMENTS THAT FAILED[1]

EDWARD II's inheritance of a reorganized army of feudal-mercenary character, a redeveloped militia, enlarged political ambitions, and a rapidly developing legal and administrative machine, is in many ways reminiscent of the situation a century before at the accession of John. In fact, the strain of prolonged warfare with a determined enemy and of mounting resentment on the part of the baronage strengthens the analogy.

Yet Edward I's later wars had been conducted in the teeth of increasing opposition, and had strained the fiscal resources, if not the economy, of the nation. The Confirmation of the Charters had rallied a large party of baronial and knightly opposition, and only wise and popular leadership could hope to overcome the twin handicap of political opposition and fiscal frailty. The onset of economic crisis, in the form of famine and of urban discontent, probably added to the opposition initiated by the leading barons, and must have made the expense of the new form of warfare even harder to sustain.

I

Edward II was ill fitted to cope with either problem. In another age, neither his anti-chivalric bias nor his psychological idiosyncrasies would have been serious flaws. In 1307, as is well known, they led to alienation from both the baronial leaders and his wisest counsellors at a time when he desperately needed both. Gaveston, who supplied the love of chivalry which Edward lacked, did not thereby bridge the gap, for his upstart manners and superior skills only increased the hostility of the barons. Besides these failings,

[1] In spite of many changes in detail, the structure and the conclusions of this chapter are substantially those of my 'Edward II and Military Obligation', *Speculum*, xxxi (1956), 83–119.

Edward lacked real military insight, though his failure to develop the arms and tactics introduced in his father's later wars was partly due to opposition on the part of his subjects.

He had had a good deal of experience as a commander in the last three campaigns of Edward I, and he showed a determined, if fitful, energy and obstinacy which led him to spend winter after winter in bleak northern castles, often at times when both comfort and political wisdom beckoned him south.[1] To implement his objectives he inherited the architectonic system developed by Edward I and his generals in the course of seemingly endless campaigns in Scotland and Wales: the recruitment of men by feudal summons, commission of array, contract; the building up of units by indenture and appointment of officers; the construction of castles; the organization of supplies; the household as a military exchequer, commissariat, and administrative centre; the tactics of combined bowmen and dismounted men-at-arms. But besides being devoid of his father's constructive and directing genius, he was faced with a huge debt and with an utterly dissatisfied baronage, and a probably no less restive community of knights, burgesses, and freemen. For all these measures had cost money, and where they saved money they pressed hard on people. But Edward refused to give way; he refused to 'stoop to conquer', the only possibly successful course open to him. He tried to go ahead without the country's support, and thereby lost both his wars and his country.

It is with Edward's efforts to maintain and develop the military innovations of his father that we are primarily concerned; his attitude to the consent of his subjects (which he almost certainly required if he was to pursue an aggressive military policy) must be left to a separate chapter. The rewards of success and victory could have been great; they might even have 'dished the Whigs'. As it was, military failure aggravated domestic disaster. On the paralysing effect of the defeat of Bannockburn most historians are agreed. But,

---

[1] On his experience in the years 1300–5 and on his character in general, see Hilda Johnstone, *Edward of Carnarvon* (Manchester, 1946). He spent all or part of the winters of 1310–11, 1311–12, 1315–16, 1316–17, 1318–19, 1319–20 in Scotland and the north of England; C. H. Hartshorne, *Itinerary of Edward II* (London, 1861), *passim*.

in addition, the less spectacular failures of all his other expeditions were disastrous for the initiative of the crown. The failure of 1307–8 led to Gaveston's trial. The fiasco of 1310–11 compelled assent to the Ordinances. Success in 1319 might well have averted the triumph of the opposition in 1320–1. The calamitous mishandling of the Scottish expedition of 1322 began the slide to the final disaster, which followed almost immediately from the miserable failure of the Gascon expedition of 1324–5.

The military tasks of Edward dictated the forces required to achieve them. He needed two principal types of force: small units for the garrison of castles and conduct of forays, and occasional large armies for campaigns.[1] The system of indenture could, and usually did, take care of the former responsibility; but it was insufficiently developed to take care of the latter, and possibly not acceptable enough to conservative minds (including Edward's) to play more than a subordinate role.[2] For large numbers of cavalry and for foot it was barely suited. But he inherited other means of raising forces for a campaign, chief of which were the feudal summons and the commission of array. The former was still the chief means of assembling the cavalry core of the army. Those summoned by strictly feudal writs (i.e. with their *servicium debitum*) corresponded so closely, and often exactly, with those personally summoned to parliament that they might well be called the 'peerage in arms'. Even those summoned *quanto potencius poteritis* were often drawn from the parliamentary or *servicium debitum* list. It would seem that the tendency noted in the last two years of Edward I's reign towards a more conservative cavalry force was continued and strengthened in that of his son, the number of summons for '*s.d.*' increasing considerably.[3] Further, the two major cavalry innovations of the great Edward, the extension of obligation to knighthood to become a duty of cavalry service, and the evolution of the 'military indenture' from the 'money fief',

---

[1] For the former, see especially J. Bain, *Calendar of Documents*, iii, *passim*, where considerable numbers of 'garrison' indentures are printed.

[2] See, for a classical example of opposition, the 'Household Ordinance' in *Annales Londonienses*, in *Chronicles of the Reigns of Edward I and Edward II* (R.S.), i, pp. 198–202.

[3] See Note A, p.162, for a fuller analysis of the writs of summons.

both appear to have been relatively neglected by his son. The neglect of the former may have arisen, in part, from the increasing use of arrayers to levy both cavalry and foot from the shires, and thereby to increase the arms and financial contributions of the local community and the individual subject.

This array of the county foot, or horse and foot, on the basis of the oath of the *jurati ad arma*, had been the chief means employed by Edward I, as indeed by his predecessors, to gather the 'auxiliary' forces in his Welsh, European, and Scottish warfare. Yet his legacy was crippled by two dangerous innovations which looked like hardening into custom: the pay of the 'militia' outside their county, or even from leaving their place of muster inside the county, and the limitation of arms and armour to those prescribed by the Statute of Winchester. Neither practice was really ancient.[1] As previous chapters have attempted to show, the period from 1066 to 1272 had seen frequent employment of the 'English' and later the *jurati* outside their counties at communal expense, while the Statute of Winchester had been utterly indifferent to military needs and arrangements. Yet the prejudice was obstinate and the class involved was approaching a new peak of influence. Edward II's attempts to increase arms and 'free' service were so persistent that they provoked the severely conservative legislation which followed his fall.[2]

These attempts can best be studied in relation, first, to Edward's wars, and, secondly, to the political crises which alternately crippled and expanded his initiative. With regard to the former, it is to be remembered that apart from the

---

[1] Stubbs stigmatized Edward II's and III's use of commissions of array as unconstitutional purveyance, *Const. Hist.* ii. 297, 569; this judgement was essentially anachronistic, for it assumed the retroactive force of the militia Statutes of 1327. It was influenced by the great seventeenth-century constitutionalists and their 'Whig' successors. For Prynne, the unconstitutionality had resided in infringements of a primitive parliamentary sovereignty; 'The Parliaments Interest in the Militia', in *The Soveraigne Power of Parliaments and Kingdoms* (London, 1643); for Henry Hallam, Edward III's measures were 'arbitrary pretensions' (*On the English Constitution*, with DeLolme's *Constitution of England*, London, Chandos Classics, p. 31).

[2] For suggestive comments, see W. Stubbs, *Constitutional History*, ii. 568–73; H. M. Cam, *The Hundred and the Hundred Rolls*, p. 192; B. Wilkinson, *Constitutional History*, iii. 208.

years when armies went into Scotland (1307, 1310, 1314, 1319, 1322) or into France (1324, 1325), troops were frequently mustered and moved to some place of assembly without actually engaging in war (e.g. to York in 1318). It will be necessary, therefore, to look at stillborn as well as active campaigns in this study. Moreover, account must also be taken of the civil wars of 1321–2 and 1326.

In the following analysis, a rather different plan from that of previous chapters has been adopted. Edward's measures before August 1318 are treated in chronological order, but it is well to bear in mind that they fall into two main categories: the arming of the militia, and the local communities' responsibilities for its maintenance and pay. Moreover, the steady increase in recorded administrative detail makes it necessary to glide over a whole range of important developments which were not such as to excite opposition. After the Treaty of Leake, which may perhaps be treated as the turning-point, when the initiative passed to the king and his supporters, an analytical approach is adopted for the noticeably fuller military reform measures.

II

Edward already knew, from his experience in the campaigns of 1300–5, that a short campaign in Scotland was of little use. His experiences of 1307 and 1310–11 confirmed this. That he could not, on the other hand, maintain a long stay in the north in the face of baronial opposition was brought home to him in 1311. Further, he discovered how difficult it was going to be to increase the militia contribution of the shires, even with their consent.

It is probable that the opposition of the barons was the main deterrent from campaigning in Scotland in 1308 and 1309. At any rate, the initial moves of an expedition were made in each year, but nothing came of them.[1] In the conflict as to the prior claims of war and reform, the former lost, and it was only when Edward had agreed to the establishment of a reforming commission in March 1310 that he was able to

---

[1] *Parl. Writs*, ii. 373–92; *Rotuli Scotiae*, i. 55–76; *Chronicon de Lanercost*, ed. J. Stevenson (Edinburgh, 1839), pp. 212–24; Walter 'Hemingburgh' of Guisborough, *Chronicle* (R.H.S., Camden Series), pp. 384 f.; *Chronicon* (E.H.S.), ii. 275; J. Bain, *Calendar of Documents relating to Scotland*, iii. 9, 12, 16, 18.

mount a campaign. But most of the leading earls were absent, due to a renewal of the quarrel.[1] This conflict may also have been responsible for the change from the summons for *servicium debitum* to a request for as powerful a force as possible. Besides this quasi-feudal force,[2] the counties of the south-west, Lancashire, Wales, and London supplied small levies at the king's wages.[3] The order that the Irish foot were to be arrayed in hauberks shows they were continuing the role of pioneers in new equipment and weapons which they had begun under Edward I as the originators of the 'hobelars', or mounted spearmen; for while hauberks had long been the armour prescribed for the ten-librate holders under the Assize of Arms, the order of 1310 was the first demand that levies should be equipped with them, heralding as such the new emphasis of Edward II on defensive armour. Edward kept these forces on duty long after the forty days' march in and out of Scotland was over.[4] But in the south the baronial opposition continued to work on the Ordinances. Hence, when spring came, the king did not summon parliament with a view to a fresh feudal summons, as prudence and tradition might have dictated, although he appears to have thought of doing so.[5] Determined to carry on his duty in the north, he embarked on the well-known 'request' for one foot soldier from each vill, whose wages were to be paid for seven weeks by the vills.[6] Stubbs did not bring out the full force of this levy. In particular, the method of payment, viz. by a special aid raised by the sheriffs from the vills, was likely to underline the oppressive nature of the order. The attempt to obtain 'consent' by a direct appeal to the vills and by a re-

[1] *Chronicon de Lanercost*, p. 214; *Annales Londonienses*, p. 174; *Vita Edwardi Secundi*, ed. N. Denholm-Young (London, 1957), pp. 10–11. Cf. J. C. Davies, *The Baronial Opposition to Edward II* (Cambridge, 1918), p. 507.

[2] See Note B, p. 163, where an attempt is made to assess the extent to which it was feudal.

[3] *Parl. Writs*, ii. 397 f. (76); B.M. Cotton MS. Nero C VIII, fols. 17d, 28d show payment was made from leaving the county. Cf. for 'hobelars', J. E. Morris, 'Mounted Infantry in Mediaeval Warfare', *Royal Historical Society Transactions* (1914), pp. 80 f.

[4] Besides the above, cf. Scotch Roll 4, Edward II, mm. 15–5; J. Bain, *Calendar of Documents*, iii. 393–434.

[5] H. G. Richardson and G. O. Sayles, 'The Early Records of the English Parliaments, II', *Bulletin of the Institute of Historical Research*, vi (1928–9), 80, n. 4.

[6] Cf. Stubbs, *Const. Hist.* ii. 569–70. The writs governing this and other measures are to be found, unless otherwise stated, in Palgrave's *Parliamentary Writs, etc.*, vol. ii.

quest for the approval and support of the magnates made on the same day, rather than by seeking the prior consent of parliament, was unprecedented and unacceptable.[1] That Edward was at least aware of the need for the consent of the *communitas* is indicated both by the writ to the magnates and by the abortive plans for a parliament. The whole project was cancelled, of course, although 'orthodox' commissions of array, with pay of levies from leaving their counties, took its place. Before this army could muster, Edward had to leave Berwick to confirm the Ordinances, which had at last been drawn up, and almost at once Bruce and his followers surged over the half-defended frontier.[2]

The three themes which run through these opening years —Edward's determination to stay in the north, and thereby finish off the Scottish business, the attempt to widen the militia obligation without adequate consent, and the baronial preoccupation with internal affairs—set the keynote of the ensuing decade. To this the Ordinances added the obligation of the king to consult the baronage in making war.

It was under the shadow of this Ordinance, which transformed the ancient tradition of consent to war into a right which the king was sworn to observe, that the military events of the next seven years worked themselves out. On the one hand, in spite of several parliaments, Edward failed to consult the earls and barons to the extent that wisdom might have decreed. On the other hand, and from our point of view most important, the possibility of further developments of the militia in the teeth of a hostile baronage was slight, though the need for them did not decrease. Another hindrance to increasing the burdens on the local communities was that these were years of economc crisis, as well as of political conflict.

At the end of 1311 paid squadrons of southerners and unpaid northern lords were drafted to the Scottish border. Similar stop-gap measures went on in 1312 and 1313.[3] In

[1] Cf. Gaines Post's very apposite comments on the legal background in 'The Two Laws and the Statute at York', *Speculum*, xxix. 2 (April 1954), 426.

[2] A thin stream of reinforcement had reached Edward, reaching its peak in May (Letters of Protection). Some Welsh infantry stayed on through winter and spring. Cotton MS. Nero C viii, fol. 104.

[3] *Rot. Scot.* i. 106; cf. E. 101. 14/15 m. 3.

spite of strenuous efforts, only small holding forces were assembled in the Marches. Gaveston's return and death, which terminated Edward's efforts to assemble a partially mercenary force in 1312,[1] may have prompted him to seek a mustering of the nation through the issue of writs of distraint of knighthood, and through the array of all trustworthy men-at-arms and foot in constabularies, centenaries, and vintenaries.[2] The distraint of knighthood, apart from being directed to forty- instead of twenty-librate holders, was simply a reissue of the 1278 writ. In the early summer the earls promised to serve in Scotland with 400 men-at-arms at their own cost for half a year, provided that consent had been obtained and that the king was present in person.[3] Moreover, Edward planned to have levies at the autumn parliament, but was unable to offer pay on what had become the usual conditions, i.e. on their leaving their counties.[4] In London, likewise, heavy expenses were incurred by the city though ostensibly repayable by the crown. Less than half the required cross-bowmen were raised, and these were led by John de Luke to Berwick by indenture with the city.[5]

The conflict of 1312 involved a struggle for the allegiance of the Londoners. Edward's request for the proper defence of London led to an instructive city ordinance. The 'arming' was to be simply *iuxta statum*, but in a later order all citizens with fifty shillings or more in 'goods and merchandises' were to find a well-armed man. The bedels were to be sworn to make a fair assessment, and not to hire any substitutes for those summoned to perform watch.[6]

The recruitment for Bannockburn—feudal, national, and contractual—was impeccably conservative, except in the lack of consent, for which good, though not generally acceptable, excuses existed. Defeat, however, brought an end to caution, and a good reason for unorthodox measures, as the whole

[1] *Parl. Writs*, ii. 416, 420; E. 101.14/15, 22; Bain, *Calendar*, iii. 48 f.
[2] *Parl. Writs*, ii. 418–19. In Sussex the earl of Warenne organized the county in hundreds and twenties, while Nicholas Aucher chose levies from these forces; cf. P.R.O. Ancient Correspondence, xlix, no. 8.
[3] *Annales Londonienses*, pp. 209–13.
[4] Ibid. In some cases pay was offered on arrival at London, in others it was not mentioned.
[5] Riley, *Memorials*, pp. 114–15.
[6] Ibid., pp. 93–98, 102–3.

north was in manifest danger. Most startling of the summer measures was the plan for the impressment of the whole Yorkshire foot to serve under Pembroke at the cost of the vills. In November the cities of York, Lincoln, Northampton, and London were ordered to supply cross-bowmen armed with aketons, coats of mail, or basinets of plate, at the king's expense. Although not oppressive, this measure shows that Edward—and probably this meant Pembroke—was attracted as early as this by the idea of heavily armoured foot. Moreover, the accounts of the city of York show that £4. 16s. of the £33 expenses were disallowed—not a large sum, but indicative of the sort of charge laid on the communities even when the payment of expenses by the king had been promised.[1] The city of Leicester hired archers on behalf of Thomas of Lancaster with money raised from an aid assessed on citizens.[2]

The year 1315 began conservatively, bringing a reaffirmation of the Statute of Winchester arms' scale. Shortly after, a special northern *tractatus* of prelates and magnates consented to the appointment of four 'wardens and captains' of the north. Though not parliamentary, this consent was somewhat more real than the consultations of May 1311. But a writ of array in August ordered levies to be ready to serve for forty days at the cost of themselves and others of their neighbourhood, and it is just possible that some service was obtained.[3] The settlement with Lancaster in January at the parliament of Lincoln made it possible to extend this idea of service at cost of the vills considerably, and to resume distraint of knighthood. In fact, the measures of 1316, although ineffectual, are worthy of closer examination than they have hitherto received.

At the Lincoln parliament, a strenuous effort was made to

---

[1] *Parl. Writs*, ii. 433–4 (10–13); E. 101. 14/33; Bain, *Calendar*, iii, no. 401, omits the detail here cited. The first order for the impressment of seamen to be printed by Nicolas dates from April 1314; N. H. Nicolas, *Royal Navy* (London, 1847), i. 403, 465.

[2] M. Bateson, *Records of the Borough of Leicester* (Cambridge, 1901), i. 344–5.

[3] *Parl. Writs*, ii, Appendix, pp. 94–95. Cf. for complaints of extortion by arrayers, ibid., pp. 460 (24). The lords were also ordered to serve at their own wages, ibid. ii. 457 (7). For other attempts to support Pembroke, who was 'holding' the north, ibid., pp. 439–40 (71, 79 f.); App., 96, 97 (12—preamble); for Pembroke's force, P.R.O. E. 101. 15/6 and E. 376. 7; E. Devon, *Issues of the Exchequer*, p. 126.

heal the breaches in national unity and send a national force into action against the Scots. The condition for this was a renewal of the Ordinances, and, in particular, of those parts which demanded consultation of parliament. Further, it was conceded that when parliament was not required a 'baronial' council must now be consulted.[1] With Lancaster as the head of the council, the various classes of the nation might unite and take the offensive. A 'full' feudal muster, distraint of all with £50 annual rents to knighthood, and a levy of one man per vill to serve for sixty days at the cost of his vill, were the three principal measures undertaken.[2] The expedition failed to materialize for two main reasons: the plans thus laid were too ambitious, and the breach between Edward and Lancaster was only superficially mended. The levy of one man per vill deserves further examination, because, while it had parliamentary sanction on this occasion, it did embody some of those features which led to the enactments of 1327. The modest customary obligations of the vill were extended to cover the maintenance of their representatives not only to the county muster, but beyond that to the national muster, and even beyond that, for sixty days in the field, in addition to supplying them with arms and armour. Of course, there was the 1311 precedent, and the 'plan' of 1315 to pave the way for this 'grant'.[3] But neither of these had been universal. Moreover, the 1316 measure proceeded much farther before being cancelled than had the earlier schemes; an order of 26 June indicated that the levy was well under way at that date.[4]

There were new measures on 20 August for a winter campaign. Among those was a very important order, which seems to have been overlooked. Instead of the resummons of

---

[1] J. C. Davies, *Baronial Opposition*, pp. 411 f. Cf. B. Wilkinson, *Studies in the Constitutional History of the Thirteenth and Fourteenth Centuries* (Manchester, 1937), p. 130, n. 1.

[2] *Rotuli Parliamentorum*, i. 351–2. *Parl. Writs*, ii. 157 (22), 461–3 (32–35), 464 (42–45).

[3] See above, and Stubbs, *Const. Hist.* ii. 570–1.

[4] *Parl. Writs*, ii. 469 (54) and E. 101. 15/10, giving vills custody of armour and wages, and returns to inquiry about same. For the cancellation of this levy in favour of a parliamentary grant to support more orthodox armies, see *Parl. Writs*, p. 470 (57); cf. ibid., Appendix 104 (47–48). The writ of 25 June summoning county representatives to Lincoln marks the decision to abandon the project. For some useful comments, see H. M. Cam, 'Shire Officials', *English Government at Work*, iii (Mediaeval Academy; Cambridge, U.S.A.: 1950), 170–1.

the lesser knights through the sheriffs, the fifty-pound land-holders of most counties were now summoned, not to take up knighthood, but to *serve* with horses and arms (and without promise of pay) alongside those receiving personal summonses. This measure, of course, constituted a serious departure from custom at precisely the point where vigorous protests had previously been made. The class affected, moreover, was the dominant 'parliamentary class', which was becoming ever more vital in the counsels of the nation. The heavy penalties but not, apparently, the service itself were authorized by the magnates staying with the king. A corollary to the writ was the array of all the 'fencibles' of the northernmost counties by parishes (an innovation) and wapentakes.[1] The most significant change from earlier measures in this order was the stress on body armour.[2] The aketon, which had been mentioned in earlier writs concerning the cities and in the cancelled plan of one man per vill, was now required of the whole of the northern militia, while the ten-pound and fifteen-pound class were to wear hauberks. This array was never mustered, some arrayers of the midland footmen being met by blunt refusals to serve. In concluding this survey of the 'extraordinary' measures of 1316, it may be noted that the justification advanced was common interest and obligation in the defence of the kingdom. In the array by vill, parliamentary consent was forthcoming, as for a tax,[3] but the array which took its place, in part equally controversial, had no such foundation. This may have contributed to the crisis which put a temporary stop to innovation. The north was left to fend for itself, and by early 1318 the Scots were raiding deep into Yorkshire.

III

In this crisis the middle party began to make itself felt, and the Treaty of Leake was negotiated. The outcome of that

---

1 *Parl. Writs*, ii. 478–9 (14–18).

2 The requirement of aketon or hauberk, according to status, was traditional enough, but had not, except in the case of the Irish, previously been set forth in writs of array.

3 Such consent was claimed in the writ for the distraint of knighthood of 28 Feb., as well as for the levy of a foot-man from each vill. As J. C. Davies surmises (*Baronial Opposition*, p. 414) this had probably been given, but escaped recording.

treaty, for our purposes, was twofold. On the one hand, the king was again bound to obtain 'parliamentary consent', or where that was not required, conciliar consent, in all great matters; thus Lancaster's point was made, and it was not to be unmade entirely, even by the Statute of York in 1322. On the other hand, and perhaps as a *quid pro quo*, Edward seems to have been encouraged to go ahead with the upward revision of the obligations of the militia. The latter part of this 'deal' would naturally never be embodied in a document. It was, after all, a betrayal of the Commons. The likelihood of this suggestion rests on two main premisses. On the one hand, and in general, Pembroke was a military man, who would appreciate the needs of army reform. On the other, and more specifically, the initial measure reforming the militia was dated 12 August, just three days after the Treaty of Leake, and must have had the authority of Pembroke, Segrave, and the bishops of Ely and Worcester, who temporarily formed the council.[1]

The levy of 12 August 1318 took the form of a request to certain cities and towns for foot-men to serve for forty days at local expense and with special arms, viz. aketons, hauberks, basinets, and iron gauntlets.[2] It claimed to have the consent of the 'prelates, earls, barons, and *proceres* of the realm', and that these had also agreed to be at the muster.[3] Such consent would have had to have come from the negotiators of the Treaty of Leake, though there is no other evidence for it.

Apart from the unpaid period of service, this request was unusual in that the foot-men were required to serve in armour—a duty confined to the wealthy (the ten-pound class) in the Statute of Winchester; the iron gauntlets had no statutory warrant, though their military usefulness had by now been established. The story of the city levies did not end

---

[1] *Parl. Writs*, ii. 505–6 (5); J. C. Davies, op. cit., p. 449. The only other recorded preparation for this muster was a request for provisions, *Rotuli Scotiae*, i. 183.

[2] The cost of each set of armour, as instanced in Exchequer Accounts, varied considerably, but was about £1 in all.

[3] The feudal muster had been prorogued to 25 Aug., on which date parliament was summoned. Presumably the Leake agreement led to the change of plans; *Parl. Writs*, ii. 504–5 (1–4), 182 f. Although there is no writ enrolled proroguing the feudal muster from 25 Aug., letters of protection issued in Sept. and Oct. show that the lords brought large retinues to York (a total of *c*. 530), and that these were intended for Scotland. Scotch roll, C. 71/6 mm. 13–12.

there. For in the face of at least some opposition (at Grantham, Lincoln, and Nottingham), part of the town levies were mustered under John Weston, and kept watch at York, along with the feudal forces and some horse and foot from the northern shires, for the required forty days.[1] The London response to these demands, which can be followed in the Letter books, is instructive.[2] An assembly of mayor, aldermen, and commonalty agreed to supply 200 armoured foot at the expense of the commonalty, each citizen 'of the stronger and better class' furnishing one soldier. An exchange of letters with the king which followed this service shows the king's satisfaction, and, more important, the actual terms of service; for the troops acknowledged royal pay from the time of their setting out from York: i.e. the city was responsible for the journey north and the sojourn at York.

These orders regarding towns and cities were to prove the beginning of a regular series of distraints. Stubbs selected some of these as examples of 'purveyance', but made no systematic analysis.[3] Morris, in his brilliant paper on 'Mounted Infantry in Medieval Warfare', examined at least one campaign—that of 1322—with some thoroughness, but dismissed too easily Edward's policy as thoroughly incompetent in its preference of armoured over mounted infantry (hobelars).[4] For, while the levy of armoured foot was indeed a major preoccupation of Edward in these years, there were many other experiments undertaken or continued in an effort to improve the military machine. We may trace some of these measures, beginning with those attempts to levy mounted infantry and armoured foot which are most germane to Morris's criticism, and then proceed to look at some other developments which serve to amplify our knowledge of Edward's intentions.

---

[1] *Parl. Writs,* ii. 507–8 (11–12, 15–16), 510 (30). Nearly a fifth of those requested (371 out of 2,045) are acknowledged (loc. cit). For the shire levies of horse and foot, see ibid. ii. 506 (7, 9).

[2] *Calendar of Letter Books 'E',* pp. 93–96; Riley, *Memorials,* p. 128. The former includes the lists of citizens and of soldiers found.

[3] *Constitutional History,* ii. 570.

[4] Cf. his *Bannockburn,* p. 95, and A. E. Prince, 'The Importance of the Campaign of 1327', *E.H.R.* l. 299–300.

IV

Every military undertaking from 1319 to 1326 involved special measures for the mounting or arming of the county and town levies. Troops summoned to Scotland from towns in 1319, and from both towns and counties in 1322, were to be protected by basinets and aketons, while in the latter year iron gauntlets and uniforms were also required.[1] Against the rebels at Boroughbridge, some of the levies were to have at least aketon and basinet. In August 1324 the implication of the 1322 Scottish measure was made clear in one of the writs concerning the Gascony levies; as the Statute of Winchester, it stated, was ordained in time of peace and freedom from fear of foreign attack, it was inadequate against sudden invasion, and a greater and stronger force of other armoured foot was needed. Hence the array was ordered of some 19,200 foot, of whom one third were to have aketons, habergeons (*hauberiettis*), or plate armour, basinets, and steel gauntlets at the expense of the counties.[2]

This force was not called out, but some of the larger southern cities and towns were directed to raise numbers of similarly armed foot and march them to Portsmouth for embarkation. The muster of city foot and county foot archers was postponed twice, and abandoned on 17 September, the day before a small expeditionary force sailed for Gascony.[3] On the 19th the 'purveyance of armour' of 6 August had to be seriously modified: the demand for habergeons or plates was dropped, and men of each hundred and vill were to be associated with the commissioners in choosing, assessing, and purchasing the arms. Similar modifications were introduced into the new orders for the array of cities and towns. While the reason given for the modification was the misdeeds of the arrayers in levying money for the buying of armour,

---

[1] *Parl. Writs*, ii. 518–19 (63–64), 524 (39–41), and E. 101. 5/27 m. 4 for 1319. Most of the towns affected in 1319 were northern and had failed to serve in 1318. London supplied military equipment to the value of £250, repayable from the current subsidy (*Cal. Letter Books 'E'*, p. 106). For 1322, see B.M. Stowe MS. 553, fo. 82ᵛ.

[2] An earlier order for archers had put part of the burden of supplying armour for archers at the cost of the vills.

[3] *Parl. Writs*, ii. 673–5 (118–20, 132–4); J. H. Ramsay, *The Genesis of Lancaster* (Oxford, 1913), p. 144. On the composition of this force see Nicholas Hugate's account book. See also P. Chaplais, *The War of Saint-Sardos* (R.H.S. Camden, 3rd series, 1954), nos. 45–46.

and in extending the array to clergy, it is probable that the extension of the obligation and the fact that it was at the cost of the people were the main causes of discontent. Indeed, although the new muster of foot had been abandoned, some at least of them were actually levied and taken to Gascony, sailing on 18 September with the earl of Surrey and his men-at-arms.[1]

At the same time as the muster of September was being cancelled new plans were being laid for 1325. The last-mentioned writs ordered the modified array of foot to be ready by 10 November. Then there quickly followed a great number of measures, which, for all their disorderliness, reveal the existence of a plan for the army in the mind of 'the government', of which the most remarkable feature, perhaps, was the revived interest in 'mounted infantry'. At the centre of the force were to be the feudal lords.[2] Next came reduced numbers of heavily armed foot, based on the array of 6 August and 19 September.[3] Thirdly, Edward called out considerable numbers of men-at-arms who did not owe military service ('qui ne soient pas de nostre retenance ne dautri ne qe service nous devient faire ne qe service facent pur autres'), and, in a given ratio to them, hobelars and archers.[4] Finally, the cities and towns were again required to supply foot-men armed with heavy armour in an order which extended considerably the array of the cities beyond what had been planned for 1324.

In addition to the preparation for armies going into Scotland and Gascony, measures concerned with defence of the north after the 'Chapter of Myton' in 1319 and after the failure of the 1322 summer expedition reflected Edward II's views on armour. In 1319 the 'five-pound' class of *jurati* had to have horses and iron gauntlets 'fit for a hobelar' as well as

---

[1] B.M. Add. MS. 7967, fos. 83d. et seq.; 300 foot were in pay till 4 Dec., and after that a rapidly diminishing number.

[2] A. E. Prince writes ('The Army and the Navy', in *English Government at Work*, i. 349) of this feudal summons as one of the causes of the petitions of 1327, but it is difficult to discover anything improper about it. In any case, Prince believes the levy was not made; ibid., note 3.

[3] *Parl. Writs*, ii. 685 (176–7). Those with the additional armour received 3d. a day instead of the usual 2d.; Gascon Roll and Hugate's Account, loc. cit.

[4] Ibid., ii. 684–9 (173–87). The ratio was one man-at-arms to ten archers, and one hobelar to two archers. The northern counties supplied hobelars only.

their 'Winchester' armour of aketon, iron cap, and sword, while the 'two-pound' class, customarily unarmoured archers, were to have aketon, basinet, and iron gauntlets.[1]

In an extensive scheme of September 1322 the horsing of the five-pound class was dropped, but now they were to have habergeon in place of aketon.[2] After the complete failure of the defence measures of which this order was part, and after Edward's own narrow escape, new orders for the militia dropped this requirement; moreover, the two-pound class, required in September to have palet and iron gauntlets, were no longer required to have the latter. As a final evidence of Edward's concern with militia revision, an order in the early days of 1326 may be noted: arrayers were told that the real value, not the old extent, was to be the basis of obligation under the Statute of Winchester, while those over sixty years old or beneficed clerks with lay fees were to find substitutes.

Measures directed at the 'knightly class' in these years varied in intent. Distraint of knighthood was ordered in 1319, and after Myton Yorkshiremen with ten pounds of rents were to be arrayed as men-at-arms. Twenty-pound landholders were required late in 1322 to have rouncies (horses worth five pounds), basinets and *aventails*, and gauntlets. In May 1324, after an inquest into the county men-at-arms, distraint of knighthood was ordered, equipment being provided; a later order stated that even if not taking up the order of knighthood, the forty-pound landholders were to have two horses, and the twenty-pound class 'horse and arms'. Two years later, knighthood was to be taken up after two, instead of the customary three, years' tenure, and defaulters to be cited to Chancery for contempt.[3]

V

There was little that could offend the most die-hard of county squires in the proposals for the pay of levies between 1318 and 1321. The main army sent against Scotland in

---

[1] Ibid. ii. 527 (79); the penalties were unusually harsh.
[2] Ibid. ii. 603–6 (19–23, 35–37), 608 (45–54), 737 (24).
[3] Ibid., pp. 527 (79), 604 (23), 316 (91–93), 657–8 (113–14), 670 (98); *C.C.R.* 1323–7, p. 191. On knighthood, see Chapter IX.

1319 was conservatively recruited, though immediately after its return the levies which met disaster at Myton were ordered to bring their own provisions.[1] Again, in 1321, some knights and squires were required to serve unpaid against the rebels, collective fines being imposed on the defaulters, and in case of open revolt a general muster without pay was expected. But it was not until the Boroughbridge campaign in the spring of 1322, when circumstances amply justified it, that anything approaching a widespread use of unpaid levies was made. To meet the Lancastrian threat, shire levies were called out on an unusually large scale. Only one of the writs included a promise of pay and perhaps we can assume that the service required by the other writs was to be voluntary.[2] Some of the writs were more explicit. Thus, the order for 200 additional foot-men to be levied by Peter Corbet from his estate of Caus stated that they were to serve at the cost of the community (*sumptibus communitatis*), a provision which presumably applied also to the order for armoured foot from Bristol. Secondly, in a writ to the mayor and sheriff of London demanding the completion of the city's grant of 500 foot, it was stated that the grant was for forty days at the cost of the community, and for forty days thereafter at the king's wages.[3] It would seem that many deserted before completing the paid forty days. The background of this writ can be followed in the Letter books and city chronicles. In the spring of 1321 Lancaster and Edward had competed for London's loyalties.[4] The Londoners sent 400 men to the siege of Leeds Castle, and, under pressure from the king and council, ordained for the defence of the city.[5] The Leeds contingent of 400 was paid by the king's sergeant, but the king attempted to get him reimbursed by the city.[6] It was presumably in connexion with the levies for Worcester, which involved acrimonious discussion in the autumn of 1321, that

---

[1] This and the following writs are in *Parl. Writs*, ii. 525–58; Appendix, pp. 176–200.

[2] Some paid retinues served, of course: e.g. that of William de Ros of Hamelak; E. 101. 15/37.

[3] *Parl. Writs*, ii. 553–4 (68). It is not entirely clear whether individuals or the 'community of the city' bore the cost.

[4] Sharp, *London*, i. 149–50.

[5] *Cal. of Letter Books 'E'*, pp. 141, 142–3. Riley, *Memorials*, pp. 142–4.

[6] *Cal. of Letter Books 'E'*, p. 153.

the king put forward his 'charter of great servitude'.[1] In fact, he obtained an increase of the contingent from 300 to 380 men, to serve at forty days at the city's expense, but granted a letter that it was not to be to their prejudice.[2] A few weeks later, 120 *hommes armez* were sent to join the king, and were present at the capture of Earl Thomas.[3] In the case of Coventry, 100 armed men were contributed to serve for forty days at the cost of the community, and special commissioners were appointed to collect their expenses, along with the separate grant of £100.[4]

The borough of Leicester was caught between two fires. In January the mayor was beset by demands from Thomas, which were frustrated by delays and bribes (Leicester's record in military service was throughout well diluted with the wining and dining of all who came to claim it). A few days after the earl's representative, the king's sheriff put in his appearance, and in response to liberal bribes, he reduced royal demands from the service of all between sixteen and sixty for fifteen days to the service of fifty men for two weeks.[5] Unfortunately the terms and methods of service employed in the counties are not revealed by the writs, though the fact that the cancellations of service were supposed to spare effort and expense of the foot indicates that the cost fell partly on the communities.[6]

With the Scottish war of 1322, when Edward was for the first time free from baronial opposition, the exaction of unpaid service became more serious. Before the May parliament London and forty other towns (rather more than had been addressed in 1318) were 'affectionately required and requested' to grant either foot-soldiers or financial aid— the former bringing exemption from the general array by

---

[1] G. J. Aungier (ed.), *Chroniques de London* (Camden Soc., 1844), pp. 42–43. Cf. the mayor's letter: 'the citizens pray to be excused from attending the king in force, as commanded'; *Cal. of Letter Books 'E'*, p. 154.

[2] The *Chroniques* say 380. In the exchange of letters, the city agreed to try to raise 500 in place of the 400 granted (they were upbraided with sending only 300).

[3] *Chroniques de London*, p. 43.   [4] *Parl. Writs*, ii. 557 (92).

[5] *Records of the Borough of Leicester*, i. 328–32. The total cost was £225. 10s. 1½d. including a £200 fine and £5 in bribes (sheriff, under-sheriff, and (indirectly) the king's confessor). Two vintenaries (*not*, as Miss Bateson, a vinter and his tavern!) and one group of ten served, under a constable.

[6] *Parl. Writs*, ii. 557 (93).

counties.[1] In the execution of the commissions of 25 March, the foot were directed to have ten shillings each for expenses, and to be well armed. Moreover, both the horse and foot of Yorkshire and small numbers of Welsh foot were to be arrayed in readiness to march against the Scots—without mention of pay. Some returns to the March arrays have survived, which show that large sums of money were in fact raised.[2] The foresters made it clear that they served with bows and arrows only, and beyond Gloucester at pay (the arrayers reported that they had neither money nor power to raise them). A London record shows that arrayers had purchased large quantities of arms—aketons, basinets, and gauntlets—for the arming of 200 foot raised in Surrey and Sussex, at a cost of approximately £240.[3]

At the May parliament the muster was postponed at the request of the lords, and several new measures were introduced. Foremost among these, of course, was the grant of one foot man-at-arms from every vill to serve for forty days after the muster at the vill's expense. Although this was clearly modelled on the grant of 1316, there were certain novel features. Both grants were parliamentary, but the present one lessened the service from sixty to forty days after the muster, did not specify the details of pay or armour, omitted the clause giving the lords of liberties command of those elected in their domains (although seeking to retain their co-operation), and warned the commissioners not to raise their own expenses from the townships or counties.

This scheme represented a relaxing of the demands of 25 March, perhaps as a result of pressure in parliament; the community of the county of Lincolnshire had complained that they could not possibly sustain the cost of supplying 4,000 foot, well armed and furnished with expense money.[4] The new assessment represented a reduction of the numbers of archers to one-third,[5] if towns are excluded. What was perhaps most extraordinary, however, was the actual quantity

[1] *Parl. Writs*, ii. 563 (124–5); cf. Spalding, ibid., ii. 568 (146–7), 581 (200).
[2] From Northamptonshire, for example, 500 marks; C. 47. 2/23 mm. 10–12, 24.
[3] *Cal. of Letter Books 'E'*, p. 170.
[4] *Rot. Parl.* ii. 400; H. M. Cam, *The Hundred and the Hundred Rolls*, p. 192.
[5] e.g. Northamptonshire, required in March to supply 500, had 212 vills.

of service supplied. Nearly 7,000 armoured foot spent four weeks in Scotland at local expense; and this was in addition to a supplementary 5,000 serving in response to orthodox commissions of array.[1] The expenditure which tells of their service also confirms the chroniclers' story of disaster; for it was an isolated payment of money and food issued at Leith on 24 August, clearly a desperate measure to avert starvation. Other records tell of opposition by ecclesiastical lords, overridden by the argument from parliamentary consent, and of negotiations with the larger towns which ended up with considerable expenditure on the part of the city fathers.[2] Altogether, Edward obtained more from the communities with less results than any previous ruler.

Beside this service of the vills, two other kinds of non-paid service were demanded by Edward: that of the Yorkshiremen between sixteen and sixty years old, both horse and foot, and that of the lords, knights, and men-at-arms. The Yorkshiremen, who had already been 'readied', were called out several times, and some may have accompanied the main army on its barren expedition. Most, however, probably served in defence under the hierarchy of county, riding, and wapentake or town arrayers, who made up the most elaborate (and therefore, presumably, oppressive) defence organization hitherto constructed.

Community-paid troops were an impossibility in overseas campaigns, so Edward's sole sins in this matter in the Gascon wars of 1324–5 were in postponing the time when he took over pay responsibilities until well after the levies had left their counties. In June 1324, about 2,000—later 1,000 —foot archers were levied from the southern and south-eastern counties to sail from Plymouth on 8 July.[3] Although

---

1 B.M. Stowe MS. 553, fo. 82ᵛ. (Cf. E. 101. 16/11, 14.) John of Trokelowe, *Annales* (R.S.), pp. 124–5. The pay of 'regular' foot is recorded in the aforementioned MS. at fos. 80–83ᵛ.

2 See the rejection of the Abbot of St. Osyth's complaint, *Rot. Parl.* ii. 413; unpaid service of cities and towns is recorded in Stowe MS. 553, fo. 82ᵛ. London supplied 161, York 60, Canterbury 20, Rochester 9 armoured foot. The Londoners had offered men in preference to money, but ended up supplying both; *Cal. Letter Books* 'E', p. 169; Riley, *Memorials*, pp. 147–8. It cost Leicester over thirty pounds to arm and supply twelve foot for forty days in the field; *Records of the Borough*, i. 340–5; cf. P.R.O. C. 47, 2/23 m. 16.

3 *Parl. Writs*, ii. 658–9 (118–21); *C.C.R. 1323–7*, pp. 199–200. Palgrave's account

these levies were to serve in Gascony 'at the king's wages', a writ concerning deserters shows that the communities of the vills were to supply at least some of their armour and to pay their wages at least in the earlier stages of their march to the point of embarkation.[1] The account book of Nicholas Hugate, the receiver of moneys and victuals at Bordeaux, bears this out.[2] A total of 1,140 foot archers received wages beginning 2–6 July. But these wages, in most cases, commenced from a point between the county of origin and Plymouth, the port of embarkation. Thus, the archers of Kent, Surrey, Sussex, and Hampshire came into pay at Winchester, and those from Oxfordshire and Berkshire at Wells. Paymasters were sent to Plymouth, but heavy desertions began from mid-July, probably because pay ceased to be forthcoming.[3]

The army of 1325 is possibly even more interesting. In December 1324 a general invitation was issued to serve at a published tariff of wages, and although at first no clerks were appointed to pay the levies between county and port, some arrangements in this direction were eventually made. A general pardon for all volunteers from Gascony, and individual pardons for some 215 criminals were issued. Some of these jail-birds, no doubt, entered into professional contracts of service, as had John de Lorteye the year before.[4] Although the levies were curtailed, and the 2 August muster cancelled, a considerable force was brought into pay and some of it sailed to Gascony.[5] The way in which this was done aroused strong resentment, and there were large-scale desertions. Stringent measures were issued to keep the army in being. After violent protests, and a ravaging of the countryside

is rendered mysterious (see his notes in the 'Chronological Abstract', p. 387) by his overlooking of the latter writ in compiling his work.

[1] *Parl. Writs*, ii. 660 (1).

[2] B.M. Add. MS. 7967, fos. 7, 7d, 82–97.

[3] Of the 180 from Gloucestershire, for example, twenty-three left without licence almost immediately, and the rest 'soon after' 17 July, when the last payment was made. Ibid., fo. 82d.

[4] *Parl. Writs*, ii. 690 (89); Gascon roll, 18 Edward II, pt. 2, mm. 12–2; *C.C.R. 1323–7*, p. 202.

[5] *Parl. Writs*, ii. 696–714; the *secunda flota* in Nicholas Hugate's account book, B.M. Add. MS. 7967, fos. 45–52d, 86d–100d. Cf. the horse inventories, E. 101/16/39, and the letters of protection (for 378 persons), Gascon roll, 18 Edward II, pt. 2, mm. 8–5.

round Portsmouth, the foot were put on board and forbidden ashore.[1] A surprising feature of this force was the large number of heavily armed foot extracted from the towns.[2] A total of 556 came into pay, and though the number dwindled rapidly until the remnant came home at the end of the year, nearly all this force (besides the county and cavalry contingents) reached Bordeaux.[3] It is certainly not the picture of complete weakness which is usually accepted. The price of this effort, besides being discernible in the constant orders against deserters, is dramatically conveyed by the 'Monk of Malmesbury', in an account which tallies with the recorded evidence. According to him, the foot were assembled and, after protesting violently at the lack of the promised wages and ravaging the countryside, were put on board under the expedition's leaders, Surrey and John of St. John. The Londoners, who had sent 140 armoured foot instead of the 300 requested, later sent their sergeant with arms and necessaries to lead and equip the contingent, about whom complaint had been made.[4] This absence of pay had caused strong accusations to be made, especially against Hugh Despenser, as the mainspring of the trouble, and even a plot against his life. At this point the 'Monk' introduces his account of the arrest of deserters. He concludes, significantly enough (after lamenting the failure of the parliaments, *tractatus* and councils to give counsel—due to cowardice and fear), by quoting the famous Roman maxim: 'For whatever pleases the king, however lacking in reason, has the force of law.'[5]

---

[1] Gascon roll, m. 2d. Only centenars, vintenars, and provisioners were to be allowed ashore. Cf. *Vita Edwardi* (R.S.), 279–80, ed. Denholm-Young, pp. 135–6.

[2] These came into pay on 5 June, a week after the men-at-arms (30 May) and three weeks after the county and Welsh foot (12, 14 May). The special arrangements for pay of the heavily armed are underlined in William of Overhampton's pay commission. Gascon roll, m. 2d.

[3] The largest contingents were the 137 from London—which still numbered over a hundred on 29 Dec.—99 from Norwich, and 78 from Lincoln.

[4] *Cal. Plea and Memoranda Rolls*, i. 7; *Chroniques de London*, p. 48.

[5] *Vita Edwardi* (R.S.), ed. Denholm-Young, p. 136. Later (p. 138) he gives a concrete example of failure to give counsel, in connexion with the proposal that the king should lead the expedition personally. The sharp opposition of Despenser and the absence of most of the barons accounted for the silence of the magnates. Later, in the midsummer parliament, they stated their approval of the plan in clear terms (pp. 138–9).

In his frantic efforts to raise an army against Isabella and Mortimer, however, Edward naturally trespassed outside the narrow confines in which custom had sought to enclose his power of conscription. Another impressive hierarchy was built up consisting of supervisors of array, advisory bishops, county custodians, and sub-arrayers of the hundreds and wapentakes.[1] One of the many writs, relating to arms and armour, has already been mentioned. Another was a 'form of array' ordained for the chief supervisors. This contained the clause that they were to ordain how wages could best be raised, and if they could not raise them, to borrow from sheriffs and escheators until they could be levied on the county.

VI

It may be concluded from the above instances that there was a definite increase in unpaid service after 1318, though mitigated by the existence of emergency or parliamentary consent. We may now turn to the third development we have noted: the increased use of the feudal lords in this period. Apart from the Welsh Marcher lords, the bishop of Durham, and earl of Chester, who had long had the privilege of levying all troops raised from their lordships or liberties, the duties of the lords had hitherto been confined to feudal service and, along with the other freemen of their counties, to assistance of sheriffs and commissioners of array. This had become rather more explicit in the abortive levy of vills in 1316, when the seignorial bailiffs were to assist in the election and to command and pay the levies (by indenture with the arrayers); and even earlier, general commissions to great lords may have concealed specific powers of array.[2]

At the end of 1318, after the reconciliation at the York parliament, it was necessary to provide for defence in the months before the agreed expedition could be mounted. This was done in a novel way, by ordering the earls of Rich-

---

[1] *Parl. Writs,* ii. 735–60, App., pp. 292–5. Cf. P.R.O. E. 101. 17/16–27. Pay was awarded according to whether the footmen wore armour, double armour, or no armour (at 4*d.*, 3*d.*, and 2*d.* per diem).

[2] In 1312 the earl of Surrey had been engaged in arraying the men of Sussex in twenties and hundreds: P.R.O. Ancient Correspondence, xlix, no. 8. His commission was to keep the peace. *Parl. Writs,* ii, Appendix, 53 (3).

mond and Lancaster, forty-two other lay lords, and many prelates in Yorkshire to array all their 'men and tenants', both horse and foot, who were between twenty and sixty years old, in readiness to serve in their retinues in case of Scottish invasion.[1] In January they were warned to be ready to serve, as the Scots were preparing to attack, although doubt as to the effectiveness of seignorial action is reflected in the clause that any tenants not in retinues must nevertheless be ready to serve. The lords were then ordered to ready their tenants and return their names by a given date, and finally the sheriffs were to order the assembly of all between twenty and sixty at York on 5 March. These levies were to be well armed and to have supplies for one month from the date of assembly. Thus both the tenants and their lords were burdened with new obligations.

After the summer campaign, when defence was again the main consideration, this 'array by tenure' was revived. On 4 September the sheriff of York was ordered to proclaim that all between twenty and sixty, horse and foot, were to be ready to go *with provisions* for fifteen days against the Scots, and that all lords of vills or parts of vills were to arm and prepare their tenants in like manner. On 27 October the earl of Richmond was ordered to raise his horse and foot tenants who were aged from twenty to sixty and array them in readiness. This latter force, at any rate, was never assembled. But once again, lords and tenants had been given new responsibilities.

The renewal of the Scottish threat, combined with civil war and later the expedition into Scotland, led in 1322 to a revival of this kind of measure. The lay barons—this time from all over England—were ordered to raise both horse and foot troops, who were to be ready to serve with them when required; and the prelates were to raise 'horse men-at-arms'. This was a precautionary measure taken, it was claimed, because the truce was ending; but no doubt was also directed against the rebels. After Boroughbridge, 'array by tenure' formed part of the military call-up against Scotland. In May the northern lay and ecclesiastical lords were ordered to arm

---

[1] For the measures described in this and the following five paragraphs, see *Parl. Writs*, ii. 511 (37)–749 (74).

and array all their tenants between sixteen and sixty years according to the Statute of Winchester. In June the lay lords were to get ready to serve all the horse and foot they could. In addition, the earl of Richmond was to arm according to their condition (*status*) any of his men not covered by the Statute of Winchester, and later to muster them.

At the end of the summer, as had happened in 1319, the lords were again called on. On 20 September the earls and thirty-three others were to muster with horses and arms and as many foot as they could raise for the relief of Norham Castle. In October the northern and midland sheriffs were to proclaim that all lords of vills and hamlets, or parts thereof, were to levy and to lead their own men, under the command of the commissioners of array.

Little use was made of this device in the French wars of 1324–5, but the magnates were ordered on one occasion to be ready with as strong a following of horse and foot as they could assemble.

Such were the principal measures in which reform and experiment were present in the years after 1318. In addition, there were several more or less isolated novelties which illustrate further the spirit of the régime. For Boroughbridge, a levy of one horse man-at-arms from each hundred was introduced. For the same muster, the mayor and sheriffs were notified that *exploratores* had been sent to 'supervise' their conduct of the levy—an early example in English history of government 'snoopers'. Another interesting development concerns the clergy. They appeared in a new role in August 1324 and February 1326, when some of the bishops were ordered to co-operate with the chief arrayers, or supervisors of array, in each county by receiving oaths and having troops ready.[1] In May they were ordered to array all the horse and foot of their households and retinues in defence of the realm.

Apart from the measures of Edward there were, of course, the inevitable abuses on the part of those who carried them out, which were not peculiar to these years but naturally added to the strength of any opposition. Thus the complaints

---

[1] There is a significant statement of the justification for calling on the clergy for military service in *Parl. Writs*, ii. 664 (13).

of prelates, magnates, and people, on the basis of which commissions of inquiry and adjudication were issued in July 1323, were directed against the occupational diseases of acceptance of bribes and impressment of the unfit. The result was the oath administered to arrayers by the prelates of each county a year later—not to spare the fit, or attempt to conscript the legally exempt. Many instances could be adduced of pay claims remaining unsatisfied; for example, the bailiffs and men of Yarmouth were still, as late as 1334, claiming repayment for the wages of eighty armoured foot whom they had sent to Berwick in 1309.[1] But complaints about the measures themselves were not advanced until the deposition of the king.[2]

In sum, the military measures of these later years were ambitious and in no way calculated to win over the people to Edward's support. Edward, aided by the Despensers, resumed the pursuit of his favourite ambition. He employed all the measures hitherto devised for the building up of an army, and invented new ones. He demanded knights, hobelars, armoured foot; he employed an unprecedentedly elaborate organization of arrayers to obtain and lead them; for the first time the lords and clergy were integrated into this organization; and if not recklessly oppressive in seeking unpaid service, he demanded enough to provoke measures against such service after his deposition.

VII

After all these innovations, it was natural that among the petitions for redress of grievances advanced in the first parliament of Edward III's reign were several which dealt with military matters.[3] These petitions give an insight, however imperfect, into the attitude of the commons to the increasing burdens laid upon them. They are yet another expression of the *vox populi* which had been invoked by the rebels of 1326–7 to help in the deposition of Edward II. They con-

---

[1] E. 159. 110/141–141d.

[2] An isolated exception was the attempt of the men of Cumberland and Westmorland to define the limits of their obligation. They went as far as to demand pay even for defensive service within the realm. Bain, *Calendar*, iii, no. 716.

[3] *Rot. Parl.* (Rec. Comm.), ii. 8–11. *Statutes of the Realm* (Rec. Comm.), i. 255–7.

sisted of grievances and of the remedies proposed to meet
them. The former should indicate the practices which the
commons opposed, while the latter may be usefully compared with the replies recorded in the rolls and embodied in
the statutes. Petition 9 embodied three complaints. The first
went quite unanswered: it requested that none be distrained
in future to serve against their will in lands where they were
not obliged to serve, contrary to their tenure; and that, in
lands where they were obliged to serve, none be constrained
to do so in any other manner than their form of tenure
allowed. The second part of this petition, that *gentz de Comune*
be not distrained to arm at their own cost contrary to the
form prescribed in the Statute of Winchester, was granted in
modified form: they were not to arm at their own cost except
as had been customary. The third request, that those *gentz*
should not be distrained to go out of their counties, except
at the cost of the king, was also modified: they were not to
go out of their counties except in case of sudden coming of
foreign enemies into the realm—and then it was to be done
as in the past for defence of the realm. The meaning of this
answer (repeated in the statutes) is ambiguous. But the most
likely meaning, if we take into account the relation between
the wording of the petition and that of the reply, is that they
were not to go out of the counties *at their own cost* except for
such invasion.[1] Petition 10 is even more obscure in wording.
The abuse was stated . . . commissions had been issued to
certain persons of the counties to array *gentz d'armes* and to
pay them and to lead them to Scotland and to Gascony at the
cost of the county (*commune*), the arrayers, and leaders, without receiving anything from the king, so that the county,
arrayers, and leaders had been seriously injured. The remedy
requested was that when the king issued commissions for
matters which concerned him, they should be carried out at
the cost of the king, and that no one be distrained to go into
Scotland or anywhere outside the realm, or to do any other
service which he did not owe by law from his tenements.

---

[1] A. E. Prince, 'The Army and Navy' in *The English Government at Work,
1327-1336*, ed. Willard and Morris (Cambridge, Massachusetts, 1940), i. 360-2,
argues against this. But the evidence advanced would merely prove that the Statute
was broken at once. It is not proof of its meaning. Cf. *Rot. Scot.* i. 217, 219, 221.

This request implies greater political sophistication, but hardly greater progressiveness on the part of the commons. The reply on the rolls of parliament and in the Statute was that the council (in the former), or the king (in the latter), wills that it shall be done no more. This, of course, was evasive. A more positive reply would probably have committed the government either to find pay or to obtain consent (whereby royal business could become common business), except in cases of emergency and defence.

It was, in short, against experiment and not against autocracy in military affairs that the first parliament of Edward III struck. There was no return to the baronial aims of 1311 and 1317. The Statute was less rigid in several respects than the petitions. But even in this modified form the attempt to put the clock back was in vain. Edward III inevitably took up the work of his father and grandfather in extending the military obligation of the communities. Only this time those communities were so strongly established as part of the *communitas regni*, whose highest expression was in parliament, that they could lift their opposition to a constitutional level, and make it a matter of consent in parliament. Thereby in the mid-fourteenth century the oppositions based on custom and on the constitution would at last be united.

VIII. *Conclusion*

This survey of Edward II's principal military problems indicates how closely related they were to the political and constitutional development of the time. Edward's determination to defend his inherited lands was in conflict with the baronial demand for reform of the realm. The initial deadlock gave way to baronial triumph after Edward's failure in 1310–11, a triumph perhaps precipitated by the king's anxiety to increase the strength of his armies at the expense of established custom—in this instance by the levy on vills. At any rate, this and subsequent efforts to develop the militia were hamstrung by the opposition. Co-operation after 1318, and royal victory after 1322, meant a rapid development of militia obligation, for while neither barons nor king sought to minimize the claims of the former to consultation in matters of war, both—and especially the latter—

were willing to see an increase in obligations which fell largely on the local communities. These 'communities', however, gained a great accession of power with the overthrow of Edward II, and used the new weapon of collective petition to secure military legislation of a cripplingly conservative nature. The impossibility of abiding by this legislation set the stage for the next development of this area of national life.

NOTE A. PARLIAMENTARY AND MILITARY SUMMONSES

IT has been argued above (p. 136) that the basis of the claims of the barons to be consulted in matters of war was the relationship between parliamentary and military summons. The interdependence of the two has been demonstrated for the reign of Edward I by Round and Jolliffe. It was continued, though not consistently, in that of Edward II. There was not only a rough identity of the names of those personally summoned, but also a direct affiliation of the lists used by the chancery clerks in issuing summonses. The nature of this affiliation can best be demonstrated by a table, with comments at points of special interest. Unqualified affiliation is attributed where names occur in the same order (without regard for individual additions or omissions). In many cases such an affiliation is not readily apparent, as the clerk must have used loose membranes, with the result that whole blocs of names got transposed. Elsewhere, a list in columns has at one time been read down, and at another time across. It has not been thought necessary, for the purpose of this table, to attempt any generalizations about the nature of the peerage which may be derived from it, or any explanation of the omission and addition of individuals.

Military summons dated:	Previous list with which directly affiliated:
21 June 1308 (*servicium debitum = s. d.*)	3 November 1306, parliament.
20 June 1309 (for readiness)[1, 2]	11 June 1309 parliament (*tractatus*).
30 July 1309 (*s.d.*)	11 June 1309 (plus ninety-seven new names inserted into old list in blocs).
18 June 1310 (*s.d.*)	First few names and some blocs follow 26 October parliament. Much enlarged.
2 August 1310 (*quanto potencius poteritis = q.p.p.*)[2]	Begins as above.
28 May 1311 (*quatinus . . . potenciori comitiva armatorum qua poteritis*)	Begins as above.
14 July 1311 (*q.p.p.*).	New list.

[1] This list was used for the next parliamentary summons, viz. that of 26 Oct. 1310.
[2] A request.

Military summons dated:	Previous list with which directly affiliated:
24 June 1312 (*q.p.p.*)	Regional list.
23 December 1313 (*s.d.*)	28 May 1311 military summons.
30 June 1315 (*q.p.p.*)	New list.
30 August 1315 (*q.p.p.*)	Largely 24 October 1314 parliament.[1]
20 February, 12 March 1316 (*s.d.*)	Largely 23 December 1313 military summons.
20 August 1316 (*q.p.p.*)	Largely 12 March 1316 military summons.
20 May, 17 June, 28 July 1317 (*s.d.*)	12 March 1316 military summons.
10 June, 20 July 1318 (*s.d.*)	20 November 1317 parliament.
20 March, 22 May 1319 (*q.p.p.*)[2]	Largely 20 March 1319 parliament (with many additions).
6, 14, February 1322 (*cum omnibus . . . tot quot habere*[2] *poteritis*)	New list.
25 March, 11 May 1322 (*s.d.*)	14 March 1322 parliament.
10 June, 30 September 1322 (*q.p.p.*).[2]	New list, much reduced.
27 November, 10 December 1322 (*q.p.p.*)	Regional, selected in part from 17 September 1322 parliament.
23 February 1323 (*s.d.*)	14 March 1322 parliament (via 25 March military summons).
3 April 1323 (*s.d.*)	14 March 1322 parliament (via 25 March military summons).
4 August 1324 (*q.p.p*)[2]	26 December 1323 parliament.
21 December, 17 February, 1 May 1324 (*s.d.*)[3]	26 December 1323 parliament (via 4 August military list).
5 August 1327	New list.
13 June 1385	28 September 1384 parliament.

NOTE B. THE ARMY OF 1322

FOR this army we have the summons list (for *servicia debita*), proffer roll, and a few protections.[4] The Wardrobe pay-book gives numbers but not names of followers.[5] A great number of tenants-in-chief made proffers, including over one-third of those receiving personal summons. As the protections are very scanty, no general comparison of proffered with protected followings is possible. However, in the few cases where comparison is possible, it is clear that a greater coincidence of names occurs than in 1310. Of the bishop of Ely's proffer of Robert, constable of Fleynburgh, with another knight and seven squires, the two knights and one esquire received protections as a group under the constable. William de Engelby was both proffered and protected as a follower of

[1] After much changing about, a parliamentary list had been established in 1311–12, which lasted till 1322.   [2] Horse and foot.

[3] This military list was employed for the *tractatus* summons of 30 Dec. 1324 and the parliamentary summons of 6 May 1325.

[4] *Parl. Writs*, ii. 568–9; C. 47. 5/10; *C.P.R. 1321–4*, pp. 184–9. Cf. I. J. Sanders, *Feudal Military Service in England*.

[5] B.M. Stowe, 553, fos. 56–61d.

John de Beauchamp. Robert FitzWalter proffered his son and two others, both of whom received protection as going with the son. Of the remaining two profferers whose retinues appear in the Patent roll, one (Peter de Mauley) had one follower common to each list, the other (John de Segrave) none. A small number of those proffering also served as captains of companies. Sir John de Botetourte, for example, proffered one knight with two barbed horses for a single fee; but he drew pay for a troop of twenty men-at-arms. Aymer de Valence, earl of Pembroke, served with a troop of 100, but proffered for his five fees. Henry Percy, with six sergeants proffered, drew wages for one banneret, eleven knights, and twenty-seven men-at-arms; while Ralph Neville came into wages as keeper of Warkworth Castle, after the main expedition was over, with a force of men-at-arms and hobelars.

The two principal conclusions which we may draw from the two armies we have considered are, then, that (1) the response of those personally summoned, while strengthening slightly, remained at about one-third of the total; (2) the retinues 'on the march' were much more closely related to the proffers, where the summons was for *servicium debitum* (in 1322) than where it was for 'as powerful a force as possible'. In neither case, however, was there any strong relationship. Many mustering lords brought one or more troops of twenty horses. It is just possible that there was a strengthening of the role of tenure reflected here, as in those commissions to lords to array their tenants which have been referred to above.

NOTE C. THE ARMS OF THE *JURATI*

THE attempts of Edward II to increase the armament of the *jurati* need to be considered against the background of the arms actually in their possession. In 1311 the Reading muster produced 8 men with sword, bow and arrows, and knife; 33 with bows, arrows, and knives, and over 235 with axes and knives. In Bridport, in 1319, a view of arms produced a muster of about 180 men, armed principally with sticks, staves, knives, and daggers, with occasional axes and swords, and no bows and arrows. These were years of economic depression.[1] In 1322 the citizens of Leicester had to find approximately nine pounds from each borough 'quarter' for arms and clothing of soldiers sent to the king.[2] These arms included hauberks, plaquets (for bacinets), and gauntlets.[3] The 1316 returns indicate a very low level of arming, but

---

[1] Mrs. J. R. Green, *Town Life in the Fifteenth Century* (London, 1894), p. 16, n. 1; *Historical MSS. Commission Report*, no. 6, pt. i (London, 1877), p. 491.

[2] M. Bateson, *Records of the Borough of Leicester*, i. 344–5.

[3] Ibid. i. 340.

they represent what was in the hands of the vills after an ineffectual plan had failed, so can hardly be considered typical; the Lose Hundred muster of 1326 revealed a high proportion of archers and also many with gisarmes, though the aketon had not penetrated below the centenar level.[1]

[1] *Parl. Writs*, ii. 744–8 (71).

IX

NOBLES, CAPTAINS, AND KNIGHTS

I

THE last two centuries of the Middle Ages saw the rise and triumph of the contractual system of raising armies. Although this might appear to be a simple matter of the feudal giving way to the commercial tie, the king's position at the head, and that of the nobles as leaders, remained unimpaired.[1] From the first it had been important for the king not only to take an active lead but also to have the support of his leading barons, whether accorded in a formal assembly or not. Kings who led poorly or with little noble support achieved little either in armies or in campaigns. The victory of Agincourt, for example, was founded on the enthusiastic support of the lords in council for Henry's plans.[2] This and the great expeditions of Edward I and Edward III make a sharp contrast with the ill-supported enterprises of Edward II in 1324–5, of Richard II in Ireland, and of Henry VI's reign. The great 'feudal' rallies of 1327 and 1385 countered the weakness of minorities exacerbated by political strife, but normally speaking popular kingship was more important than feudal tradition in these centuries.

The disappearance of the *servicium debitum* from the military scene was an extended process, beginning as early as the twelfth century and not ending until 1385. What took its place was the muster of lords or captains who had contracted to serve in war with a certain number (not always, but usually, agreed to in advance) of knights, men-at-arms, and archers. This system of war contracts was supported, and possibly anticipated, on the one hand by sub-contracts

---

[1] For an extreme example of 'commercial contract' viewpoint see B. L. Manning, *Cambridge Medieval History*, vii. 437.

[2] See J. H. Wylie, *History of England under Henry IV* (London, 1884–98), i. 455 f.; J. H. Ramsay, *Lancaster and York* (Oxford, 1892), i. 194 f.

between the king's followers and the men in their company, and on the other by indentures or grants of life retaining fees between king and lord, lord and follower. The early history of this complex of relationships is obscured both by the probability that early war contracts were oral and by the lack of good documentation in the period prior to the super-session of Wardrobe by Exchequer supervision in mid-fourteenth century.[1]

The feudal 'system' of military service had probably from the first been supplemented by the grants of annual fees in return for military service: fees which, like later retaining identures, were usually for life.[2] A very large number were granted to continental allies. In addition, there must have been many oral contracts with mercenary knights and foot 'taken on' at the Exchequer.[3] The granting of *fief-rentes* by lords in order to make up their feudal levies must have been a natural consequence of maintaining part of their *servicia debita* in demesne, while the existence of specific war or campaign contracts is implicit in Matthew Paris's account of the making up of the St. Albans military contingent in mid-thirteenth century.[4] However, while written contracts grant-ing retaining fees in return for service in war date from the twelfth century, the first extant written war contracts be-tween king and followers date from 1300, and the first written war contract between lords or captains and followers (or sub-contracts) dates from 1287.[5]

It is probable, as J. E. Morris has shown, that the

[1] G. A. Holmes, *The Estates of the Higher Nobility in XIV-Century England* (Cambridge, 1957), p. 81.

[2] Bryce D. Lyon, 'The Money Fief under the English kings, 1066–1485', *E.H.R.* lxvi (1951), 161–93; Dr. Lyon adopts the term *fief-rente* in preference to 'money fief' in his book *From Fief to Indenture*. The distinction between *fief-rente* and indenture is that the former involved homage and possibly some feudal incidents. Cf. also J. O. Prestwich, 'War and Finance in the Anglo-Norman State', *T.R.H.S.* (1954), pp. 19–43.

[3] J. O. Prestwich, op. cit., for the mercenaries. These contracts are hypothetical but can hardly be dispensed with.

[4] *Chron. Maj.*, vi. 373.

[5] N. B. Lewis, 'An Early Indenture of Military Service, 27 July 1287', *B.I.H.R.* xiii (1935), 85–89. Cf., however, the reference to a 1213 contract between John and Robert Berkeley in K. B. MacFarlane, 'Bastard Feudalism', *B.I.H.R.* xx (1943–5), p. 162, n. 1. War contracts between lord and follower may be deduced from twelfth-century evidence concerning such men as John Fitz Gilbert and John the Marshal, cited above, Chapter II.

contingents serving in Edward I's wars, even in response to a feudal summons, were largely indentured, or contracted, troops. The feudal summons, i.e. summons for service *cum servicio debito*, increasingly gave place to summons *quanto potencius poteritis*. However, the former remained a valuable supplement, or inducement, to contractual service long after it had lost its full legal force.[1]

The problem of creating a 'reserve' of troops for levy by contract was met in two ways; first, by the well-tried method of the Statute of Winchester and orders for distraint of knighthood, and secondly, by the granting of fees or annuities to knights, men-at-arms, and archers, in return for service when summoned. The latter system produced the social form known as 'bastard feudalism'.[2] It steadied rather than disturbed society by underpinning specific contracts with lifelong relations.[3] Even when the fiefs in money or land gave place to mere lordship, it remained a strengthening influence.[4] The retainer was frequently bound to serve not only in person but with as many 'friends, tenants, or "well willers"' as he could raise or as accorded with his rank'.[5] Hence they operated as 'arrayers', or in the words of W. H. Dunham, as 'a skeleton staff'.

The methods by which 'contractual' armies were raised and paid have been explored by A. E. Prince and R. A. Newhall.[6] Suffice it to note here that the Exchequer and Wardrobe, both directly and through special officials, made

---

[1] N. B. Lewis, 'The Last Medieval Summons of the English Feudal Levy, 13 June 1385', *E.H.R.* lxxiii (1958), 1–26.

[2] It was the solution not only to a military problem but also to the legal quandary in which *Quia Emptores* placed many nobles. G. A. Holmes, *The Estates of the Higher Nobility*, p. 83.

[3] N. B. Lewis, 'The Organisation of Indentured Retinues', *T.R.H.S.* xxviii (1945), 36 f. A late, but vivid, example is in *Paston Letters* (ed. Gairdner), no. 861.

[4] W. H. Dunham Jr., 'Lord Hastings' Indentured Retainers 1461–1483', *Connecticut Academy of Arts and Sciences, Transactions*, vol. 39 (1955), 7–14 and *passim*.

[5] Ibid., pp. 28, 39–49.

[6] A. E. Prince, 'The Indenture System under Edward III', in *Historical Essays Presented to J. Tait*, ed. J. G. Edwards (Manchester, 1933); 'The Strength of English Armies', *E.H.R.* xlvi (1931), 355–71; 'The Payment of Army Wages', *Speculum*, xix (1944), 137–60. R. A. Newhall, *The English Conquest of Normandy* (Harvard, 1917); *Muster and Review* (Harvard, 1940). An important aspect is treated well in D. Hay, 'The Division of the Spoils of War', *R.H.S. Trans.*, 5th series, iv (1954), 91–109.

strenuous and on the whole successful efforts to keep the armies in the field efficient and contented. We may ignore the will-o'-the-wisp of 'national' *versus* 'household' departments.

Three features concerning the leadership of these new armies tend to receive inadequate attention. First, it can hardly be over-emphasized that here, as in earlier periods, the element of royal leadership remained central; whether to mount a large royal expedition or to license a *chevauchée* by prince, noble, or captain. Secondly, as the council and, to a lesser extent, parliament won a share in the making of decisions, their co-operation became extremely important. It was through parliamentary statute, in fact, that royal control achieved its apex in 1439, when breach of contract was made felonious; the way for this happy development was paved by a long history of parliamentary regulation.[1] Thirdly, the descendants of the old feudal nobility were as successful here as in economic affairs in adjusting to the new contractual society and emerged as its leaders; no upstart captains rivalled the mighty hosts of Lancaster or, in the next century, York and Beauchamp.[2] A divided or apathetic nobility was as destructive of national welfare as a weak monarchy.

Fundamental as was the indentured retinue for the successful working of the contractual military system, it was not entirely adequate. As K. B. MacFarlane and G. A. Holmes have demonstrated, the permanent retainers only provided a fraction of the forces required for, and taken on, military expeditions.[3] The remainder, raised for a particular war, must be drawn from the general body of the armed populace. The Statute of Winchester still had its place, and levying

---

[1] This development is discussed in Chapter XII. See also *Rot. Parl.* iii. 213 (no. 35), 434 (no. 106); ibid. iv. 178 (no. 36), 351 (no. 14; refused).

[2] Cf. G. A. Holmes, *The Estates of the Higher Nobility, passim*; W. H. Dunham Jr., 'Lord Hastings' Indentured Retinues', indexed s.v. 'Peers of the Realm'; both A. E. Prince ('The Indenture System', p. 283; 'The payment of Army Wages', p. 169) and K. B. MacFarlane ('Bastard Feudalism', pp. 170–2) seem to underestimate the importance of noble status in the leadership of late medieval armies. The tenurial link, it is true, was no longer at the root of this, and changing fortunes were commoner than in the classical feudal age. But the great age of (more or less) upstart captains—Hawkwood, Knollys, Calverley, Chandos—was soon over.

[3] K. B. MacFarlane, 'Bastard Feudalism', *B.I.H.R.* xx (1943–5), p. 165; G. A. Holmes, *Estates of the Higher Nobility*, p. 80.

an army could involve compulsory or 'suasory' arrays as well as the mustering of retainers.[1]

Even knighthood and knightly arms must have retained some reality as belonging to the caste of mounted heavily armed troops who had to finish battles begun by archers, gunners, or sappers. Compulsory arms and arms practice for the lower orders became equally important, but are discussed in a later chapter; an attempt must now be made to survey the puzzling records concerning late medieval knighthood.

II

Edward II was as little interested in chivalry as any medieval monarch, and it would appear that no great effort to obtain knights was made until the end of his reign. Orders for distraint of knighthood were issued, it is true, in 1312, 1316, 1319, 1324, and 1325.[2] The first and last two laid the obligation on all with forty librates, but those of 1316 and 1319 raised the census to fifty pounds. In 1316 parliamentary sanction was claimed. The administrative practice varied. In 1312 security was to be taken and enrolled by view of two lawful knights of each county; fines of some variety were allowed, though £5 for a respite of two years was common.[3] In 1324 equipment was available to those coming to London to take up knighthood at the Wardrobe as a gift from the king, and fines at the Exchequer were invited. The land was to have been held for three years. The writ of enforcement eighteen months later reduced this limit to two years, and in May 1326 defaulters were ordered to appear in Chancery to answer for contempt. The respite of Walter de Traylly from knighthood on condition that he find two armed men when needed is good evidence that the measure was not merely a fiscal device.[4]

Edward III, of course, presents a complete contrast. He was the military monarch *par excellence*. Chivalry meant even more for him than for his grandfather. Knighthood received

---

1 Cf. below, Chapter XI.
2 *Parl. Writs*, ii. 418, 464, 523, 657, 735.
3 Ibid. ii. 419.
4 Ibid. ii. 741, 751; cf. J. C. Davies, *Baronial Opposition*, p. 239.

a great reinvigoration. The knights were to have an enhanced role both in war and government. In warfare, they were the *élite* among the men-at-arms, with additional horses, esquires, and pages, a special *esprit de corps*, and a still not over-developed armour.[1] They were thus the ideal partners to the bowmen in the unbeatable tactical formation which was evolved after 1330, and which men like Warenne and Harcla had already anticipated. In politics it is clear that the king and his advisers, as well as the commons, considered that it was highly desirable to have belted knights as shire representatives when warfare was being discussed.[2] Knights were in fact more active militarily than esquires or men-at-arms, while the baronage were most active of all. Such was the effect of the passing of feudalism! The superior activity of the baronage may be seen in their heavy attendance at the wars, culminating in 1415 when every active baron was present.[3] A most striking piece of evidence for the superiority of knights dates from 1338, when certain returns from Yorkshire indicate that, though there were twelve men-at-arms to every knight, the ratio among those militarily active was only four to one;[4] but this superiority was not maintained throughout the period.

There were three traditional avenues to knighthood—military tenure, royal service, and wealth. Royal service was probably the major route; judges were to become knights, as were leading household officials. Above all, on the eve of a campaign, on entering enemy territory, at the beginning of, during, or after battle, knights were created in large numbers.[5] Knighting to the soldier in the field meant immediate benefits in the form of the doubling of wages. At what point this was offset by the requirement of added armour and

---

[1] On armour see C. H. Ashdown, *Arms and Armour*, chap. x, and Sir H. Mann, 'Arms and Armour', in A. L. Poole, *Mediaeval England* (Oxford, 1958). There are valuable lists of 'full' armour in W. Hudson, *Records of the City of Norwich*, i. 395, 402–3, and *Sir Gawayne and the Green Knight*, ed. J. R. Tolkien and E. V. Gordon (Oxford, 1955), i. 567 f.

[2] K. Wood-Legh, 'Sheriffs, Lawyers and Belted Knights in the Parliaments of Edward III', *E.H.R.* xlvi (1931), 372–88; W. Stubbs, *Constitutional History*, iii. 410–16.

[3] Ramsay, *Lancaster and York*, i. 199.   [4] *Rot. Scot.* i. 527.

[5] See, for examples usefully gathered from the *Chronicles*, Joshua Barnes, *Life and Times of King Edward III* (Cambridge, 1688), pp. 95, 112, 140, 184, 355.

retinue is unfortunately not clear. The cost of the added military burdens and of the much increased political and administrative duties might in turn be met, at least in the long run, by grants of money fees or of land. The latter was preferred, and was frequently promised, even where the former were granted. Thus Hugh de Wrottesly was given £40 in farms on 21 May 1351 until lands could be provided; in other cases the grant was to last until the death of the grantee's father or until other provision was made.[1] There was nothing quite so desirable as a few substantial manors to sustain the honour of knighthood. At the centre of the retainer system, moreover, there remained the body of knights of the household, or king's knights.

The programme to make knighthood a desirable and enviable status must have been necessary to offset its obvious burdens. Various developments illustrate this programme. The founding of military orders, in particular that of the Garter, was closely associated with the holding of Round Tables and tourneys, while these outward trappings of chivalry were regulated by the 'Court of Chivalry' and enriched by the continued growth of knightly literature and the writing of history in chivalric guise.[2] In an even more direct way, the sumptuary laws of 1363 sought, incidentally, to elevate the caste by declaring that one required an income of £200 in land or of £1,000 from trade in order to rank as a knight; at the same time a sharp line was drawn between poor and wealthy knights. A petition of 1379 that only knights or those with £40 of rents should wear certain clothes, though unsuccessful, was clearly motivated by a similar concern. A century later a similar, though longer, petition was successful.[3] In Edward III's reign, knighthood

---

[1] C.P.R. 1351-4, p. 112; ibid. 1354-8, pp. 314, 320. Besides numerous enrolled grants cf. Barnes, Edward III, pp. 11-12, 140.

[2] See, in general, L. Gautier, La Chevalerie (3rd ed., Paris, 1895), pp. 89-100; G. D. Squibb, The High Court of Chivalry (Oxford, 1959); H. Nicolas, History of the British Orders of Knighthood (London, 1842), vol. i. On the Orders, Round Tables, and tournaments, cf. Cornish, Chivalry, chaps. v, x. An outstanding literary example of the vigorous Edwardian chivalric idealist is Laurence Minot, on whom see Cambridge History of English Literature (1933), i. 356-9.

[3] R.P. ii. 278-82; ibid. iii. 66; ibid. v. 504 f.; S.R. i. 278. The initial, but perhaps not the most long-lived, concern was with prices. The 'archer' class were similarly protected in their privileges, e.g. S.R. ii. 65; R.P. v. 505.

and the ways of the nobility were becoming somewhat ornate and unreal, but the complete divorce of form from reality was still far in the future.

Orders for distraint of knighthood now settled into something like a routine. Seven were issued by Edward III, all directed at the class with forty librates per year held for three years prior to the order.[1] No explanation for the orders was offered in the writs themselves, and it might be tempting to assume that their sole objective was to raise revenues by way of fines for respite. In view of the political and military importance of knighthood in Edward III's reign, however, it would seem wiser to reason that the aim was to exercise a continuous pressure on the wealthier landholders to take up knighthood, with the fairly expensive alternative of buying oneself out of the honour. These fines, though not as severe as in the reign of Edward I, remained heavier than they had been in the days of 'half a mark into the Exchequer'; they ranged from £1 to £2.[2] In later years they were to become established at a sum of £3.[3] Moreover, the orders for knighthood continued to be related to military activity. The first, issued in 1333, seems to have been connected with the muster for Scotland of that year,[4] and several of the others were similarly related.[5] As the income yielded by these orders was infinitesimal, we may conclude that their objective was, in the first place, to encourage knighthood.

The *Lytell Geste of Robin Hoode*, whose ballad source may well date from this period, throws valuable light on the practice of compulsory knighthood.[6] Commenting on his sorry condition, Robin says to Sir Richard-at-the-Lee (vs. XLV)

---

[1] *C.C.R. 1333–7*, p. 93; ibid., pp. 362, 418; *C.C.R. 1341–3*, 134; *C.C.R. 1343–6*, p. 450; *C.C.R. 1354–60*, p. 319; *C.C.R. 1364–8*, p. 266. Several of these are printed *in extenso* in Rymer's *Foedera*.

[2] Fines were entered in the Memoranda rolls under that title—e.g. E. 159. 111, fo. 190; E. 159. 118, fo. 277.

[3] *Foedera*, x. 656, 685 (1410); E. 159. 188 *sub titulo 'Fines'*.

[4] A. E. Prince, 'The Army and Navy', in *The English Government at Work*, i. 352.

[5] Notably those of 1344 and 1356. No such relationship links the writs with parliamentary summons of belted knights (cf. Miss Wood-Legh's list, 'Belted Knights', p. 385).

[6] Ed. F. J. Child, *English and Scottish Popular Ballads* (New York, 1883–98), vol. ii. Cf. W. H. Clawson, *The Gest of Robin Hood*, University of Toronto Philological Studies (Toronto, 1909).

> I trow thou wert made a knight of force
> Or else of yeomanry

to which Sir Richard indignantly replies (vs. XLVII)

> I am none of them, said the Knight
> By God that made me
> A hundred winters herebefore
> My ancestors Knights have be.

The fact that knights 'of force' were, like jumped-up yeomen,[1] a recognized and not altogether respected class in the popular literature of the period is of first-rate importance as evidence for the aims and effects of orders of distraint. The *Geste*, moreover, tells how the equipment for a knight was, in this case, six yards of scarlet and green, a courser, saddle, palfrey, boots, gilt spurs, and a yeoman attendant, without whom it would be a disgrace to be seen. (vv. LXX–LXXI.)

The proceedings in the Exchequer which frequently terminated in fines enable the student to elaborate the picture. They were consequent on an innovation introduced in connexion with the 1333 distraining order. A chancery letter to the Treasurer and barons of the Exchequer stated that the writs and shrieval returns had been sent to the Treasury with instructions for the punishment of remiss sheriffs, fines from those who had disobeyed the writ, and further inquiry into the names of men with forty pounds of land who had not been returned.[2] This order was repeated in connexion with the 1334 distraint, and no doubt the later ones also.[3]

The returns themselves were kept much more carefully than they had been in the past.[4] The immediately striking thing about them is that of the 2,000 potential knights only 150 were returned as not being knights in 1333 and only 170 in 1366—both sets of returns being complete. Most of the forty-pound class were already knights or had taken up

---

[1] Cf. Ad. Usk, *Chronicon*, p. 28 (a knight *infimi generis*); cf. Sir Gilbert de la Haye, *The Buke of Knychthede*, p. 14, ll. 26–31.

[2] *C.C.R. 1333–7*, p. 144.

[3] Ibid., p. 418; *Foedera*, II. ii. 912.

[4] E. 198. 3/18 (1333); C. 47. 1/13 (1334); E. 198. 3/19 (1335); E. 198. 3/20 (1341); C. 47. 1/14, 15, 16 (1344, 1356, 1366). The writ of 15 Oct. discussed above was attached to the returns of 1333. Original, but not enrolled, returns survive from Edward I's reign.

knighthood in response to the writ. The completeness of
these returns is, of course, open to question; as we have seen,
it was doubted by the royal officials. But entries to the effect
that certain individuals were invalids or otherwise unable to
take up knighthood, and other circumstantial shrieval notes
as to the number of inquests made, &c., discount hopeless
corruption, especially in view of the extremely active Exchequer supervision.[1] On the other hand, there were certainly
occasions when knights were not obtainable for civil duties.
F. M. Nichols records that in 1328 esquires were to be admitted to the Grand Assize if there were no suitable knights;
on another occasion, a sheriff could only find two knights
who were not related to one of the parties to serve on a writ
of right.[2] The sheriff of Northumberland reported in 1360
that there was only one knight available in his county, and
that he was unfit for work.[3] At the end of Edward III's
reign it was ordained that sergeants or esquires were to be
known as knights of the shire in parliament.[4] Nichol's evidence as to the lack of knights is, however, not all conclusive.
The first case he cites refers to an hypothetical situation and
the second to the absence of non-relatives in a local area
where two parties were claiming a castle; a situation per-
fectly compatible with a fairly large body of knights in the
county as a whole.[5] The Northumberland knights who were
not available to the sheriff would be largely occupied in
garrison duty; at any rate, the sheriff reported in 1356 and
1366 that there were only six and eight esquires respectively
with forty pounds rents who had not taken up knighthood in
accordance with the distraints of those years.[6]

The operation of these writs of knighthood must have
been largely hidden: men who 'took up the order' (the preferred phrase at this time) in anticipation or as a consequence
of the writs usually earned no place on the records. The exceptions perhaps prove the rule. In 1333 William Morant of

---

[1] This is evidenced in the Memoranda Recorda, discussed below.
[2] 'Obligatory Knighthood', p. 225, from the *Year Books*.
[3] Wood-Legh, 'Belted Knights', p. 383.
[4] Made into a statute in 1445; ibid., p. 384.
[5] It is to be remembered that the number of forty-pound tenants in a given
county rarely rose above one hundred.
[6] C. 47. 1/15 m. 11d; C. 47. 1/16 m. 24d.

Kent was noted as having taken up knighthood in the feast of Holy Trinity from Richard de Grey of Thodenore by reason of the proclamation;[1] John of St. Clair produced witnesses that he had 'taken up knighthood in accordance with the writ' of 1333. In the same year John de Vaus of Nottinghamshire or Derbyshire was returned as being liable, but a note was added to the effect that he took up knighthood as recorded in the *Memoranda* rolls.[2] The latter may well have been the result of action taken on the returns by the Exchequer. Such action consisted of an attachment of the individuals concerned who would then appear or send an attorney, and either acknowledge or deny the allegation. In the case of denial, he must show that he had in fact taken up knighthood—a rare event, as the sheriffs almost certainly erred on the side of the subjects in making their returns. Occasional cases do occur, however, in which individuals pleaded that they had received knighthood from some baron. John de Harsyk of Lincolnshire, who had been returned in 1333, brought a writ of privy seal to the effect that he had been made a knight by Robert de Morley at the siege of Berwick.[3] In the same year and county John Shleyth and William de Friskeney stated that they had received knighthood at Whitsuntide; William de Kyme confirming with witnesses that he had conferred the order on them at his manor of Kyme,[4] while Gilbert Bridsdale of Barrow and Ralph de Mauley pleaded that they had received knighthood on the occasion of the first assault on Berwick, at the hands of Henry Percy.[5] Henry Gernet of Essex likewise pleaded he had received knighthood from Richard de Grey at his Thurrock manor.[6] Such pleadings had normally to be substantiated by the personal testimony of the lord, or by the view of a jury of eighteen.[7] In the case of a plea that knighthood had been conferred by the king, a writ of privy seal was usually called

---

[1] E. 198. 3/18. This return, along with other evidence discussed elsewhere, disposes of Nichol's view that subjects ceased to confer knighthood after 1313.

[2] Ibid.   [3] E. 159. 110, fo. 166d.

[4] Ibid., fo. 143.   [5] Ibid., fo. 144.

[6] Ibid., fo. 159.

[7] In 1335 Thomas de Hertford's knighting by John de Mowbray was attested by the latter and by others of the king's council. E. 159. 111, fo. 179. Cf. E. 159. 118, fo. 191 (knighting of John Ferinband by Sir Ralph Basset), where a letter from the lord was required.

for.[1] After Creçy and Calais there were naturally several pleas of being knighted abroad.[2]

The usual plea of those cited before the Exchequer, however, was that they had not taken up knighthood, but had less than forty pounds per annum in lands, or had held it for less than three years. There followed an inquiry by a jury of eighteen neighbours (not necessarily knights) and a return—after delays running often into years—to the court. Either in anticipation of an unfavourable verdict or to avoid seemingly endless costs, many would come and fine or purchase a writ of pardon and respite and so bring the case to a close.[3] Others would plead that although they had forty pounds of land, it was exempt at least in part. From these pleas and their fate we can build up a picture of the common law on knighthood. In the assessment itself allowance came to be made for reprises and outgoing rents. Lands held in dower were held exempt;[4] lands held in right of one's wife, on the other hand, were frequently pleaded but not accepted as exemptions.[5] Other pleas regarding tenure were that the land was only held for life, i.e. the holder had no 'estate' in it (no judgement recorded);[6] and, later, that the land was held for the use of others.[7] Some of these pleas referred back to the decisions of Edward I's reign regarding burgage and gavelkind tenure. The former, it will be recalled, had been exempted by the 1278 *Statutum de Militibus*, and the latter by a writ of the following year. Gavelkind tenure as well as land held in the wife's right were pleaded in 1411 by William de Notebem of Kent.[8] Burgage lands were a more popular plea, especially by Londoners, whose attorneys presumably were well acquainted with the *Liber Horn*. Such pleas were successfully

---

[1] e.g. E. 159. 110, fo. 164. (The evidence required for knighting at Creçy and Calais is not made clear in Wrottesley's Calendar, *Creçy and Calais*, pp. 137, 147.)

[2] Wrottesley, *Creçy and Calais*, pp. 136, 137, 147; cf. also E. 159. 121, fo. 228; E. 159. 122, fo. 175d.

[3] Of course, at each of the four exchequer terms, the attached person had to pay an attorney's fee or incur a fine for contempt, so there can be no presumption of guilt.

[4] E. 159. 110, fo. 65.

[5] E. 159. 134 (1357), Michaelmas Recorda, fos. (unnumbered) 'ii' and 'iii'; William de Nevill was convicted in spite of the plea that of his £53. 13s. 4d. of lands, over £22 were in common with his wife and her heirs.

[6] E. 159. 118, fo. 205.

[7] E. 159. 207, Michaelmas Recorda, fo. 'xxx'.

[8] E. 159. 188, Michaelmas Recorda, fo. 'x'.

made by Richard the Lacer, Henry de Gisors, and Benedict of Folsham in 1341–2.[1] Benedict's case came up again in 1345, when he pleaded that his London land was not liable *iuxta libertatem* of London; this was finally allowed 'on account of the Statute'.[2] In connexion with this plea, it is worth noting that the city of London, in its official returns, gave no names in view of the fact that all land was held 'by free burgage', but clearly had not regarded this reason as adequate: the costs arising from damage by storm and fire made valuation uncertain, they added.[3] Other citizens did not claim the protection of the Statute, either because they were making the safer plea of insufficient lands, or because it was not held to apply outside London.[4] However, in 1358 a Yorkshire tenant successfully claimed the protection of the Statute which stated that impleaded lands could not be burdened with compulsory knighthood;[5] though it was ruled that as £20 had been the limit for knighthood in 1278, his remaining lands must not be worth more than that.

Besides tenurial exemptions, personal claims such as military service (especially if followed by knighting, even long after the day appointed), old age, long service, and the position of king's sergeant-at-law were all allowed at one time or another.[6]

After Edward III's reign, knighthood began to decline. In military matters, the ratio of knights to men-at-arms steadily decreased, and men-at-arms as a whole declined in relation to mounted archers.[7] This was partly due to the elaboration of armour to the point where it was too cumbersome and ornate to be really practical. In politics the requirement that representatives be belted knights was, at least for a while, formally relaxed.[8] Yet the passion for knighthood

---

[1] E. 159. 118, fos. 201, 226, 247.   [2] E. 159. 121, fo. 228d.

[3] E. 198. 3/18; C. 47. 1/16 m. 17; cf. *Cal. Letter Books* 'F', pp. 105, 289.

[4] E. 159. 122, fo. 87; cf. Benedict's plea, above; Humphrey de Scovill had lands in Bristol, E. 159. 134, fo. 16; cf. E. 159. 207, Michaelmas Recorda, fo. 'xxx'.

[5] Aylmer Burdet; E. 159. 134, Hilary Recorda, fo. 4.

[6] e.g. E. 159. 110, fo. 144 (Malcolm Wasteneys); E. 159. 118, fo. 194 (Thomas Weston); Nichols, 'Obligatory Knighthood', p. 225.

[7] J. H. Ramsay, *Lancaster and York*, ii. 157–8; C. Oman, *Art of War*, ii. 379; H. L. Gray, 'Incomes from Land in England in 1436', *E.H.R.*, xlix (1934), 609–39.

[8] *Dignity of a Peer*, iv. 674–982. The years of relaxation were 1447–60.

did not decline; it became, in fact, 'one of the most striking follies of the day'.[1] The ideals of knighthood received their definitive statement in the 'Books of Knighthood' and in the prose of Malory. Most public careers were crowned with knighthood, and the ritual of the joust and tourney, whether as a peacetime frolic or an eve-of-battle gesture, was more prominent than ever before.[2]

The Paston family illustrate very well the ways in which knighthood could be assumed in the fifteenth century. John I paid a fine to avoid knighthood; later, when it was rumoured that Edward IV planned to confer knighthood on him at his coronation, it appears that he had his son, John II, substituted. John III was knighted for his services at the battle of Stoke.[3] An interesting example of knighthood conferred by a great lord is that of Sampson Meverell (1387–1462) whose epitaph in Tideswell church, Derbyshire, tells how he fought under Salisbury and Bedford, and after eleven battles 'the said duke [of Bedford] gave him the order of knighthood'.[4]

The ceremonial knightings at coronations continued with possibly increased ritual, and the first handbooks began to appear. These knights of the coronation, because of the ceremonial bath which had long figured in the proceedings, came to be known from Henry V's reign as 'knights of the Bath'.[5] An important element among them were the 'king's

---

[1] J. Burckhardt, *Civilisation of the Renaissance in Italy* (Phaidon), p. 221; cf. J. Huizinga, *Waning of the Middle Ages* (London, 1937), chaps. iv–vi; S. Painter, *French Chivalry* (Baltimore, 1940); and A. B. Ferguson, *The Indian Summer of English Chivalry* (Indianapolis, 1960), *passim*.

[2] Cf. E. Vinaver, *Malory* (Oxford, 1929), chap. i; Sir Gilbert de la Haye, *Book of the Order of Knighthood* (E.S.T.S., vd. 62, 1914); F. H. Cripps-Day, *The Tournament* (London, 1918), chaps. 3–5; see the valuable analysis by S. Thrupp, *The Merchant Class of Medieval London* (Chicago, 1948), 275 f.

[3] H. S. Bennett, *The Pastons and their England* (Cambridge, 1922), p. 13; *The Paston Letters*, ed. J. Gairdner (London, 1940), nos. 457, 1016 and note.

[4] Quoted by K. B. MacFarlane, *Bastard Feudalism*, p. 171.

[5] The name dates from 1423, *Rot. Parl.* iv. 275. Cf. for 1399, *Archaeologia*, xx. 275. F. H. Winkler, 'The Making of King's Knights in England, 1399–1461' (unpublished Ph.D. thesis, Yale, 1943), has studied these knights and their careers from the printed records without adequately distinguishing (1) those knighted at the coronations from (2) those receiving robes and fees in the household (king's knights proper)—a confusion unfortunately repeated in W. H. Dunham, 'Lord Hastings' Indentured Retinues', p. 108.

knights', the household retainers who had figured strongly in English warfare and continued to do so.

There is no reason to doubt that the reissue of orders for distraint of knighthood continued to exercise some pressure on the wealthier classes to adopt the order.[1] At least as late as 1414 the Exchequer was pursuing the recalcitrant term by term, extracting fines both for respite and for the initial transgression.[2] A list of defaulters in 1430–1 numbered about 300—about twice the number averaged in the returns of Edward III's reign. Fines in that year varied from £2 and a mark to £5.[3] Nevertheless, the returns to the parliamentary oath of 1434 (against peace-breaking) reveal that only a handful of knights were resident in each county— Rutland, 3; Wiltshire, 5; Sussex, 6. That this handful of knights were on almost perpetual public service is to be deduced from the fact that they were nearly all drafted to form the leading element among the arrayers of 1436.[4]

Distraint of knighthood became a matter of parliamentary petition in the reign of Henry VI. In 1439 the commons, stating that some lieges had been fined for not taking up knighthood in 1430 and again for the same offence in 1439, even though some of the land was held in the right of their wives, so that they and their heirs were liable to unending payments, petitioned that such as had paid their fines should thereafter, for themselves, and their heirs, be discharged in perpetuity.[5] The petition, of course, was rejected, thereby preserving a source of revenue and irritation for some centuries. In 1450 the commons made it a condition of a tax that those paying it should have two years' exemption from knighthood.[6]

---

[1] Most of the orders, enrolled as was customary on the Close rolls, are printed in *Foedera*, ix. 180; x. 449–50; xi. 389; xii. 181, 185, 770.

[2] This provision in the writ of 1411 was repeated in 1430; cf. Michaelmas Recorda, E. 159. 207, and A. Steel, *The Receipt of the Exchequer* (Cambridge, 1954), p. 175.

[3] The returns filled both sides of two folios in the Memoranda roll for Michaelmas. In 1438–9 the numbers making fines were about 150—by implication a far larger number were returned; E. 159. 215, Trinity Recorda and Fines.

[4] *C.P.R. 1429–36*, pp. 519–24; H. L. Gray, op. cit.; cf. the good showing of the knights in the parliament of 1422; J. S. Roskell, *The Commons in the Parliament of 1422* (Manchester, 1954), pp. 92–93.

[5] *Rot. Parl.* v. 26–27; cf. Nichols, 'Obligatory Knighthood', p. 225.

[6] Ibid. v. 173; *Foedera*, xi. 389.

We may conclude, then, that the system of compulsory knighthood, the array according to wealth under the Statute of Winchester, and new orders regarding archery practice and sumptuary laws, were continued or introduced with a view to providing a reservoir of troops for use by means of contracts, personal summons, and commissions of array. The 'cavalry' aspect of those measures has been considered in the foregoing pages; it remains to inquire, in the following chapter, into the arming and array of 'foot' troops.

X

EDWARD III: THE FAILURE OF COMPULSION

THE political circumstances within which the military measures of Edward III's reign were undertaken have been clarified to a remarkable degree by the work of constitutional historians. The dominating political condition was one of co-operation, probably achieved as a result of a conscious compromise in 1330 which was not effectively broken even by the crisis of 1341.[1] This co-operation was in the first place between king and lords, and as a result Edward was able to pursue his military ambitions with their co-operation. Both in parliament and in the field the lords supplied leadership and support; in fact, there was a counter-influence of war on politics, for successful military campaigns on the territory of others helped to win for Edward the support of the sons of men who had been uncompromisingly hostile to his militarily ineffectual father.

The commons, however, were not to be left out of either the political or the military scene. That, as communities, they would gladly have withdrawn from the latter is seen by the Statutes of 1327 and their reply to the demand for counsel in 1348. As it was, Edward needed the constant help of the communities to supply the taxes, to furnish the defences, and to reinforce the expeditionary forces. The price which he paid even for a moiety of this 'programme' was the greatly enhanced political power of the communities; ironically, this power was used to destroy or, at least, to cripple severely the other half. In brief, the right of consent to taxes and customs was used by the commons to secure legislation reinforcing the limitation set by the Statutes of 1327 on the use of their military forces outside the realm.

---

[1] B. Wilkinson, *Constitutional History*, vol. ii; cf. M. McKisack, 'Edward III and the Historians', *History*, xlv (1960), 1–15.

That the economic and social development of the reign affected the history of military obligation there can be no doubt. Here, however, only a few tentative suggestions may be made—partly because the subject remains even more controversial than that of political history. In spite of the crises of the second, fifth, and seventh decades of the century, the economy remained buoyant enough to support larger taxes and larger armies than ever before. The uneven nature of the changes in prices and incidence of depression was such as to counter the natural tendency towards a more plebeian army. On the one hand, the difficulty encountered by the lords in changing from demesne to tenant farming on favourable terms, combined with the tendency of luxury articles to rise while staple foods fell in price (with consequently declining receipts and rising expenditures), must have constituted a pressure on them to enter royal service for fees and wages. Conversely, the advantages of declining rents, rising wages, and falling food prices must all have combined to make the peasant less willing to leave his peaceful occupations for the hazards of war. It may well be that their success in drastically limiting their obligation to serve except by consent, culminating in the Statute of 1352, was in part the result of a sharp tilt of the economic scales in their favour administered by the Black Death. Whatever the causes, the lords and captains were obliged to bargain for the service of archers and spearmen just as they had long learned to do for that of knights and men-at-arms, and the array of fencibles declined into a purely domestic measure.

Quite apart from general political and economic influences, the traditions of the past centuries continued to be effective in moulding the use of obligation. Never had the king's leadership been more important than at this time, when it was decreasingly arbitrary. The distinction between forces led by the king and those led by others was all important. In the campaigns which Edward headed in person, the general obligation to serve under commissions of array played an important if declining role.[1] In later years, when great nobles

---

[1] On the fascinating question of compulsion and contract, see J. E. Morris, Introduction to 'Northamptonshire Musters' (ed. J. Wake, *Northamptonshire Record Society*, vol. iii, 1926), pp. xl–xliv; cf. also H. S. Bennett, *English Manor*, p. 124;

or military captains led forces encouraged and sanctioned by royal letters, the militia were confined increasingly to those defensive tasks which had always been their principal vocation.

There was, in fact, an increase in the number of 'total' mobilization orders in Edward's reign, and the justices of the peace were, until 1359, regularly endowed with power of array. Special powers of array were added to the original commissions on several later occasions.[1] In short, the army reserve remained in being, though the form of its mobilization changed rapidly.

The creation of this reserve may well have been in part the result of contract, but G. G. Coulton's basic proposition that 'behind these [professionals and volunteers] he [Edward III] had a whole nation in arms' must be allowed to stand. This nation in arms was the product of the ancient Assize of Arms fortified by such new regulations as that enforcing archery practice on feast days and Sundays.[2]

I

A. E. Prince's thorough study of the strength of English armies in this reign may be endlessly extended, but is not likely, in its principal conclusions, to be substantially modified.[3] What may usefully be attempted here is an estimate of the relative strength of the contribution to the different armies by the national obligation. This is possible because the pay books normally divide their entries into personal retinues and county (and urban) contingents.[4]

J. H. Ramsay, *Genesis of Lancaster*, p. 70; and G. G. Coulton, *A Strong Army in a Free State* (London, 1900) pp. 8–11.

[1] On the increased levies of all '16–60', cf. H. Bennett, *English Manor*, p. 124; A. E. Prince, 'Army and Navy', pp. 351–2. On commissions of the peace, cf. R. Sillem, *Records of Some Sessions of the Peace in Lincolnshire 1360–75* (Lincolnshire Record Society, 1936), pp. xxiii–xxiv; and B. H. Putnam, 'The Transformation of Keepers of the Peace into Justices of the Peace', *T.R.H.S.*, 4th series, xii (1929), 34–35, 43, 45, and *Proceedings before the Justices of the Peace*, Ames Foundation Publications (1938), pp. xxviii, xxxix, &c.; on commissions of array, see W. Stubbs, *Const. Hist.* ii. 571–3; C. Oman, *Art of War*, ii. 118–21.

[2] The first order was in 1363, *Foedera*, iii. 2, 704; *C.C.R. 1360–4*, pp. 534–5; not in 1337, as Coulton, loc. cit. See also *S.R.* ii. 57, 163; *R.P.* iii. 643.

[3] A. E. Prince, 'The Strength of English Armies in the Reign of Edward III', *E.H.R.* xlvi (1931), 353–71.

[4] This method, however, weights the evidence in favour of contract; in 1337, for example, commissions of array were issued for the levy of troops to go in the retinues

In the first place, there were one or two campaigns where the county and urban levies made up the whole army, with the exception of a few household or garrison troops. Such were the Scottish wars of 1346 and 1355; in each case, the campaign was primarily defensive, the army's task being to hold off the Scots while the main armies attacked France.[1] In other armies got together for 'defence against the Scots', levies of 'foot' vastly outnumbered retinues; in June 1337, by eleven to one; in the mighty army of 1335, by four or five to one; in January 1338, by four to one; and in August 1336, by three to one.[2] After 1338, apart from exceptions already noted, a ratio of five to two in favour of the levies seems to have been usual. This was true for such widely different armies as the Scottish force of Christmas 1341, the Calais force of 1347, and the Irish army of 1361.[3] However, the great army of 1359 shows that the wind was blowing in a new direction, for in that year the retained 'foot' (including mounted bowmen)[4] outnumbered those levied by three to two; the first occasion on which this had happened in a royally led force.

The cavalry forces had always been predominantly assembled by the lords, and this continued to be the case. There was a decline in the practice, common under Edward II, of levying men-at-arms by compulsion. For great defence efforts, such as the army for Scotland in 1355, the counties were expected to contribute horsemen; London occasionally supplied men-at-arms for France and many mounted leaders

of various lords; these appear as personal retinues in the wage books; *Rot. Scot.* i. 486–509. Moreover, as the registers of the Black Prince show, the retinues of palatine lords might well be made up of arrayed as well as indentured troops; *Register*, iii. 199–200, 204–5, 224, 331, 449.

[1] Accounts have survived for the Neville's Cross campaign, but not for 1355. Cf. J. E. Morris, 'Mounted Infantry', p. 99. In 1355 the local levies who made up the force appear to have been largely unpaid; but cf. the financial aid by the inactive, and appointment of war treasurers.

[2] B.M. Cotton MS. Nero C VIII, fos. 261–261d; ibid., for 252–4d; E 101. 388/5; Nero C VIII, fos. 259–60. The ratios in each case are approximate, though they may well reflect definite ideas of the king and his advisers similar to those suggested in some writs of array.

[3] E. 36/204; Wetewang's accounts printed in G. Wrottesley, *Crecy and Calais* (London, 1898); E. 101. 28/21.

[4] The reader is reminded that for the purposes of this book, 'infantry' or 'foot' includes mounted bowmen, spearmen, &c.; 'cavalry' includes men-at-arms whether they fought on horseback or not (they usually did not).

—constables, millenars, and centenars—must have been drawn from the upper class of the *jurati*. Moreover, there were many calls on the tenants-in-chief to raise troops before 1342, and occasional ones thereafter; the late medieval summons is a sadly neglected topic.[1]

Mounted infantry proved a special problem. In spite of many efforts to increase their contribution, counties and towns remained sluggish in their response. In 1336, for example, the foot archers supplied by counties outnumbered those in retinues by three to one; but the mounted archers of the counties were only twice as numerous as those in retinues. By the end of the reign it was normal for the 'unit' in a contractual force to be a knight with men-at-arms and horse archers in attendance.

The steady increase in the system of indenture, uneven as it was in incidence, had some precedent even in the matter of strictly infantry service. As early as Edward I's first Welsh campaigns, the lords of the Welsh Marches had been expected to supply foot from their estates; in Edward II's reign other lords had been expected on occasion to see to the array of the men on their estates. The change in Edward III's reign, of course, is that the retinue took the place of the estate. However, a rigid line cannot be drawn between contractual retinues and territorial levies. The local official might be bound by a sort of contract to carry out his part of the bargain, and local communities might hire a captain to raise their contingents.[2] On the other hand, the war contract was never considered a purely private or commercial matter; it might be the result of a royal mandate, and the recruitment of retinues was both licensed and stimulated by royal orders, the resulting forces coming under royal 'review'.[3] Neverthe-

---

[1] Cf. N. B. Lewis, 'The Last Medieval Summons of the English feudal Levy, 13 June, 1385', *E.H.R.* lxxiii (1958), p. 1, n. 3. Cf. also such orders to selected northern nobles as serve *cum . . . toto posse quam potencius poteritis* as that of December 1355; *Rot. Scot.* i. 785 f. Many of the later summonses must, however, have been privy seal orders.

[2] See, for example, the security given by Robert Hamburg, treasurer of North Wales, to lead a contingent to Carlisle; E. 159. 111/182.

[3] e.g. in 1342 the king of Scotland entered into a contract for his force, and was given power of array and of pardon in order to fulfil it; *Rot. Scot.* i. 630–5. B. Manning's characterization of indentured companies as private armies is misleading; *Cambridge Modern History*, vii. 437.

less, strong as was the survival of compulsion, the trend towards contract was unmistakable. Even in strictly defensive forces, contracted troops proved necessary; in June 1339, for example, the failure of the Hampshire militia was cited as the cause of an increase in the forces retained by the warden of Southampton. In estimating the cause of the change, the influence of the royal household, which for some time had been employing both foot and mounted troops, must not be overlooked. Even more significant, perhaps, was the effect of opposition to the levies on the part of the commons in parliament.

II

The terms on which the levies were to serve had rarely been a subject of national debate prior to Edward III's reign. It is not surprising that the combination of almost continuous large-scale wars with an increasingly active and self-conscious body of lords and commons in parliament should have changed all this. Some of the discussions about military matters, and the institutions with which they were associated, are examined in the final chapter; but to understand the terms on which service was sought, some idea of the issues is necessary.

The crux of all legislation on military obligation was the question of limitation or extension of the king's demands. Several related royal practices received condemnation: foreign service contrary to tenure, in 1327; arming contrary to the Statute of Winchester, in the same year; service beyond county boundaries at the cost of the county, in 1327, 1344, and 1346; the provision of troops, or fines for the pay of troops according to the value of one's lands, in 1346, 1347, 1348, and 1352; similar exactions contrary to tenure, in 1352; money levies on counties or other local communities for the support of troops, in 1344 and 1348; prise of victuals in 1344, 1346, 1347, and 1348.[1] We may note, too, the charge against Mortimer that he had tricked the parliament

---

[1] *Rot. Parl.* ii. 8–11, 149, 159–60, 165–6, 170, 239; *Statutes of the Realm*, i. 255–7, 301, 321, 328; cf. W. Stubbs, *Const. Hist.* ii. 571–3. In addition, note the role of parliament in bringing the farce of scutage to a close; H. M. Chew, 'Scutage in the Fourteenth Century', *E.H.R.* xlix (1923), 19–41.

of March 1330 into granting one man-at-arms from each vill, to serve in Gascony for a year at the cost of the vill.[1] Most of the later petitions demanded parliamentary consent rather than a complete cessation of these practices. Moreover, until 1352, the king tended in his replies to justify the exactions on grounds of necessity and to make what had often proved a worthless concession, that they would not be a precedent. With the unequivocal concession of the 1352 request, however, the era of discussion ended, and the limitation of levies to defensive tasks seems to have been accepted.

The Statutes, based for the most part on these petitions, ordained that none were to be compelled to serve outside counties at their own cost except in case of invasion, when custom was to decide; that arrayers and leaders were in future to have the king's wages for the troops they raised for service in foreign parts;[2] that arrayers should not hold on to money levied for arming and mounting hobelars and archers;[3] that men-at-arms, hobelars, and archers should be at the king's wages outside the kingdom.[4] The complaints of 1346 and 1348, as has been seen, received fair words but no legislation. Finally, in 1352, it was ordained that no one was bound to find men-at-arms, hobelars, or archers unless holding by such service, except by common consent and grant in parliament.[5]

The Statute of 1352 has rightly been considered a turning-point in the history of conscription.[6] Even in Edward III's reign, however, the levy of troops at local or county expense (forbidden in 1348) was again the subject of complaint in 1371, when the commons put forward a petition, later vacated, that if no subsidy was granted for war, and men-at-arms, hobelars, and archers were arrayed in the counties, they should be at royal charges to the seaport or other place of muster 'issint qe les ditz communes plus outre ne soient

---

[1] Rot. Parl. ii. 52.

[2] Statute of 1327, clauses 5 and 7. Ibid., clause 7.

[3] Statute of 1336, S.R. i. 278: a concession which occasioned the false alarm that the king was to pay troops from leaving their counties.

[4] Statute of 1344, clause 7.

[5] S.R. i. 321.

[6] B. Wilkinson, Constitutional History, iii. 209; N. B. Lewis, 'The Last Mediaeval Summons of the English Feudal Levy, 13 June 1385', E.H.R. (1958), pp. 14–15; cf. J. H. Ramsay, Genesis of Lancaster, p. 70.

grevez ne chargez durant celle aide et graunt susdit'. The likelihood is that the proposed, or rumoured, array at county charges was abandoned and, with it, the petition.

III

Those features of the levies which contravened these laws or provoked protest deserve first consideration. A major question facing any king was the need to experiment in equipment and tactics, and this meant attempts to revise the arms obligations of his subjects. The notions of Edward II had required armoured cavalry and foot, so he had consistently promoted such a revision of the Statute of Winchester as would produce such troops. Edward III, on the other hand, is famous for the introduction on a large scale of the slowly evolved tactics of using dismounted men-at-arms and archers in a closely organized, integrated, battle line, and mounting them for transport and pursuit.[1] Mounted, rather than heavily armoured, 'foot' were the order of the day. In addition, he required a strong 'chivalry' to adorn and lead his forces and to give him prestige in other countries. The preferred ratio of the former to the latter was two to one.

To achieve these objects he sought, like his father, to modify and elaborate the terms of the Statute of Winchester. There were two phases to this endeavour. First, personal-arms assessment might be stepped up; secondly, orders might be given to find, rather than to serve as, the required kind of troops.

The second type of order was more significant in Edward III's reign. Although it satisfied what may be regarded as a natural preference to supply troops or their pay rather than to undergo the rigours of service in person, it proved no less obnoxious, and eventually led, as we have seen, to petitions and statutes.

In seeking to modify the 'Statute', it proved less provocative, and probably more useful, to demand the special array of a selected group rather than a change in the assessment of the whole community. Such a special array might well presage a wider order, but might escape hostile attention. Thus,

[1] J. E. Morris, 'Mounted Infantry', pp. 9 ff. C. W. C. Oman, *Art of War*, ii. 111–12, 146, &c.

there is no record of protest at the order for the arming in iron gauntlets of a selected hundred hobelars from Lancashire in the autumn of 1332.[1] Such levies, however, and among them must be included all orders for mounted archers, and in fact all levies of archers which bore on others than the £2 to £5 class, must be regarded, strictly speaking, as infringements of the Statute of Winchester, or for that matter of the 'custom' upheld in the Statute of 1327.

The first demand for arms without regard for statutory or customary sanction was the levy of mounted troops on the towns in 1327. In 1332 followed the demand for hobelars to which reference has been made. In 1334–5 the first full 'Writs of Arms' of the reign were issued.[2] In December 1334 each man with forty pounds of lands or rents 'although not a knight' was to have horse and arms for himself and for one other; if with twenty pounds he was to provide himself with these; if with less, he was to be assessed and arrayed in accordance with the Statute of Winchester. An important feature of this writ was the definition of *iuxta statum* as the arming of forty-pound and twenty-pound landholders in the above terms, for this cryptic phase was perhaps the commonest feature of all arms orders; this 'definition' of 1334 perhaps enables us to give a little more precision to its fourteenth-century usage.[3] The following January a writ of enforcement was issued, in which the form of the array was included.[4] In August 1335 and February 1336 it was enacted that all of *jurati* age were to be armed according to the Statute of Winchester, including knights and esquires.[5] The latter provision must have referred to the provisions for forty- and twenty-pound landholders made in the previous December. In May 1336 the array was ordered again along these lines, the holders of lands with forty and twenty pounds

---

[1] *Foedera*, ii. 846. Other troops were arrayed at the same time.

[2] A. E. Prince, 'Army & Navy', pp. 351–2, 355–6; *Foedera*, ii. 900. The assessment of forty-pound tenants, discussed here, involved the finding of the arms of another; such levies led to the distraint to provide troops according to the value of one's lands, which caused parliamentary protests in 1345–6, a problem dealt with at a later point.

[3] Another phrase frequently used was 'according to the quantity of their goods'; e.g. *Rot. Scot.* i. 216.

[4] Ibid.; *C.P.R. 1334–8*, pp. 137–9.

[5] *Foedera*, ii. 916, 931; *C.C.R. 1333–7*, pp. 516, 647–8.

being armed *iuxta statum* and in accordance with the recent proclamation.[1]

An order for the array of the forty- and twenty-pound class in the Isle of Wight in February 1339 was to provide a precedent for an important innovation.[2] This time each additional twenty-pound unit was to be assessed to provide one man-at-arms, no ceiling being set; a provision which proved to be the direct precedent of the 1345–6 measures. This revised obligation does not appear to have become a regular, or even common, feature of arming writs. It may be, of course, that the definition of *iuxta statum* in these terms continued to hold good in the innumerable arrays *iuxta statum* which occurred throughout the following century. In fact, this assessment may have been more widespread than the Chancery orders suggest. A 1339 muster roll for the Rape of Hastings, for example, assessed those with twenty librates at one man-at-arms and those with thirty (unfortunately none with more than thirty was listed) at one man-at-arms and one hobelar.[3]

After the 1330's references to the Statute of Winchester grew much less frequent, and in 1359, when provisions for resistance to invasion were being made after the long truce, the terms of the Statute had to be recited in the writ of arms.[4] The Council met later and was taken aback at the anomaly that no one with more than fifteen pounds of lands was assessed to arms in the Statute; but instead of re-enacting the 1334–6 order, it was content with a general comment that each, if fit, should be armed according to his estate.[5] Most of the ordinance was concerned with the assessment of these richer groups to supply money or arms, a subject discussed at a later point.

It has been noted that Edward II attempted to ensure that the mounted *jurati* should be armed as hobelars. This policy,

---

[1] *Rot. Scot.* i. 422–4. For the associated *forma parandi ad arma*, cf. below.

[2] C. 76/14 m. 18d.

[3] Printed in C. Dawson, *Hastings Castle* (London, 1909), i. 175 f., and J. G. Nichols, *Collectanea Topographica et Genealogica*, vii (1841), 118–26; cf. Bennett, *Life on a Mediaeval Manor*, p. 121.

[4] *Foedera*, iii. 449. The last promulgation of the Statute had been in 1344; *Rot. Scot.* i. 657.

[5] 16 Nov.; *Foedera*, iii. 455–8; W. Longman, *Edward III*, ii. 45.

with the addition of mounted archers, was continued under
Edward III. In 1344 hobelars selected from the cities and
towns were to be 'armed according to the Statute of Winchester'.[1] This, of course, was in a year when the infringe-
ment of the law about arms and arraying was a major public
issue. Now, while it is true that the statutory arms of a fifteen-
pound landholder could provide the basis of a hobelar's arms,
they certainly did not amount to the full prescription. The
arms of a hobelar were laid down in an order of 27 March
1335—viz. horse, aketon or plates, basinet or palet, gorget
(*pisa colerettum*), iron gauntlets, sword, knife, and lance. As
in 1332 the gauntlets were perhaps the principal departure
from the arms of the fifteen-pound class, though aketon or
plates had replaced the haubergeon,[2] and visor, gorget, and
lance were also additional.[3] Somewhat earlier in the same
year, a writ had ordered the array of all men 'who had lands
by reason of which they ought to be armed as hobelars'.[4] In
1338 certain hobelars were to be arrayed with arms and
horses 'according to their estate'.[5]

The same approach was made to the partial substitution
of mounted for foot archers. On the one hand, the writs for
arms either neglected this basic change or simply added a
phrase, so that many orders were phrased: 'armed with bows
and arrows and other arms according to their estate'.[6] There
is strong evidence that, without changing the terms of the
Statute of Winchester, the mounted archers and hobelars
were felt to fit in at the five-pound to fifteen-pound level of
assessment. Thus a man with thirty pounds of land could be
assessed to provide a man-at-arms and a hobelar, and in 1339
all with less than five pounds of land were excused from
assessment to serve as mounted archers.[7] The scheme of
1345, discussed below, assessed those with five pounds as
mounted archers and those with ten pounds as hobelars.

It is quite possible, however, that there was some difference between the requirements of an archer selected for

---

[1] C. 76/19 m. 9; *Calendar Letter Books 'F'*, p. 100.
[2] Which appears again in 1359, however.
[3] *Rot. Scot.* i. 328–9; A. E. Prince, 'Army & Navy', p. 339, n. 5.
[4] *Rot. Scot.* i. 324–5.   [5] Ibid. i. 532.
[6] e.g. 2 May 1338 (*Rot. Scot.* i. 529); 6 Mar. 1340 (C. 76/15 m. 29d), and 23 Jan.
1347 (*Rot. Scot.* i. 682).   [7] *Rot. Scot.* i. 573–5.

foreign service and one arrayed for home defence. The latter, at least in the early years of the reign, might be armed fairly strictly in accordance with the Statute of Winchester. Thus the order of October 1336, agreed to 'after mature debate in the great council', stated that levies were to have arms *iuxta statum*, and went on to say that the archers were to have 'bow, arrows, sword and knife'—the weapons of the two-pound class of Winchester—and others likewise (the minor weapons of Winchester being defined as staves and poleaxes).[1] An indenture between the arrayers and chief constables of a Norfolk hundred shows that the two- to five-pound class did in fact supply the bulk of the archers, of whom only one had more than five pounds of land, while the great majority had swords, knives, and staves or axes.[2] The chief addition in the order was armour—the aketon and burnished helmet (*bacinettum splendidum vel politum*). In 1355, when horse archers had become standard troops, those selected from Yorkshire were to serve *cum albis caputiis et nigris tipettiis*, but such precise additions were infrequent.[3]

We may perhaps conclude that Edward III's reign witnessed a more subtle approach to the arms question than had Edward II's. While the selection of men-at-arms, hobelars, and archers continued to be the principal mode of array, the orders for arming, or writs of array, tended to fall back on vague phrases or on such ambiguities as 'hobelars arrayed according to the Statute of Winchester'.

A strong reason for the absence of a vigorous policy of revising the arms of the *jurati* was the concentration on special levies of arms, or of money for arms, when selected forces were arrayed for foreign service. The need for such measures is quickly appreciated if the actual arms in the possession of defence levies are studied. Suffice it to note that in the array of Norfolk in 1336 few but the vintenars pretended to as much as spear, sword, and knife, most having merely staff or axe, and knife.[4] The archers were a small select body apart, consisting, as has been noted, mostly of two-pound landholders. The problem that arose, therefore,

---

[1] *Rot. Scot.* i. 459–61.
[2] P.R.O. E. 101. 19/37. The Hastings muster fully corroborates these points.
[3] *Rot. Scot.* i. 785.   [4] P.R.O. E. 101. 19/37.

was how to bridge the gap between the arms held according
to the Statute of Winchester and the full equipment for a
'pisa', gorget, 'aventail', body armour, 'wambras', 'rerbras',
armoured gloves, shoulder pieces, or most of these.[1]

IV

The second kind of royal 'purveyance' to be considered is
the levy of troops and of arms according to the value of one's
lands, or of the fines consequent on such an assessment. This
'abuse' conveniently links the complaints against infringements of the Statute of Winchester with those against fiscal
levies for the support of county arrays. It followed naturally
from the fact that once one went beyond the twenty-librate
holding of land, it became desirable to assess each additional
unit to greater quantities of arms rather than to more
elaborate arms.[2] The principle had been initiated in 1298
by Edward I, when an individual with a multiple of thirty
librates of land was to be assessed to the supply of more than
one man-at-arms.[3] Hence in the assessment of 1334 and
later, as we have seen, those with forty pounds were assessed
to two men-at-arms, and the assessment of ten-pound units
to provide a hobelar was anticipated in 1339.

Another precedent for the assessment of lands to supply
service was the custom of requiring the old or sick, or otherwise disqualified from personal service, to find substitutes.
In 1335 one John de Bukton was distrained to provide a
hobelar from his Lincolnshire lands.[4] The *forma parandi ad
arma* of May 1336, already referred to, began with a clause
to the effect that the weak should find others to serve in their
place with the arms to which they were assessed.[5] Two years
later, in April 1338, the clergy were to find men-at-arms,
hobelars, and archers according to the value of their lands

[1] One view of the full 'armour' is to be found in the 1355 Norwich muster roll;
W. Hudson, 'Norwich Militia', pp. 271, 276; Cf. *Rot. Scot.* i. 328.

[2] The continued distraint of forty-pound tenants to knighthood does not seem
to have affected this issue as much as might be expected.

[3] *Parl. Writs*, i. 320 (1*b*).

[4] *Rot. Scot.* i. 346. He obtained relief because he found sureties that he would serve
in person in Scotland.

[5] Ibid. i. 419–20; cf. ibid. i. 422 f. The levy of money to provide arms was forbidden.

for the defence of the Isle of Wight.[1] In May, on the other hand, the weak were to be assessed to find expenses and equipment if liable to service as men-at-arms.[2] The finding of substitutes was also enjoined in July 1337, August 1340, May 1344, and November 1345.[3] In February 1339 it was agreed in parliament that the 'rich' (prelates and magnates) were to serve in person and also to bring men-at-arms according to their wealth, and in 1340 certain lords brought men-at-arms, hobelars, and archers to Scotland *iuxta statum*.[4] On other occasions those liable to serve were to be distrained to find the *expenses* of others if unable to serve in person.[5]

The extension of the Statute of Winchester and the principle of substitutions for personal service provide the background for the highly contentious experiment of 1346, when troops were levied according to the value of lands for service in France. The kind of army required—a balanced force of men-at-arms, mounted infantry, and archers—had been evolved in the experiments of the previous ten years. The need to extend obligation and the certainty of opposition alike may be traced to the vigorous assertion of parliamentary control of war subsidies in 1339 and 1340, and the extension of this to special levies for war wages in 1344.[6] For the next great effort in France, Edward and his ministers would attempt to escape some of these stringent controls and restrictions.

The first step in the 1346 plan was, in fact, taken in October 1344, immediately after the explosion in parliament of the opposition to levies for war wages. On 20 October commissioners were sent out to find, by inquisition, the names of all laymen with 5 pounds, 10 pounds, 25 pounds, 100 marks, 100 pounds, 150 pounds, 200 pounds, and so on

---

[1] *Foedera,* ii. 1027–8 (cf. ibid. ii. 1061).

[2] *Rot. Scot.* i. 527.

[3] *Foedera,* ii. 987; P.R.O. C. 76/15, m. 9; *Rot. Scot.* i. 649, 665. There were several orders, such as that of Aug. 1340, in which Isle of Wight or Southampton inhabitants were given the alternative of returning to defend the island or sending substitutes.

[4] *Foedera,* ii. 1070; *Rot. Scot.* i. 600.

[5] e.g. in 1327, 1338, 1339, 1346, 1355, 1359: *Rot. Scot.* i. 221–2; *Foedera,* ii. 1025; *Rot. Scot.* i. 573, 673, 779–80; *Foedera,* iii. 455. The problem of the local community's contribution to expenses is discussed below, p. 199.

[6] Stubbs, *Const. Hist.* ii. 400–2.

up to 1,000 pounds of rents per annum, deducting all necessary services and reprises, and to send in their returns by
6 January.[1] On the 9 January a writ of arms based on this
went out, ordering that all with five pounds of land should be
assessed to *be* a mounted archer; ten pounds, a hobelar with
specified arms; 25 pounds, a man-at-arms. In addition, those
with 50 pounds were to serve with one other man-at-arms;
those with 100 pounds with three others, and so on, up to
1,000 pounds, proportionately.[2] The principle of this assessment did not itself go beyond those measures which had
already been taken. But while the duties of the twenty- and
forty-pound classes were relaxed (as compared with the
1334–6 scheme), the obligations of very rich individuals were
enormously increased. Moreover, the measure of 1344 was to
apply to the whole country, not to particular regions.

Logically, one would expect the new assessment to have
been the basis of the array of men-at-arms between sixteen
and sixty, ready for overseas service, which was issued seven
months later.[3] Yet the evidence of the returns suggests rather
that the Statute of Winchester was still the basis. A fair
number of the original returns have survived, and give a con-
vincing demonstration of the thoroughness of the commissioners.[4] It would appear that the assessment of the wealthy
and the array in arms of the rest were undertaken together.
A typical hundred would be arrayed under the title of
arrayers, constables, the wealthy, centenar, vintenars, and the
landless. Thus in Bosmere hundred, there were two arrayers,
one being assessed, at twenty pounds, to one man-at-arms;
the other, at ten pounds, to hauberk, iron cap, sword, knife,
and horse; the constables were two-pound men assessed to
axe, sword, and knife; of four men-at-arms, one with thirty
librates was assessed to one man-at-arms; the other three,
each with five pounds, were assessed to aketon, basinet,
sword, and knife (likewise two 'five-pound' clergy); two 'two-
pound' tenants were to have bow, arrows, sword, and knife;
a ten-mark tenant was to have one *homo armatus*; then follow

[1] *C.P.R. 1343–5*, pp. 414–16; B. Wilkinson, *Constitutional History*, iii. 208–9.
[2] *C.P.R. 1343–5*, pp. 427–8.
[3] G. Wrottesley, *Crecy and Calais*, p. 58. Cf. the postponements of 12 Nov.,
20 Jan., and 5 Mar. (French roll, 19 Edward III, mm. 8, 4, 2; 20 Edw. III, m. 32.)
[4] C. 47. 2/38–41, and *passim*.

the vintenaries of those with less.[1] The last group have a variety of weapons, of which *gisarme*, sword, and knife were most common. Thus only in the matter of the ten-pound tenant's horse was the statutory obligation seriously exceeded.

So far there had been no attempt to levy a large overseas conscript force assessed on the new scheme of 1344–5. On 26 February 1346 a writ addressed to the sheriff of Devon, who had failed to make a return to the earlier order, altered the assessment significantly.[2] Those with 5 pounds of land were each now to *provide* (not *be*) an archer; with 10 pounds, a hobelar; with 20 pounds, two hobelars; with 25 pounds, one man-at-arms; with 30 pounds, a man-at-arms and an archer; with 40 pounds, a man-at-arms, hobelar, and archer; with 50 pounds, two men-at-arms; and so forth. The troops so raised were to be at Portsmouth by mid-Lent.[3] On 21 March arrayers were appointed in all southern counties, with powers to choose replacements for the unfit and inadequately armed.[4] This meant that what had begun as a revision of the Statute of Winchester along well-explored lines had turned into an order to find certain kinds of troops for overseas service. It was this aspect of the measure which, as Murimuth points out, aroused such fierce opposition: the whole country considered it extremely burdensome and unprecedented, especially the part about going overseas.[5] As a large number of the troops so provided were inadequate in both physique and arms, orders to reject such, and to take fines from those who preferred not to go, were quickly promulgated.[6] It should be noted, however, that though personal service was commutable, the assessment (Murimuth to the contrary) was not.[7] Only two weeks later the coroners of

---

[1] C. 47. 2/49 mm. 35–39; cf. C. 47. 2/49 mm. 14, 17 (Blything Hundred) for a similar return.

[2] Ibid., p. 66 (French roll, 20 Edward III, m. 35).

[3] Postponed later, with Shropshire, to the quindene of Easter; ibid., p. 70 (Fr. roll, m. 32).

[4] Ibid., pp. 78–79 (Fr. roll, m. 21).

[5] Adam Murimuth, *Continuatio Chronicarum* (R.S., 1889), pp. 192–8.

[6] Above, note 4; the preference for home was at times expressed forcibly; see *C.P.R. 1345–8*, p. 112.

[7] The true situation was correctly reported in Sept. in the reply to the commons' petition.

Bedfordshire were receiving orders to supervise the assessment in that county and to warn those arrayed to attend a muster, while the treaty rolls continued to be sprinkled with orders to individuals to find men-at-arms, &c., as assessed, or to the Treasury, to cease levying fines from those who had proved their service. There were also many exonerations because of service, and reductions in assessment.[1] Moreover, the array of the *jurati* of coastal shires, and the supply of men-at-arms and quotas of archers by counties and towns, armed and supplied to the port at local cost, increased the sense of oppression in the commons.[2] In September, when parliament assembled, the commons protested against this levy, as also against *archeries* charged on the community (*le commune*), as being contrary to the promise made in the last parliament not to impose *mises* and tallages; they also petitioned against such charges on the people as *gentz darmes, hobelars archeries et vitailles* without parliamentary consent.[3] All that the king (or rather, council) would promise was that such levies, made as they were out of necessity, would not constitute a precedent. In spite of which, the sending of men-at-arms, *armati*, and archers to Calais was ordered in November to be expedited.[4]

In the following six years there were no major levies except defensive ones, and a lesser expedition to Scotland. The new arms regulations must have remained in force, however, and continued to rankle, for in 1352, the commons again petitioned that no man should be obliged to find men-at-arms, hobelars, or archers other than those who held by such service, except by common consent and grant in parliament. This time the petition was granted, and a Statute embodied the concession in almost the same terms.[5] Now, strictly speaking, none except those recipients of land grants which had

[1] *Creçy and Calais*, pp. 80 f.

[2] These arrays began as early as Aug. 1345, with a commission to choose archers in the counties, to provide with arms, and to lead to Portsmouth; similar levies were made on towns (Feb.); cf. also the levy of victuals, and of bows and arrows; ibid., pp. 58 f.; *Rot. Parl.* ii. 194, 399 (pleas for exemption from finding men-at-arms, &c., because of coast defence duties).

[3] *Rot. Parl.* ii. 159–60.

[4] *Foedera*, iii. 95, 96.

[5] *Rot. Parl.* ii. 239 (no. 23); *S.R.* i. 321 (*c.* 8). Cf. the certificates of exemption because of service, C. 81/1760.

specified such service would 'hold' by any such terms. In applying the formula of 1215 and 1327 to the conditions of 1352, the Statute was bringing to a close a century of great experiment. For it seems to have marked the end of such assessments, and to have led to a marked increase in new grants of land to be held by military service, and also, possibly, to the revival of the forms of *servicium debitum* in the war of 1385.[1]

Although hobelars and mounted archers continued to be levied, the former together with foot archers being increasingly to the fore, the burden of service presumably fell on the classes assessed to such arms under the tacitly 'revised' Statute of Winchester. As for the 'wealthy' they were burdened more with assessment to find money than with the responsibility for actual service.

v

Money levies for the support of troops, constituting as they did unparliamentary taxation, early received the attention of the commons in parliament. In 1344 they said that commissioners for the array of men-at-arms, hobelars, and archers had been levying on the 'people' twenty shillings or one mark for each archer (besides extortions made in the manner of arraying), and asked for remedy. The answer was favourable: if the troops went outside the county (*terre*) they were to be at the king's wages and not at the county's.[2] Ambiguities in this reply were clarified in the Statute embodying it: men-at-arms, hobelars, and archers chosen to serve outside England were to receive king's wages from leaving the counties in which they were chosen.[3] This left the crown free to levy wages for expenses within the county when service was foreign, and for expenses to the muster and even beyond if service was on the coast or in the marches.

In January 1348 the matter was again raised in parliament. Besides alleging failure to keep the concession of 1346, noted above, concerning the levy of troops on lands of

[1] N. B. Lewis, 'The Last Medieval Summons', pp. 14–15.
[2] *Rot. Parl.* ii. 149. Cf. the 'hobelar silver' withheld by the men of Harwich; D. Hughes, *Early Years of Edward III*, p. 197.
[3] *S.R.* i. 300–1.

a certain value, the commons petitioned against extortionate levies of money for archers, hobelars, and men-at-arms on the value of lands (£10, £20, &c., up to £100) [and also against the levy of sums of 20 marks and £20 on small towns which were neither cities nor boroughs]. To which it was replied, as in 1346, that such levies were made of great necessity and would be no precedent; consent was also alleged.[1] It should be noted that illegal money levies for the support of troops were not necessarily the work of unscrupulous arrayers; complaints against the latter formed a separate category. The question of illegal levies and pay to the muster, however, were inextricably connected.

Edward III inherited from his father the tradition of expecting the counties to pay their levies either to the muster where the king's marshal took over, or at least part of the way towards it. One of the aims of the Statute of 1327, as has been seen, was to curtail this 'abuse'. Nevertheless, the great costs of war and increasing frequency of expeditions to Scotland and France were sufficient to prevent the Statute having much force.

In addition to the burden of wages, the counties might be expected to provide other things: in particular, arms and armour, horses, and victuals. Both with these and with wages, it should be carefully noted, there were good lawful reasons why some levies should be made: the local communities had an ancient duty to support their representatives at least within the county, and it was also a well-established tradition that those who did not serve should support those who did. As has been noted, it was only a series of small steps from personal service to finding substitutes, thence to finding arms, and finally to finding money for the hire of substitutes. If, at the end of this process of concessions, the crown were to find itself accused of extortion from those not serving, it might well feel inclined to reject the charge!

For the decade 1327–36 most of the evidence on this topic has been carefully expounded by A. E. Prince.[2] It will not be

---

[1] Rot. Parl. ii. 166 (no. 16), 170 (no. 44).
[2] 'Army and Navy', pp. 360–2. Cf. also, for paymasters before and after the muster, J. H. Johnson, 'The King's Wardrobe and Household', English Government at Work, i. 224.

necessary, therefore, to discuss it in any great detail. One of the commonest types of levy was also one of the first—in which the county was to bear the cost of arming and arraying a large number of foot, and probably of finding the wages of these to the muster, no pay being allocated for the journey.[1] The 'commutation' principle was used in the Holderness array of 13 July, wherein those who did not serve were to contribute to the expenses of those who did.[2] Further possible distraints of wages were implicit in the order for men and horses from the cities, with only vaguely promised recompense, and the 'free grant' of men from Chester.[3]

In 1333 wages or victuals to the muster were to be provided at county expense.[4] Two other orders may be noted in which pay to the muster was ignored and those too ill to serve were to pay for the equipment of others.[5] In the majority of arrays pay to the muster was accorded by the crown.

For the winter of 1334–5 many commissions of array promised pay only from the point of muster, or not at all. Later, Welsh troops were accorded pay to the muster, and northerners from it.[6] Writs issued during this campaign ordered pay from a point intermediate between county and muster—for the Nottinghamshire levies, Boroughbridge and York.[7] Complaints about assessment brought to light the fact that arrayers were apparently free to choose the manner of levy for wages and expenses which suited them.[8] On the other hand, the plea of Lancashire deserters that they had not been able to get their pay from their *villati* probably referred to their wages inside the county.[9] We may note, finally, that

[1] 9 June 1327; *Rot. Scot.* i. 213; 'Army and Navy', p. 361.
[2] *Rot. Scot.* i. 217. The community was also to find the expenses of the leader-centenar. Ibid., p. 219.
[3] *Foedera*, ii. 188–9; *Rot. Scot.* i. 209; cf. ibid. i. 213; ibid. i. 211–12. On pay by London, see *Cal. Plea and Mem. Rolls*, p. 41.
[4] 'Army and Navy', p. 363.
[5] Lancashire and East Riding; *Rot. Scot.* i. 226, 227–8, 239.
[6] Ibid., pp. 279–80, 289, 294–5 (Wales); 291–2, 293, 294 (the North). The latter, however, were to bring victuals (ibid. i. 302); cf. 'Army and Navy', pp. 361, n. 6, 363.
[7] *Rot. Scot.* i. 299, 301. On the payment of wages, cf. B.M. Nero C VIII, fos. 181, 181a.
[8] *Rot. Scot.*, i. 316.
[9] Ibid. i. 319.

men pressed for service on warships also were to receive pay only after mustering.[1]

For the great Scottish expedition of 1335 a large number of writs were issued which thrust the burdens of pay and of supply on to the local communities. Some of these measures went beyond previous orders in their explicitness, if not in their actual effect.[2] No pay was promised to the mounted and other infantry ordered in March from thirty-three counties.[3] In May it was made clear that hobelars and archers were to be led to the king *sumptibus comitatus*.[4] Some levies were reduced because of the burden of their expense on the communities.[5] As in 1334, and as in fact was normal (though many difficulties arose), the Welsh were accorded pay from leaving their home parts. When many of the county and city forces had been commuted or reduced in the York parliament, the arrayers were ordered to return the money which had been levied for their equipment with arms and other necessities.[6] At the end of the year Yorkshire levies (foot and horse archers) were to be armed at the cost of the county, but, in spite of ambiguity in the writ, were clearly paid from leaving the county to the muster.[7] Ships' crews were this time to be paid, after an initial order to the contrary, though some ships served at the cost of the towns.[8]

In 1336 the county hobelars and archers were to be paid by the king only from Newcastle. As a punishment (so it would appear) for their refusal of these terms, it was ordered that many were not to get wages till they reached Berwick.[9] Parliament, in the meantime, was the scene of complaints about arrayers retaining money levied for the arms and expenses of hobelars and archers, as a result of which the return

---

[1] *Rot. Scot.* i. 317.

[2] 'Army and Navy', pp. 334–5, 351, 361–3. Prince deals very little with the advances in demands on local communities, though other features of the array are fully analysed.

[3] *Rot. Scot.* i. 328–9 ('Army and Navy', p. 339, n. 5).

[4] Ibid. i. 346, 347, 348, 353.

[5] Ibid. i. 339–40.

[6] Ibid. i. 348.

[7] Ibid. i. 383, 390; B.M. Nero CVIII, fo. 257d.

[8] *Rot. Scot.* i. 364, 367; Lynn, for example, supplied a ship for two months at the cost of the town—ibid. i. 337, 338, 342–3.

[9] *Rot. Scot.* i. 408, 418. For the autumn muster, see ibid. i. 456, 458–9, 462.

of such moneys was ordered.[1] A distorted version of these
events appears to have reached the counties in the form of
a rumour that parliament had ordained that the cost of arming and sending to the muster was to be borne by the king as
in old times. This rumour was scotched in a letter to the
arrayers, which emphasized that the previous order was in
full accord with past usage.[2] A writ to Yorkshire, where
there had been opposition, gave an interesting justification of
the royal demands—when the king was staying in the north,
all were bound by their allegiance to defend the kingdom.[3]

In the coast-defence arrays of the same year, the problem
arose, not whether pay should be forthcoming before the
muster, but whether any pay at all was due. Here the centre
of the problem was the pay of the Berkshire and Wiltshire
levies who owed service in Hampshire. This year the Berkshire men-at-arms and archers chosen to serve in Portsmouth
refused to go until paid wages; all they got was an enforcement order.[4] In the general defence array, already referred to
in its arms provisions, supplies and transport for three weeks
were enjoined on the communities.[5]

The strong opposition of 1336 must have had its effect,
for the following year there was a tendency to rely on small
foot forces levied by lords.[6] When these were afforced by
northern county detachments sent at the cost of the counties,
the order was most carefully based on a parliamentary grant.[7]
The costs, moreover, were apportioned in a way clearly based
on the idea of commutation of personal service, those with
forty shillings of land and less supporting the archers, and
those with more, the men-at-arms. Later in the year, mixed
personal and county groups were ordered to the muster
without provision for wages: but they were small in numbers.[8]

In 1338 the Yorkshire men-at-arms who were not strong
were to pay the expenses and equipment of the men-at-arms

---

[1] S.R. i. 278.   [2] Rot. Scot. i. 430.
[3] Ibid. i. 439. A sizeable Yorkshire force was already in the field when this writ was
issued.
[4] Ibid. i. 435.   [5] Ibid. i. 459–61.
[6] Cf. also the investigation of complaints of misuse of funds levied for the array
of hobelars and archers in Middlesex, C.P.R. 1334–8, p. 340.
[7] Rot. Scot. i. 495–6, 501–3. Many levies originally intended for France were
switched to the north.
[8] Ibid. i. 503–6.

selected for Scottish service. Yorkshire archers were paid
only on reaching the muster, and even a garrison force drawn
from that county had to be supported *en route* (to Perth) by
the men of the county.[1] The first arrays of county troops for
French service included no provisions for wages before the
embarkation muster (excepting, of course, for the Welsh),[2]
which may account for the conspiracies to desert against
which measures had to be taken.[3]

In the following year there were again both Scottish and
French arrays. The pay of the forces was negotiated in parliament, where it was agreed that wages should be paid by the
localities (*pais*) to Newcastle and thence by the king.[4]
Assemblies, with the instruction to spare those with less than
five pounds rent, were called to implement this. Their task
was to appoint commissioners to array, raise funds, and lead.[5]
The levies of archers for France were not promised any
wages before reaching embarkation, or possibly disembarka-
tion, point.[6]

A commission for both Scotland and France shows that
the arrays did not differ,[7] and the payment of wages to the
muster port was on one occasion at least specifically imposed
on the county.[8] In Sussex, money was being levied for the
arms of archers.[9] Ports again supplied ships for three weeks,
and marine archers were paid from going on ship, not from
leaving their counties.[10] In the defence arrays, the clergy were
to provide men and their wages.[11]

In 1340 the lords were called on to send contingents at
their own expense to Newcastle, and the arrayers of county
levies, summoned to serve under Angus, Percy, and Nevill,
raised expenses as well as troops; in their case, too, royal
wages began at Newcastle.[12] As in 1339, the levies for France
were on one occasion promised wages after landing, but on
another were clearly to receive them from embarkation;

---

[1] *Rot. Scot.* i. 529, 541, 543.
[2] *Foedera*, ii. 1018; P.R.O. C. 76/13 m. 6d.
[3] *Foedera*, ii. 1045.   [4] *Rot. Parl.* ii. 110.
[5] *Rot. Scot.* i. 573–5, 577–8.
[6] P.R.O. C. 76/14 mm. 19, 11d.   [7] *Rot. Scot.* i. 560–1.
[8] P.R.O. C. 76/14 m. 10d (Worcestershire archers).
[9] Ibid. m. 6d—an inquiry into abuse.
[10] Ibid. mm. 13d, 18.   [11] Ibid. m. 17.
[12] *Rot. Scot.* i. 592–4, 600–1, 603–4.

probably the latter represented the normal practice.[1] Perhaps the lax rule of the *custodes regni* explains the pay of coast-defence units out of county revenues this year.[2] It is possible, on the other hand, that the terms of the county-archer levies of 1341 were affected by the explosions which Edward had faced on his return; for the first time, wages were to be found from the county revenues for the archers on their way to Winchelsea, 'to spare the expense of the men of the county'.[3] When switched to Scotland, however, those forces were to receive king's wages only from the muster.[4] In other cases, the Scottish wardens were given power to decide when wages should begin.[5] The border counties, however, were apparently to be ready to serve in Scotland without wages.[6] The following year the arrayers had to be instructed to arrest those men who had absconded with wages received from the county for the journey to Scotland and from the king for service outside England. Others had got as far as Newcastle before being discharged, and were required to return wages received from the men of the county to take them farther.[7]

The preparations for Brittany and Gascony in 1342–3 involved no special charges on the counties.[8] In the defence orders of those years, however, it is possible to discern a renewed attempt to enforce tenurial obligation. Orders were issued for the defence of the southern coast (Isle of Wight) by those who were bound to do so by reason of their tenures, and for the withdrawal of those grants of land in Berwickshire for which recipients had not performed defence duties in Berwick.[9] In the commissions of array for the Loghmaben relief force, moreover, no provision was made for payment of wages.[10]

In 1344 planning for the renewed assault on France began, and the levies of the following two years undoubtedly

---

[1] P.R.O. C. 76/15 mm. 29d, 7.
[2] Ibid. m. 7.
[3] P.R.O. C. 76/16 m. 15d. (for the levies, cf. ibid., m. 17, where the men of Chester had already been promised such wages).
[4] *Rot. Scot.* i. 616–17.   [5] Ibid. i. 611 (13 Aug.).
[6] Ibid. i. 609, 611 (1 Aug.).   [7] Ibid. i. 622–3.
[8] For these arrays, see especially the Treaty rolls, *passim*.
[9] *Foedera*, ii. 1194 (cf. 1210); *Rot. Scot.* i. 639.
[10] Ibid. i, 641.

provoked the petitions and enactments of 1344, 1346, and 1352. There is no extant order which explicitly contained the demand for the levy of twenty shillings or one mark per archer which aroused the ire of the commons in 1344. Perhaps the writ of 13 May for the muster of 9,000 county archers on 24 June contained some such demand.[1] That the Statute of that year was designed to remedy such an abuse appears from the commissions of array which went out within a few weeks, which promised wages from the moment of leaving the county and stated that the array was to be in accordance with the Statute of Winchester. The muster date was put back from 24 June to 22 September.[2] However, no arrangements for this pay were made, and in August the arrayers had to be warned not to assess the lands of the religious and others to contribute, nor to make levies on *communes bones vills* and counties to find men and arms, nor to raise anything (*de rien lever*) from them—a decision made on complaints, 'with the good advice of the council'.[3]

The arrayers may well have been confused, for on 18 August arrays for 3,000 archers and 3,500 hobelars from the northern counties ordered that the counties, wapentakes, &c., were to find the wages of these troops until the muster at Newcastle.[4] However, at the end of the year special supervisors were appointed to see that nothing in the array contravened the Statute of Winchester,[5] and in 1345 pay was to be drawn from county revenues.[6] In the latter year was launched the ambitious scheme, already discussed, for assessing all lands to provide men-at-arms, hobelars, and archers according to their value. Other commissions ordered the array of all men-at-arms and quotas of archers first from the counties and subsequently from the towns. Nothing was said of wages being supplied by the government, and arms were specifically a local responsibility.[7] However, the London

---

[1] C. 76/19 mm. 15–14; cf. ibid. m. 13, for the levy of Welsh Marcher foot to be equipped and paid out of county revenues.

[2] C. 76/19 mm. 11–5; in May, from southern and midland counties only.

[3] Ibid. m. 1d.

[4] *Rot. Scot.* i. 652–3.

[5] Ibid. i. 657.

[6] Ibid. i. 666–7.

[7] *C.C.R. 1343–6*, pp. 569, 573; *Crecy and Calais*, pp. 58–60.

archers, while armed and 'treated' by the city, were marched to Sandwich at the king's wages.[1] In other cases, however, the provision of wages must have been a local affair.[2]

For the campaign of Neville's Cross and for the large coastal arrays of 1346, county supply was a matter of course. For the former, Yorkshire and Lancashire each paid eight days' wages to their forces, and the rich were admonished to contribute to the cost.[3] In his reply to the complaint of the commons in the September parliament (i.e between Crécy and Neville's Cross) Edward referred to wages only in order to point out that the men produced by the contested assessment went out at the king's wages. He carefully avoided the fact that these began at the muster, and not as the law required, on leaving their counties!

Early in the following spring, forces for Calais were levied 'to go at the king's wages'—to begin where, the writ did not state.[4] However, a case for the recovery of a small surplus many years later shows that the county arrayers levied substantial sums (in Essex, 200 marks) for the expenses of leading these troops.[5] Later reinforcements for Calais were to be paid from leaving the county out of county revenues.[6] In the same year northern levies of horse archers were to go at the cost of county or riding to the Scottish Marches.[7]

What must have occasioned the renewed outburst of the commons in January 1348 was the continued levy of fines for failure to serve in person in accordance with the 1346 assessment.[8] This time it was claimed, somewhat brashly, that parliamentary assent had been given, some of the commons being present. There is no likelihood of truth in either claim, for the writs themselves would certainly have contained some reference to consent if it had been given. The crown clearly felt under no compulsion to redefine its concessions regarding pay for troops outside their counties.

[1] *Cal. of Plea and Memoranda Rolls*, i. 221–2. So also were the Cheshire levies; H. J. Hewitt, *The Black Prince's Expedition of 1355–1357* (Manchester, 1958), p. 16.
[2] *Crécy and Calais*, pp. 66 f.
[3] *Rot. Scot.* i. 668–74; J. E. Morris, 'Mounted Infantry', pp. 98–99.
[4] *Foedera*, iii. 107 f.
[5] E. 108. 159/134, fo. 'xiv' (the folios are not numbered).
[6] *Foedera*, iii. 135.
[7] *Rot. Scot.* i. 682–3.
[8] *Rot. Parl.* ii. 166 (16), 170 (44). 'Great necessity' was also pleaded.

For the naval defence against Spanish naval forces in 1350, Edward called on county volunteers (men-at-arms, hobelars, and archers) and also demanded small quotas of *armati* from each town.[1] The following year considerable numbers of county archers were levied by arrayers for a royal expedition, and some may have sailed with the earl of Warwick for the relief of St. Jean d'Angely.[2]

In the next major 'foreign' expedition involving county levies, the Scottish war of 1355–6, the government had no hesitation in levying the wages of the forces (almost entirely northern) from county to muster, first on those of their fellow *jurati* who were unfit to serve, and second 'by rational distribution on the men of the county'.[3]

Nor were the levies for France normally paid before embarking. Although the writs of array were not always explicit in this matter, the incentive value of king's wages to the muster or port was so potent that they would almost certainly have been mentioned if they were being accorded. Thus the abortive levies of 1350 were to be at wages from Sandwich.[4] The Cheshire and Welsh levies for the prince of Wales's expedition of 1355–6, on the other hand, were paid for a fixed period of march to the muster; but when, three years later, King Edward took the field in person with one of the greatest armies of the reign, he levied archers armed at the cost of the counties, 'in view of the pressing necessity', and led at the same charge to the muster.[5] Kentish reinforcements for Calais in 1362 were to be paid on arrival, but in 1368 were to be armed and paid out of county revenues.[6] In the latter years the London contingent, as in 1345, was armed by the city and paid in transit by the king.[7]

---

[1] French roll, 20 Mar.; from G. Wrottesley, 'Military Service of Staffordshire Tenants', in *Collections for a History of Staffordshire*, viii (1887), 93.

[2] Ibid.; cf. Longman, *Edward III*, i. 331. The same numbers were again called for in 1352; 'Staffordshire Tenants', p. 94; *Foedera*, iii. 243.

[3] *Rot. Scot.* i. 750–85. The few archers from Essex were to have wages from county revenues; ibid. i. 784. These may have been 'retained', as they were summoned by name. No pay arrangements were made for the Forest of Dean archers; ibid. i. 785.

[4] *Foedera*, iii. 194.

[5] Ibid. 415–16; *Black Prince's Register*, iii. 199 f., 331 f. On the 1356 force, see H. J. Hewitt, *The Black Prince's Expedition*, pp. 16–17, and G. Wrottesley, 'Military Service . . . by Staffordshire Tenants', p. 102.

[6] *Foedera*, iii. 675, 853. In 1368 there were also detachments from Surrey, Sussex, and Essex.   [7] *Cal. of Letter Book 'G'*, pp. 242–5.

The pay of levies for the great non-royal *chevauchées* of
1366–76 arouses interest. In 1366 archers sent to the prince
of Wales and to John of Gaunt were to go at the cost of those
princes.[1] The same was true of William of Windsor's Yorkshire archers (for Ireland) in 1368, and of the volunteers for
service under Knollys in 1370. But in Lancaster's expedition of 1369 and the smaller force of Warwick and Suffolk
the following year, county archers and *armati* were levied to
go to the ports of embarkation at the costs of the counties.
These chancery orders may be compared with the procedure
in the case of levies by the great palatine princes.

Defence arrays were frequent in these years of growing
Franco-Spanish sea-power. Undoubtedly, the men who
served were in most cases armed and paid out of local resources, while the arrayers themselves, besides having extensive coercive powers, were threatened with forfeiture of
life and limbs.[2] When, as in 1360, pay was accorded to
defence troops leaving their counties, it was probably because they were to leave the country as a sea-borne force.[3]

VI

It appears from the foregoing analysis that the statute
against finding men according to the value of one's lands was
more effective than the one against money levies to support
county troops. In the former case, the Statute of Winchester
(tacitly modified to require arming as men-at-arms, hobelars,
and archers) came back into force. This was a victory for the
divitii, who had been the chief target of the 1345–6 reassessment. In the latter case, however, the responsibilities of
the counties, on occasion of a royally led expedition, appear
to have been kept up in their extended form, in spite of a
brief period of compliance with parliament's wishes. But the
real success of the *communitates* is to be sought not so much
in the form of such arrays as were made as in the supersession
of the arrays altogether. In their place was substituted the

---

[1] The arrays discussed in this paragraph are to be found in *Foedera*, iii. 797, 799,
854, 863–5, 890, 895; the expenses of messengers bearing these commissions are on
the Issue Rolls; M. C. Hill, *The King's Messengers* (London, 1961), p. 91.

[2] See, for example, the commissions of Feb. 1370; ibid. iii. 887.

[3] Ibid. iii. 478.

system of big professional or princely forays which made little use of compulsion.[1] The negative attitude to conscription was a contributory cause to the change in the method of assembling armies after the initial decade of the Hundred Years War.

NOTE A. CORRUPTION AND OBSTRUCTION

I T is hardly necessary to stress the ubiquity of what J. E. Morris called 'Falstaffs and Shallows' of real life. The Chancery rolls abound in inquiries into corruption on the part of the arrayers and also, be it added, to desertion and obstruction on the part of the levies. It would be misleading, however, to concentrate on the Falstaffs and Shallows and ignore the Bardolphs and Bullcalfs. Nothing is more tedious than a recital of abuses; it will perhaps suffice to note that peculation of funds levied for arms, wages, and supplies, extortion of such funds without good cause, and bribery to choose the unqualified (the 'Feebles'), were perhaps the most frequent subjects of inquiry and (very occasionally, as in 1336) of parliamentary complaints.[2] The profitable French wars occasioned less abuse than had the unpopular Scottish expeditions. Where profit waned and compulsion rose, the opportunities for corruption and the temptation of desertion also increased.[3] The taking of securities to serve, and the use of careful exposition and negotiation were clearly more constructive, if less frequent, solutions than the piling up of commissions of enforcement.[4]

NOTE B. WAGE RATES

T H E wage rates of the upper categories—earls, bannerets, knights, and *scutiferi*—remained fairly constant. Variations are highly significant. The double rates of Flanders in 1338–9 (with rate and a half if living in the household) were perhaps the product of over-confidence and novelty; those of 1370, of desperation.

Below the 'upper crust' were the skilled and semi-skilled artisans of

---

[1] See on this B. Wilkinson, *Constitutional History*, iii. 209.

[2] Cf. A. E. Prince, 'Army and Navy', pp. 359–61, on both desertion and corruption. Rival or bogus arrayers are there noted as a frequent problem. Cf. also *Rot. Scot.* i. 316, 573; C. 76/14 m. 6d. For the contrary abuse—commissioners kept waiting for years to recoup their expenses, cf. D. L. Evans, 'Principality of Wales', p. 58, n. 4; and for similar troubles, J. G. Edwards, *Calendar of Ancient Correspondence Concerning Wales*, pp. 191, 235–6.

[3] A. E. Prince, loc. cit.

[4] In addition to Prince's references, cf. *Rot. Scot.* i. 244, 494. Commissions for the arrest of deserters continued throughout, however: *Rot. Scot., passim.*

war—from the proud *armatus* of London to the humble Welsh spear-man. The *armati* were paid 6*d.* a day in 1338, 1343, 1360, 1380.[1] Hobelars drew either 6*d.* or 4*d.*, usually the latter. They drew 6*d.* from the warden of Edinburgh Castle in 1335, although only allowed 4*d.*, and 4*d.* in 1340 when without horses.[2] Most of the county hobelars in 1334–5, 1336, 1337, 1339 drew 4*d.*, but in 1341 a few drew 3*d.* and the rest 6*d.*[3] Mounted archers, who were roughly the equivalent of hobelars, were paid 6*d.* on special occasions, but ordinary county levies drew 4*d.* in the Scottish wars, 1334–6. Sixpence was paid to those on the way to Scotland *quia in terra pais*, in 1334–5, to Cheshire and bodyguard archers, and to a few of those serving prior to the king's arrival, and in 1335 to those *de retinentione*.[4] The drop in pay was not normal, but occasioned by the promise of all the lands and goods they could seize when in Scotland.[5] Normally on foreign soil pay increased or stayed the same.[6] In 1341 the horse archers, like the hobelars, received either 6*d.* or 3*d.*, possibly the latter being without horses. In Europe, 6*d.* was paid, even when, as in 1338–9, men-at-arms drew two shillings; when the rate was again doubled at the end of the reign, however, they drew one shilling.[7] *Valetti regis*, who may at this period have been archers, hobelars, or *armati*, drew 6*d.* In the fifteenth century the rate for mounted archers and spearmen serving in France went up to 8*d.*[8]

Foot archers and Welsh foot spearmen normally drew 2*d.*, but received 3*d.* when they were part of a company in which a mounted soldier earned 6*d.*; i.e. wages were halved if one was not mounted.[9] In 1359 the archers of the royal household were, surprisingly, the only ones to draw 3*d.* This may have been because they were 'living in' or because they were foot troops.[10] Welsh archers also drew 2*d.*, even on occasions when their English confreres drew more.[11] The reason for the lower pay of Welsh archers has eluded students of the subject. Perhaps the main reason was lack of armour—the characteristic of the Welsh

---

[1] These and the following figures, principally from Exchequer and Household Accounts, are intended to constitute a 'fair sample' and a record of exceptions.

[2] A. E. Prince, 'Army and Navy', p. 339 n., who states erroneously that 6*d.* was the normal rate. Sixpence was the general rate in 1333 and for the Nottingham levies in 1334–5.

[3] *Rot. Scot.* i. 611; E. 36/204, fos. 103d–104.

[4] B.M. Nero C VIII, fos. 253d–8; E. 86/294, fo. 104.

[5] *Rot. Scot.* i. 284.

[6] e.g. in 1338–9, for foot archers going to Flanders—E. 36/203, fos. 131, 144 f., and E. 101. 21/21.

[7] E. 36/203, fo. 131 (the rates), 142 f.; Ramsay, *Genesis*, 7–8.

[8] *Proceedings*, v. 26, 172.

[9] B.M. Nero C VII, fos. 253d–8; *Rot. Scot.* i. 580.

[10] e.g. E. 101. 373/11, fo. 115.

[11] D. L. Evans, 'The Principality of Wales', p. 55.

which attracted attention was their weird clothing; but in 1339 the pay clerk noted that they received 2*d*. (after drawing 3*d*. at first) *quia in Anglia*.[1] It is perhaps helpful to observe that it was rather a matter of the Welsh not sharing in the general increase which took place in the late 1330's, than of their being 'downgraded'.

NOTE C. SUPPLY OF VICTUALS

I n the Scottish wars and in the coastal and naval-defence measures of Edward III, the counties (in the first case, those of the north only) were occasionally expected to supply their forces with victuals for a given number of days. This 'purveyance' amounted to the provision of troops with wages—if we may consider wages as essentially a means of recouping the cost of supplying *victualia*![2] Of such measures, those for the Scottish force of 1327 and 1334–5 (for six days' victuals from joining host, and fifteen days from the county) were the most drastic.[3] This form of supply of victuals for coastal and naval forces can be observed in 1336, 1337, and 1340.[4] The normal method of obtaining supplies, however, was to order or invite merchants to bring victuals to the place of muster for sale, or to demand that certain counties send given quantities, independently of any possible contribution in troops.[5]

[1] D. L. Evans, 'The Principality of Wales', pp. 56–57; E. 36/204, fos. 143d, 144. For the higher pay of armoured foot, cf. E. 101. 16/14 (for 1322), analysed by J. E. Morris, 'Mounted Infantry', pp. 89, 96.

[2] This is made explicit in the order for the supply of *either* wages or *victualia nomine vadiorum* on one occasion; *Rot. Scot.* i. 585. On the standard *dietae*, see *Red Book of the Exchequer* (R.S.), III, 835–9.

[3] *Rot. Scot.* i. 220, 301–2. In 1333 five days' victuals from the county muster were required; ibid. i. 246–7. The numbers of days are those required of the Yorkshire levies.

[4] Ibid. i. 459–61, 472–5, 477, 583. Needless to add, there were innumerable orders for the purchase of victuals (on more or less acceptable terms) in the counties.

[5] A. E. Prince, 'The Army and Navy', pp. 365–76.

XI

COMPULSORY CONTRACT, ARRAY BY LORDS, AND COMMISSIONS OF ARRAY IN THE YEARS 1377–1485

THE last century of the Middle Ages witnessed a considerable decline in England's military stature, offset only by the brilliant recovery under Henry V and John Duke of Bedford. In spite of many recent important advances in our understanding of the period, there is still no agreement whether economic, political, or personal factors were at the root of this decline. The view that it was a case of a healthy society suffering from long bouts of poor leadership has recently gained ground at the expense of the idea that the new feudalism was essentially anarchic and the economy depressed.[1] An inquiry into the role of government in military recruitment may throw some light on this problem.

The recruitment and organization of armies in this last medieval century have not received intensive study except in the case of the French wars of Henry V and Bedford. Those wars suggest that for important decisions the Privy Seal rather than the Great Seal had become the principal instrument of the crown. The unenrolled writs of this office have not yet provided as firm a foundation for a study of obligation as the earlier writs of chancery, which are both enrolled and printed.

One thing is clear: the feudal lords retained, and possibly increased, their leadership in matters of war. Not only did they receive privy seal letters to array troops for important

---

[1] For recent attempts at a synthesis of the specialist literature, see V. H. Green, *The Later Plantagenets* (London, 1955), chaps. one, three, and thirteen; and S. B. Chrimes, *Introduction to the Administrative History of Medieval England*, Epilogue. The present writer is well aware that this chapter constitutes a foray into virgin territory, and that the conclusions are more than usually provisional.

campaigns, but also they received an overwhelming majority of commissions for the array of communal troops against invasion. The former practice can be illustrated from the recruitment of the 1417 army for France, when writs of privy seal to leading lords and knights ordered them to state what troops they could bring; they were subsequently to come and make their indentures before the Council.[1] The predominance of the great lords among the arrayers is even more marked, as may be quickly observed by a comparison of the arrayers in a given area of the middle of the fifteenth century with those of the thirteenth and fourteenth.[2]

The summons of lords to serve with the king was by no means a regular feature of the assembling of armies in this century. However, the revival of the feudal levy (in form, though not in effect) in 1385 was not completely isolated. The summons of those holding fees or lands from the king was a noteworthy element in most war preparations. Henry IV's Welsh and Scottish armies were largely composed of fee-holders summoned by chancery writs addressed to the sheriff; these forces appeared again in the French expeditions of 1406–7 and of 1415–20.[3] These life-retainers of the king had first been so summoned under Richard II, and may have owed their prominence to the absorption of first the Cheshire and then the Lancashire fee-holders in the royal establishment. One group, those granted lands in Normandy, were expected to serve without pay;[4] but all were marked off from the true feudal levy by the life term of their contracts. It is curious that the summons of fee-holders seems to have declined under Henry VI, but in 1470 the king's *ffeodmen* were called out.[5]

Whom did the lords and fee-holders bring with them? Many would have their own retainers, the consequent muster

---

[1] R. Newhall, *English Conquest*, pp. 190–1; cf., for 1419, ibid., p. 206.

[2] Cf., for example, *C.P.R. 1429–36*, pp. 71, 360, with *Parl. Writs*. ii. 736, 738.

[3] *C.C.R. 1402–5*, p. 185 (the term 'county levies', as in Wylie, *Henry IV*, i. 470, is misleading); *Foedera*, viii. 336 f., 456 f.; *C.C.R. 1409–12*, pp. 240–1, 309; *Calendar of Letter Books 'I'*, xxiv. 134, 174; *Foedera*, ix, *passim* (see esp. p. 355), *C.C.R. 1413–19*, pp. 433–4.

[4] R. Newhall, *The English Conquest of Normandy*, pp. 209–12; *Muster and Review*, pp. 116 f.; for a 1429 view, cf. *Proceedings and Ordinances of the Privy Council of England* (Record Commission, London, 1834–7), iii. 349.

[5] *Paston Letters*, no. 753.

being as a result not unlike those of primitive feudalism. From the palatinates, writs calling out a lord's retainers survive.[1] The lords might be requested to bring as many men as they could, as in 1415; or to array men-at-arms *d'auncestrie*, as in 1419.[2] On the other hand, the number of followers to be brought might be negotiated at the council table or with commissioners. In 1459 the lords were summoned individually to serve with as many men 'defensibly arrayed' as they could assemble, bringing money and supplies for two months, and in 1471 Oxford summoned the Norfolk lieges 'with as many men as ye may goodly make' to a military muster.[3]

It may be assumed that in many cases the sphere of recruitment open to a lord was limited only by his influence, but on occasion the array of a particular estate or fief was clearly in question. John of Gaunt called out 10 men-at-arms and 60 archers from the lordships of Knaresborough and 98 men-at-arms and 460 archers from all his estates.[4] In a force raised by the city of York, the lords were clearly responsible for their own tenants, while Sir John Howard's troops included men raised and supplied by the towns and villages on his estates.[5]

It may be concluded that the function of lordship was varied in the extreme: a potentially powerful instrument of array had grown out of the feudal era, in which the call out of retainers holding money or land fees, the array of tenants, and the assembly of forces whether tenants and fee-holders or not, were all acceptable demands. Moreover, when the lord of far-flung estates acted as county commissioner of array for a defensive levy, it must have been hard for the local inhabitants to distinguish his 'communal' from his more frequent lordly quasi-feudal activities.[6]

---

[1] e.g. John of Gaunt's *Register*, 1379-83, i, nos. 357, 642, 662.

[2] *Foedera*, ix. 307.

[3] *Paston Letters*, nos. 277, 770; cf. ibid., nos. 235, 430, and W. H. Dunham, 'Lord Hastings' Indentured Retinues', pp. 45-46.

[4] *Register*, nos. 560-2; cf. the array of the bishop of Winchester's tenants, *C.C.R. 1402-5*, pp. 82-83.

[5] R. Davies, *Extracts from the Municipal Records of the City of York* (London, 1843), pp. 113-15; W. I. Hayward, 'Economic Aspects of the Wars of the Roses in East Anglia', *E.H.R.* xli (1926), 188-9.

[6] See, for example, Thomas Beaufort's levies against the Scots in 1417 as reported in Thomas Walsingham, *Historia Anglicana* (R.S.), ii. 325-6.

Besides recruitment by lords and fee-holders, commissioners might be sent out to excite support and negotiate indentures. In 1419 and 1436, for example, commissioners were to raise knights and esquires at a given number from each district, and in 1437 archers were to be 'purveied' for Guisnes Castle.[1]

I

After 1377 county and city levies returned to their auxiliary and local role of the days before Edward I. The Statute of Winchester continued to be reissued to form the basis of law and order as well as of obligatory weapons, while the limiting Statutes of Edward III were kept before the government by the watchful commons. The request of 1371 about service at the king's expense was repeated with greater definition in 1384, when the commons requested that Edward III's ordinance against service outside counties at other than the king's cost be observed. This petition claimed that in spite of the ordinance against making men-at-arms, hobelars, and archers go armed in the king's service at their own costs or that of the counties, unless by their own goodwill and grace, commissions enforcing such service had been issued from Chancery of recent times. To the request that such commissions should stop, and that any already issued should be repealed, it was replied: 'Let the Statute of 1 Edward III be held and kept.'[2] The occasion of the petition had been the array under John of Gaunt against the Scots. In December 1383 the arrayers in northern counties and in the towns of Lincoln and Hull had been given powers to array and lead to the Wardens of the March all aged sixteen to sixty, equipped as men-at-arms, hobelars, and archers, and to proceed against the recalcitrant by means of prison and distraint of lands and tenements.[3]

It was undoubtedly against the execution of these arrays,

---

[1] *Proceedings*, ii. 246–8; Newhall, *English Conquest*, p. 206; *Foedera*, x. 647, 648; *Proceedings*, v. 26; cf. also the arraying powers of the Wardens of the Marches cited by R. L. Storey, 'Wardens of the Marches . . . towards Scotland', *E.H.R.* lxxii (1957), 598.

[2] *Rot. Parl.* iii. 201.

[3] *Rot. Scot.* ii. 57–58, cf. ibid. ii. 59–61. The writs were *per consilium*.

extending as they did well to the south of the Marcher counties proper, that parliament struck.[1] Nevertheless, the crown was eventually to win on what was essentially a matter of interpretation: the county troops were to be treated as serving against invasion of foreign enemies in defence of the realm, when mustered for wars directed against the Scots and the Welsh.[2]

The verbal pledge of 1384 was transferred to the Statute book in the autumn of 1402, when Henry IV's wars in Wales had led to parliamentary protest against service in that country without pay—a protest not averted by the thanks for recent service done *ex eorum benivolentia et sincera affectione* issued to the counties at the same time as the offending writs of array.[3] These arrays had borne most heavily on the northerners, who supplied 'the whole array of the county', when others only supplied 'knights and other fee-holders'.[4] Moreover, this time the commons secured the enactment of the Statutes of 1344 (that service outside the realm be at king's wages) and of 1352 (against finding men-at-arms, &c., contrary to tenure unless by parliamentary consent), as well as that of 1327. The new Statute modified the demands of the commons in two respects. On the one hand, it omitted all reference to service in Wales, which in point of fact was to continue, with like service in Scotland, to be considered defensive; on the other, it went on to reserve the military obligations of lords marcher, feudal tenants, and holders of retaining fees and lands.

Two years later the commons followed up this success by petitioning for, and securing the acceptance of, a new form of commission of array for use when pay for service outside the county was not required.[5] The grievance may well have

[1] The arrays extended to Derbyshire, Nottinghamshire, and Lincolnshire. Gaunt led the resulting force into Scotland, hurrying back to the parliament where the levies were condemned.

[2] On this point, cf. the complaints in 1407 of the men of Shrewsbury at repeated service in Wales at their own cost, *Rot. Parl.* iii. 618–19; cf. also Stubbs, *Const. Hist.* iii. 286–7. The abusive verdict of Stubbs that this was 'part of a general policy of an irresponsible government' is perhaps to be attributed to nineteenth-century politics (cf. his reference to Hallam, ibid., note 1).

[3] *Statutes of the Realm*, ii. 137; *Rot. Parl.* iii. 501; *Foedera*, iv. 33 (31 July).

[4] J. Bain, *Calendar of Documents*, iv. nos. 617–18; cf. ibid. iv, nos. 548, 614.

[5] *Rot. Parl.* iii. 526–7; cf. *C.C.R. 1402–5*, p. 205.

been increased by the heavy arrays against Scots, Welsh, French, and northern English rebels.[1] The procedure was that a draft form of commission was submitted to the commons and amended by them. Particular attention was drawn this time to the oppressive penalties of forfeiture suffered by arrayers, and the writ, as amended, was approved. In the new form, the preamble stated that, for the defence of king and kingdom, invasion in defiance of a truce was to be repelled; all were to be armed according to their estate, the weak providing arms and armour. Those staying at home in *patria sua* were not to draw wages; those arrayed were to be mustered and led to the coasts as occasion demanded, under penalty of imprisonment.[2]

Perhaps the first question to be asked of militia service in the fifteenth century is how well the consolidated Statute of 1402 and the parliamentary form of 1404 were observed. In the first place, it may be noted that as the parliamentary form of array was concerned with the specific case of invasion from the sea by a truce-breaking nation, it lacked the universal characteristics which might have given it greater currency. Nothing was done to define 'defence of the realm' in a way that would be helpful in interpreting the duties of northern counties in times of Scottish unrest. Nevertheless, the parliamentary array did provide a norm. Within a few weeks of its issue, commissions of array were drawn up which followed it in requiring the old and unfit to find substitutes, or imposing the penalty of prison.[3]

Few commissions of array which were issued in the following years made any departure in principle from the requirements of 1404.[4] There was a broad distinction, it is true, between those which followed the parliamentary formula and those which either reverted to older tradition or arrayed all those between sixteen and sixty.[5] The former writs did not mention the duty of the infirm to contribute arms and

---

[1] *Foedera*, viii. 291–344; *C.C.R. 1402–5*, pp. 185–6, 222, 225, 245, 478.
[2] Array in another's arms was to bring amercement.
[3] *C.C.R. 1402–5*, pp. 359, 478, 503.
[4] *Foedera*, viii. 400–1, 402–3, 406–7, 414–15, 679–80; ibid. ix. 255–6, 350–1, 568, 793; ibid. xi. 461, 624, 649–50, 655–6, 677–8.
[5] The enrolment of the 'formula' arrays often tailed off *ut in consimili casu* or some such phrase; for an example, cf. ibid. ix. 793. For the older model, cf. ibid. xi. 677–8.

armour or the penalty of imprisonment, unless these details
were included in the sections enrolled merely as *ut in consimili casu*. Such, for example, was the form taken by the
writs for the defence of the northern coasts in 1430.[1] Four
years later commissions issued to large numbers of arrayers
in the northern counties followed the parliamentary *forma*
closely enough and in sufficient detail to make the variations
significant.[2] These, in order of importance were: first, the
restoration of the forfeiture penalty for default by the
arrayers, and secondly, the addition of a clause to the effect
that not only those with property to sustain arms *but also
those without it* were to be armed by the arrayers. This defiance of the very feature stressed by the commons in 1404—
the punishment of arrayers by forfeiture—was not repeated.
In the writs of December 1435, January 1436, and March
1443 the variations from the 'model' were insignificant.[3]

The use of commissions of array in Henry VI's reign was
essentially for defence and civil war; Jack Cade's followers
set a notable example of the use of the machinery of array by
rebels in 1450.[4] The Statute of Winchester was reissued in
1437 and 1442; proclamations for the practice of archery
were frequent, and custodians of the north were frequently
nominated as chief arrayers in the call-out of the northern
counties in defence against Scottish raids—such commissions being issued in 1427, 1430, 1434 (coastal regions),
1448, and 1460.[5] However, London, Sussex, and Kent were
put under demand in 1436, the leaders of the city having to
turn to the livery companies to raise troops for Calais.[6] The
southern counties were arrayed in 1443, when the Council
sent commissioners into the counties to negotiate for 'an aide
of men, vitaille and ships'.[7] But the 1440's must have been
a very 'low' period; symptomatic, perhaps, was the allegation

---

[1] Patent roll, 8 Henry VI, m. 1 (*C.P.R. 1429-36*, p. 71, giving the addresses only).

[2] Ibid. 12 Henry VI, part i, m. 2d. (*C.P.R. 1429-36*, pp. 359-61).

[3] Ibid. 14 Henry VI, part i, mm. 20d-19d; 21 Henry VI, part ii, m. 40d (*C.P.R. 1429-36*, pp. 519-24; ibid. *1441-46*, p. 199).

[4] C. Dawson, *Hastings Castle*, pp. 269-73.

[5] *C.P.R. 1422-29*, pp. 405-6; ibid. *1429-36*, pp. 71, 359-61; ibid. *1446-52*, p. 238. *Foedera*, xi. 461.

[6] Sharp, *London and the Kingdom*, i. 297; *C.P.R. 1429-36*, pp. 519-24.

[7] *C.P.R. 1441-46*, p. 199; *Proceedings*, v. 414-17.

in parliament that the Isle of Wight's fencibles had dwindled from 10,000 to 1,200. In the 1450's more activity was manifested. Sussex was again organized for defence in 1452.[1] In 1453 parliament devised its well-known scheme for the supply of archers and their upkeep by the counties, a scheme which was put in motion four years later, though it is hardly likely that it proceeded very far.[2]

The Wars of the Roses brought a revival of both county and town militia which reveals itself in writs of array, accounts by chroniclers, and in muster rolls. The Lancastrian use of this kind of force was particularly notable, and occasioned the Yorkist propaganda that such orders were an attempt to introduce French-style conscription, 'which impositions . . . wol be the worst ensample that ever grewe in England'.[3]

Writs of array, as has been noted, did not, in the main, depart far from the rules laid down in the first decade of the century; nor, indeed, could much complaint be raised if they did, for they were not defence measures against external enemies.[4] The whole *posse* of some counties was summoned on several occasions. William Paston recorded commissions (from the Lancastrians), in January 1460, that 'every man be redy in his best aray' to rally to the king's banner; others were issued in August of that year.[5] Two years later the Yorkists were preparing to call out the *posse*; a proclamation ordered all between sixteen and sixty to be prepared to serve with the king.[6] In June 1463 the Nevilles were under commission to raise 'all lieges and subjects' in the Marches, and the following year an array similar to that of 1462 was ordered in twenty counties, 'under the peyne that shall fall thereupon'.[7] In 1464 also a Paston letter referred to a rising of 'the comenys' in Lancashire and Cheshire 'up to' 10,000;[8]

---

[1] *C.P.R. 1446–52*, p. 540.

[2] *Rot. Parl.* v. 230–1; *C.P.R. 1452–61*, pp. 406–10; see below, p. 244.

[3] *Chron. Davies*, pp. 86–90; cf. J. H. Ramsay, *Lancaster and York*, ii. 225; W. I. Hayward, 'Wars of the Roses', p. 185. See, for Yorkist arrays, P. M. Kendall, *Warwick the Kingmaker* (London, 1957), pp. 88, 281–2.

[4] *C.P.R. 1452–61*, pp. 489, 557, 606, 656; *Foedera*, xi and xii, *passim*; Hayward, 'Wars of the Roses', p. 186, n. 1.

[5] *P.L.*, no. 400; *Foedera*, xi. 461; other arrays had to be ordered against Scottish attacks; e.g. J. Bain, *Calendar*, no. 1308.

[6] *P.L.*, no. 529. [7] *Foedera*, xi. 501–2, 523–4. [8] *P.L.*, no. 560.

a report which is echoed five years later in Warkworth's reference to the rising of Yorkshire knights, squires, 'and comeners' to the number of 20,000 under 'Robin of Redesdale'.[1]

When the second bout of major campaigning began in 1469, the role of the commons seems to have been even greater, though the leaders and principal victims were still the great lords. Late in 1469 the dukes of Suffolk and Norfolk, along with Earl Rivers, were to array all lieges and subjects in Suffolk and Norfolk according to 'gradus', and to lead them to Edward if called. As the crisis of spring 1470 approached, similar arrays (with less august arrayers, except for the duke of Gloucester) were ordered by Edward in many other counties.[2] The rebel arrays were addressed to all 'manere of men', and now the death penalty was invoked against the recalcitrant.[3] The autumn of 1470 brought similar arrays of the whole population, as well as the well-known assemblies of fee-holders and 'fellowships' of the lords; it is probably to this season that we must assign the joint summons by Clarence, Pembroke, Warwick, and Oxford of all between sixteen and sixty, on pain of death and forfeiture.[4] On Edward IV's side the duke of Gloucester was given power to array the militia between sixteen and sixty, the cost to be levied from the *lieges* by their assent.[5]

The return of Edward IV in 1471 engendered similar arrays of the 'whole population'.[6] In the preparations for Barnet and Tewkesbury, it seems possible to discern a greater reliance by the Lancastrians on the commons, and by the Yorkists, in spite of their traditional 'popular' support, on such 'fellowships' as that of Hastings. The author of the

[1] John Warkworth, *A Chronicle of the First Thirteen Years of King Edward IV*, ed. J. O. Halliwell (Camden Society, vol. 10, 1839), p. 6.
[2] *Foedera*, xi. 649–50, 655–6. Cf. *Hall's Chronicle* (London, 1809), pp. 272–4.
[3] See the orders of Robert Welles and of Clarence and Warwick in *Chronicle of the Rebellion in Lincolnshire* (Camden Society, Miscellany I, 1847), p. 6; cf. also Warkworth, *Chronicle*, p. 8, where Welles levied 'alle the comons of the schyre to the nowmbre of thirty thousand'. Edward IV's counter-proclamations confirm; ibid., pp. 52–59 (*ex* Close rolls, 10 Ed. IV).
[4] Warkworth, notes, pp. 60–62.
[5] *Foedera*, xi. 658 (26 Aug.); cf. Edward IV's commission to John Neville, Marquis Montagu, ibid., p. 10.
[6] Ibid. xi. 677–8; *P.L.* v, no. 770; *Hist. MSS. Comm.*, *12th Report* (London, 1888), part iv. 3 (array of 'fencibles' by Henry Vernon).

'Arrivall' testifies to the assembly of the 'people of the countrie' against Edward in the north, while Warwick raised troops in Warwickshire at first by goodwill and later 'upon payne of deathe'.[1] In the second campaign, the 'people' and 'powere' and 'hoole myghte' of the south-western counties were called out by Margaret and her supporters, and Edward's strategy was said to be designed to prevent her from assembling more than one county at a time, i.e. to keep her from moving inland.[2]

This increasing role of the local communities in the later years of the civil wars was also reflected in the followings of lords. Sir John Howard's household troops, for example, were reinforced between 1462 and 1481 by men from the towns and villages on his estates, supplied by those communities with pay, clothes, arms, and even horses.[3]

Muster rolls of the period confirm the increased readiness of urban, if not of rural, levies. All the Norwich militiamen, for example, were expected to have *jakke* (a rough defence tunic, lineal descendant of the aketon), *salet* (a form of helmet), bow and arrows; a century before, the emphasis on archers had been much weaker.[4] The most noteworthy example of this development is that of Bridport, cited by Mrs. J. R. Green.[5] In that town not a single archer could be mustered in 1319, whereas in 1458 there was assembled an armoured force equipped with bows and arrows, bills, poles, axes, spears, and even a hand-gun. Archers had once tended to be countryside troops;[6] what was new, perhaps, in the fifteenth century, was the increased number to be found in the towns. This is confirmed by the fact that London was

---

[1] *Arrivall of King Edward IV*, pp. 3, 8, 15; cf. Warkworth, *Chronicle*, p. 13. However, Warwick did not have enough 'middle class' support to enjoy much success; P. M. Kendall, op. cit., pp. 294, 302, 309.

[2] *Arrivall*, pp. 23, 24; a similar 'popular' element appears among Fauconberg's supporters in the south-east; Warkworth, *Chronicle*, p. 19; *Chronicles of London* (ed. C. L. Kingsford, London, 1905), p. 185.

[3] W. I. Hayward, 'Wars of the Roses', pp. 188-9.

[4] W. Hudson, *Records of the City of Norwich* (London, 1910), pp. 390-410. However, the numbers actually levied did not show much of an increase; ibid., pp. 402-6.

[5] Mrs. J. R. Green, *Town Life in the Fifteenth Century* (London, 1894), i. 16, n. 1; *Hist. MSS. Comm.*, part VI, i (London, 1877), 491, 493.

[6] Cf. the fourteenth-century commissions of array; and such musters as that of Hastings in 1339, when archers were more plentiful in the hundreds than in the boroughs; C. Dawson, *Hastings Castle*, i. 175.

assessed to supply more archers than any other county in the defence scheme of 1453.[1]

We may conclude tentatively, pending a more definitive study, that by 1450 the militia, armed under the terms of the Statute of Winchester, had declined into a role of defence levies regulated by a series of parliamentary statutes; but that, during the Wars of the Roses, there had been a marked revival of service frequently at the cost of the local communities and, occasionally, under pain of death. By the end of Edward IV's reign a well-armed force, somewhat heavily concentrated in the towns, was in being.

[1] See below, p. 244; cf. also Bristol's revived military importance, extending even to the possession of artillery; *Adae Usk Chronicon*, p. 82; and *Arrivall*, p. 24. There is similar evidence for Coventry; *The Coventry Leet Book*, ed. M. D. Harris (E.E.T.S., London, 1907–13), ii, *passim*.

XII

CONSULTATION IN MAKING WAR AND IN LEVYING ARMIES

No problem has engaged the minds of medievalists more than that of liberty and order. It has certainly underlain the selection of material in the foregoing pages. It is hoped in this last chapter to confront the problem squarely and to reach some conclusions. The basic question is simple: how great a share did the various social and political groups have in decisions about peace and war, and in the measures taken to implement those decisions? In England, the king's initiative and leadership in war were never in doubt. The question was, in the first place, whom should he consult, and what force should be allowed to his counsellors' views? Behind this question lay a further one: when war was embarked on, who should decide the terms of service? Here custom, and later, petition, might very well circumscribe the initiative of the king. The subject-matter to be considered falls, therefore, into two parts: that concerned with the making of war and that concerned with the levy of troops.[1] In the following pages this division of interest will be subordinated to the larger question: what progress, if any, was made in the definition of the line between royal and subjects' rights in both of these areas? Is there any significant pattern of growing or fluctuating participation by the subjects in decisions concerning war and concerning military forces?

I

Evidence for the need for consultation, let alone consent, is rare indeed in Anglo-Saxon times. We may only guess that

---

[1] William Prynne, *The Soveraigne Power of Parliaments and Kingdoms* (London, 1643), pt. ii, pp. 1–40, may be considered the father of this subject. His preoccupation with parliamentary sovereignty and the sanctity of precedent led, of course, to manifold distortions; but for the first time the marshalling of the testimony of chroniclers and parliamentary rolls was opposed to the monstrous claims of the Stuart house.

consent was usually asked before customary rules of service were waived. Among consultations of the witan the best known are Burghred of Mercia's obtaining of consent before asking the help of Wessex against Wales, and Æthelred II's repeated requests for the advice of his witan.[1] The significance of the Anglo-Saxon contribution arose rather from the distinction between the royal mounted fyrd and the local infantry forces, for the latter were only available to the king on the most circumscribed terms in defence of their immediate localities. A second legacy of importance was the beginning of limitation on the length of service of the fyrd proper, as manifested in the famous two-month rule of Domesday Book. For in the Middle Ages custom, by providing a block to arbitrary decisions, was the begetter of consent, by which alone custom might normally be overridden.

The Normans brought over the tradition of feudal counsel, and the years between the Conquest and Magna Carta are notable for an adaptation of this tradition to the needs and customs of England. Counsel and consent are to be found in three major kinds of decision: the planning of defence, discussions in the field, and the preparation of foreign expeditions.

Defence of the realm against foreign invasion occasioned widespread consultations throughout the Middle Ages. Presumably the reason for this was that local levies and interests were most vitally involved and local counsel most likely to be of value in these matters. An added incentive in this century was that defence of English territory usually arose only when an element of civil war was present; the king was therefore appealing to loyal groups of subjects against rebels when he called assemblies for defence. Most famous of these consultations were those by William Rufus in 1088 of a 'great council' of bishops, earls, and English and by Henry I in 1102 of his barons and knights. When the barons objected in 1185 to Henry II's plans for a crusade, their plea was

---

[1] The army assemblies discussed by Freeman, Liebermann, Oleson, and Wilkinson seem to have been concerned with 'state trials', lawmaking, or conveying land rather than with military policy; Freeman, *Norman Conquest*, ii. 105, 616 f.; Liebermann, *The National Assembly in the Anglo-Saxon Period* (Halle, 1913), p. 43; Oleson, *Witenagemot*, p. 30; Wilkinson, 'Northumbrian separatism', *B.J.R.L.* xxiii (1939).

based on the view that his primary duty was defence of the realm—a concern which they had an opportunity to demonstrate in 1205, when the defences were organized with the consent of the lords, and possibly again in 1213, when the *jurati* were called out on the counsel of the king's subjects. A further element of consultation took place in the course of organizing defence, when the king or local leader consulted with his assembled troops or provincial lords. Thus the Yorkshire *provinciales* met with Archbishop Thurstan before the battle of the Standard and were persuaded by him to fight;[1] likewise in 1141 Stephen debated with his lords before embarking on the battle of Lincoln.[2] In 1174 the Yorkshiremen again debated on what action to take against Scottish invasion, this time after already demonstrating their martial frame of mind by marching to Newcastle,[3] and Henry took counsel before embarking on the siege of Bigod's castles.[4] Such special consultations in the North were a persistent feature of the Middle Ages.

The preparation of foreign expeditions was the occasion of similar, if less dramatic, consultations. The Council of 1089 at Winchester has been made famous by Round's attack on Freeman for treating it as a national rather than a feudal assembly.[5] In view of the recent emphasis on royal powers in this period, it is now desirable perhaps to stress the remarkable frequency of such 'feudal' consultations.[6] Henry II must receive credit for seeking advice most frequently about royal expeditions; we may note his Northampton councils of 1157 and 1164 (about Wales, the latter going into a discussion of the raising of military forces); his obtaining of permission (*licentiam*) to go to Normandy in 1170;[7] and his great council at Argentan to discuss the invasion of Ireland.[8] The

---

[1] Richard of Hexham, iii. 159–61; Cont. Sym., p. 291; John, Cont. of Flor. of Worcester, p. 111. This, unlike the ensuing examples, was followed by the military muster.
[2] Ord. Vit., *Hist. Eccles.* v. 126–7.
[3] William of Newburgh, *Historia*, p. 183.
[4] Rad. Diceto, *Imagines*, p. 384.
[5] *Hist. Eccles.* iii. 315–17; J. H. Round, *Feudal England*, p. 371.
[6] e.g. in J. E. Jolliffe, *Angevin Kingship* (London, 1955).
[7] Gervase of Canterbury, *Chronica*, i. 163, 165; William FitzStephen, *Vita S. Thomae* in *Materials for the Life of Thomas Becket*, iii. 70; *Gesta Henrici*, p. 6.
[8] Robert of Torigny, *Chronica*, p. 252.

year 1177 is particularly interesting from our viewpoint. In the first place, four prelates and the earls and barons of the realm treated of the peace and order of the realm; then at Windsor the earls and barons and knights of the realm met in arms ready to go wherever the king ordered; finally all earls, barons, and knights, who held directly of the king, assembled to hear the king's orders and agreed to meet again in July, and eventually (perhaps after another assembly) sailed for Normandy.[1] The practice of consulting the military leaders prior to an expedition might involve consent to taxation (as in 1164, 1193, and 1204), and it undoubtedly fostered the habit of bargaining which in John's reign turned military summonses into the occasion for collective opposition.[2]

By 1216 the tradition of consultation about war, and occasionally about military levies and plans, as well as the tendency for the opposition to seize on such occasions to bargain, were already clearly discernible. Moreover, one of the demands of the opposition was for the limitation of military service, with the result that a general form of limitation found its way into Magna Carta in the form of clause 16 (from 1225, clause 10): 'No one shall be distrained to the performance of greater service for a knight's fee, or for any other free tenement, than is due therefrom.'[3] Thus the less conspicuous form of consultation—about terms of service— bore fruit in legal rights a century before the older practice of discussion of the making of war was temporarily elevated into a privilege.[4]

II

The tendency of the barons to close ranks and to endeavour to make consultation mandatory was resisted by Henry III; though he was willing to consult the barons, he refused to be bound by their views. Great councils were

---

[1] *Gesta Henrici*, pp. 160, 167.

[2] See especially the famous assembly of 1197, and the *colloquia* of 1201 and 1213; Hoveden, iv. 40, 169; *Magna Vita S. Hugonis*, pp. 249–50; Coggeshale, pp. 152, 167. J. H. Round, *Feudal England*, pp. 528–38; H. M. Chew, *Ecclesiastical Tenants-in-Chief*, pp. 31, 39–42.

[3] W. S. McKechnie, *Magna Carta*, p. 260. For the particular demands of the barons, see ibid., p. 486 ('The Unknown Charter').

[4] See below, p. 233.

consulted about French expeditions in 1224 and 1229 with positive results.[1] In 1242, 1252–4, and 1255–8, as is well known, Henry's requests were refused, and he attempted to proceed alone.[2] The two French expeditions failed and the Sicilian venture was abandoned. On the other hand, in the writs for his Welsh and Scottish expeditions, Henry claimed to have the consent of the magnates. When consulted, the magnates usually consented to the place and time of muster; in 1257 they agreed to the dividing up of the army of Wales, and later those with the king in Wales agreed to a fresh expedition in 1258. In 1264 a military assembly was to gather at Oxford for both counsel and aid.[3] It may be because the most circumstantial reporter of royal-baronial conferences was not anxious to record matters so creditable to Henry that we know so little of the outcome of these summonses. It is often not possible to say just what the baronage discussed beyond consenting to 'aid' and, in the cases where the ensuing military summons mentioned it, to the muster. In contrast to our uncertainty about what happened at these councils, we have a very clear idea of what the barons would like to have happened.[4]

The insistence, in 1258, on more regular parliaments, and the addition of representatives to parliament on several occasions, were further legacies of Henry's reign to the future development of military consultation. Though it was about war aid that representatives were called before the council in 1254, it is not certain that they were ever consulted about the making of war or the levy of troops in this reign. We may conclude that before 1272 the consultation of subjects on war and armies was increasing, that the barons seemed intent on making it necessary, and that the king's efforts to preserve freedom of action were limited by the events of 1258. If we ask why this failure occurred, attention must be drawn

[1] Wendover, *Flores Hist.* iv. 94, 126; S. K. Mitchell, *Studies in Taxation*, pp. 181–6; H. M. Chew, *Ecclesiastical Tenants-in-Chief*, p. 44; *C.R. 1227–31*, p. 248; *Royal Letters*, i. 358; *Lords Report on the Dignity of a Peer*, iii. 5.

[2] Matthew Paris, *Chron. Maj.* iv. 178, 181–8; v. 324–47, 373–5, 383, 423, 440, 445, 520; *Annales Burton*, pp. 305, 333, 336, 360; *Dignity of a Peer*, iii. 12, 13.

[3] Ibid., iii. 9, 11, 14–16, 21, 29.

[4] M. Paris, *Chron. Maj.*, vols. iii–vi, *passim*; *The Song of Lewes*, ed. C. L. Kingsford (Oxford, 1890), ll. 483 f.

to the happy coincidence of an unwarlike king and continued dependence on baronial military leadership.

In his Welsh wars, Edward I resumed and strengthened the policy of seeking the co-operation of the barons and even, on occasion, of the knights. Their consent was requested in parliamentary summons and sometimes claimed in military ones. Before the first Welsh war a great council heard the case against Llewelyn and authorized Edward to proceed against him with full feudal forces.[1] In 1282 a great council at Devizes and a parliament at Worcester discussed the situation and provided for the muster.[2] It was here that the opposition, in the persons of Bohun and Clare, first began to appear, in a quarrel over the Constable's privileges and possibly over the form of summons.[3] The order of that year for the provision of war-horses by those with thirty librates of land was *de consilio nostro*; and in November the summons of assemblies of all twenty-pound tenants and also of shire representatives stated both the royal concern with the Welsh war and the fact of consent to the royal expedition by both nobles and 'the whole community of the realm'.[4] The assembly which dealt with David was summoned on the principle that those who had borne the burden of the war should have a say in the miscreant's punishment.[5] For dealing with Rhys ap Mareddud's rising of 1287, when Edward was out of the country, there is, curiously enough, no evidence of consultation. When, in 1294, a Welsh revolt wrecked Edward's plans for Gascony, a great council at Worcester was the setting of a well-known quarrel over Bigod's service as Marshal (he objected to service away from the king and in a subordinate position); a quarrel which, as Morris has shown, was a direct antecedent of the 'go or hang' scene.[6] Thus by 1294 the Welsh wars had provided Edward with military and political victories, but also with a habit of seeking consent which it would be hard to disavow.

[1] *Parl. Writs*, i. 5 (1).
[2] Ibid. i. 222, 224–5; *Chronicon T. Wykes (Annales Monastici, iv)*, pp. 287 f.
[3] *Welsh Wars*, pp. 155, 158.
[4] *Parl. Writs*, i. 10–11.
[5] Ibid. i. 15. This was the first time that the principle had been formally enunciated that leadership in war-making carried with it the right to decide policy.
[6] *Welsh Wars*, p. 250.

This element of consent disappeared from the writs for Scottish service. On the other hand, the French war figured frequently in the summons to the parliaments of 1294–6.[1] There followed a recrudescence of opposition to the king's military ambitions, which, as in John's reign, sought to make conditions about where service was owed, and found support in the Great Charter principle of service according to tenure.[2] As his father had done previously, Edward pressed ahead without solid baronial support. Possibly it was because he was unable to claim consent in his military summonses that he was led to make increasing use of such justifications as necessity, common utility, and defence of the English language. Another effect may have been the couching of some writs in the form of a request rather than an order.[3]

The Scottish wars of 1297–1307 revealed the ambiguity of Edward's position. He never mentioned the wars in his parliamentary summons, and showed no disposition to seek consent to them. The military writs, likewise, rarely referred to counsel, the only exceptions being those of December 1295 and March 1301, the first of which did not refer to baronial consent.[4] This meant head-on conflict, as a result of which the king was forced to postpone nearly all his campaigns until long after the first muster date, and to concede the current demands of the 'opposition' before he could assemble his forces.[5] The nearest he came to a campaign based on consent was in March 1301, when individuals were summoned *de consilio nostro* and the counties *de communi consilio*. The chroniclers, however, remind us that if Edward did not seek consent, he had nevertheless to accept criticism.[6] This was the real beginning of the age of Edward II.

Edward I's greatly increased use of the military levies of

---

[1] *Parl. Writs*, i. 25, 31, 47–48.
[2] Cf. the documents and references in B. Wilkinson, *Constitutional History*, vol. i.
[3] B. Keeney, 'Military Service and . . . Nationalism', *Speculum* (1947), pp. 536 f. Cf. the similar development in France, elucidated by J. R. Strayer, 'Defense of the Realm and Royal Power in France', in *Studi in Onore di Gino Luzzato* (Milan, 1949), i. 289–96.
[4] *Parl. Writs*, i. 275, 349.
[5] *Welsh Wars*, pp. 292–304.
[6] Cotton, *Historia*, p. 339. In the Lincoln parliament of 1301 the purveyors of victuals, it was agreed, were to negotiate with county assemblies for supplies; Bain, *Calendar*, no. 1192; *Parl. Writs*, i. 400 (46).

county and borough raised the question whether they would be simply conscripted on terms advised by the administration or whether some form of negotiation was to be undertaken. There was certainly no general negotiation, nor, with the great exception of the crisis of 1297, were there any general complaints about the terms of service. Possibly this was because Edward usually paid his levies, and in the Scotch wars made it clear in his writs that they were going to be paid, from leaving their counties; nor did he make any increased demands concerning armour and weapons. Hence though the frequency and numbers levied may have seemed burdensome, there was no legal ground for complaint. It is an old theory that by respecting the constitution in these matters Edward avoided trouble. But did he really follow antecedent custom? While it is hard to find any constitutional or customary precedents, levies had, in the main, been expected to serve outside the county for forty days or two months. Edward was, in fact, giving away a strong claim, just as his predecessors had given away the old *servicium debitum*. Where he did not give way, in Durham and Northumberland, he became involved in the same sort of hard bargaining as characterized his relations with Bohun and Bigod. The centre for this debate was in each case the county (or palatinate) court in its fullest expression; in the case of Durham it went up to parliament in 1300 and 1301. These precedents for negotiation between king and commons were fraught with significance for the future.

The period to 1307, then, was one of but sporadic consultation, in which the right of counsel and consent was implicit rather than explicit. Military writs present a marked contrast to those issued for taxation in their lack of reference to the advice or consent of the community. They relied rather on the argument of utility and necessity to reinforce the primary duty of allegiance. Yet, as the chroniclers inform us, the wars were discussed, and military aid as well as taxation subjected to baronial consent; occasionally the writs of conciliar and military summons confirm this. Moreover, the tendency to base the list of parliamentary lords on that of military summons, together with the key role of the lords even in subsidized warfare, provided, with the development of consent to taxation, a basis for military consultation.[1] But the story of 1242, 1253, 1294, and 1297 made it abundantly clear that the tradition of hostility to European wars remained very potent.

III

The most momentous development of the next period was the definite triumph of the principle of prior consultation on war, expressed in the Ordinances of 1311, opposed unsuccessfully by Edward II, and adopted with great success by Edward III. The idea made its way into the form of parliamentary writs and was also reflected in the writs of military service. Almost as significant was the attempt of the commons to use their new position as fairly regular members of parliament to fight for the freezing of the terms of their service in the form generously awarded by Edward I. In the third place there was a remarkable extension of negotiation about service, particularly in defensive wars, which reached its apogee in the years 1335–40. Lastly, London, and to a lesser degree the other large cities and ports, joined Cheshire and Durham as privileged enclaves in which the royal command was tempered by local powers.

It is perhaps surprising that in Edward II's time the decline in the effectiveness of the feudal force was not automatically followed by the decline of baronial leadership.[2] The baronial leaders, however, were fortified by their experience as opposition since 1297, by the institution of regular parliaments wherein they were becoming established as a peerage, and by the successful association of the interests of the commons with their own. Moreover, the weakness of the king as a person and the emergence of a baronial leader of the royal blood encouraged the opposition to be more radical in its demands. Perhaps the real tragedy of the reign was very close to the subject we have undertaken to review: the king

[1] J. H. Round, 'The House of Lords and the Model Parliament', *E.H.R.* xxx (1915), 389; J. E. A. Jolliffe, *Constitutional History of Medieval England* (London, 1938), p. 348 and note; cf. Stubbs, *Const. Hist.* ii. 213, n. 2.

[2] For this section, see my 'Edward II and Military Obligation', pp. 95–96 and *passim*. The most informative contemporary on this subject is the author of the *Vita Edwardi Secundi*, now easily consulted in N. Denholm-Young's spirited translation (Nelson's Medieval Texts, 1957).

was too weak mentally to enter into full consultation with his barons, and too weak materially to manage without them. His frantic efforts to lead armies into Scotland in the teeth of opposition only led to disaster and surrender.

The first three years of the reign were spent by the baronial leaders in fighting for and obtaining the Ordinances. The key feature of these was the increased power allotted to the barons in parliament. One of the clauses, which represented the aspirations of a century, was to the effect that the king was not to make war or go out of the realm without the common assent of his baronage, and that in parliament; and that if the king summoned 'his service' for a campaign without consent the summons was to be null.

If Edward had then set out to rule with the barons, and if the latter had shown some reasonableness in interpreting their ordinance, the situation might have been saved. But neither side learned, and the fiasco of the Scottish campaign of 1310 was repeated with greater or less disaster in all subsequent military undertakings.

It would seem that Edward, shaken by the death of Gaveston, made a real attempt to obtain baronial assent in parliament before the 1314 campaign. He had, indeed, sought such assent in the preceding year, but there is no evidence that he obtained it, while the parliament planned for the spring of 1314 was never assembled. It was not until January, 1316, with the 'parliamentary settlement' at Lincoln, that consultation could again become real.[1] This time the council's right to be consulted in all matters touching the realm was recognized, though its personnel and powers were thenceforward to be as much of a problem as those of parliament. It was Edward's failure to consult Lancaster in making his plans for 1317 which led to the latter's withdrawal and famous letter of protest. It was no use, wrote Thomas, arguing that his counsel was wanted, when the writs of summons which he had received showed clearly enough that the king was taking counsel elsewhere; and in any case the business concerned parliament.

The triumph of Pembroke brought hope of better things,

---

[1] The Lincoln parliament had been summoned to discuss Scotland and the March; besides the political settlement, new military levies were agreed to.

and parliament was fully consulted before the great Scottish expedition of 1319. The failure of that expedition was fatal, and the country again fell apart. However, although Edward did consult parliament before his Scottish campaign of 1322 and the French war of 1324, it would seem there was some truth in the charge that these parliaments and *tractatus* (i.e. irregular parliamentary assemblies) were terrified into acquiescense. Clearly this *modus vivendi* achieved by king and parliament could not last. The instrument designed to ensure consultation had become a weapon of autocracy.

Besides the consultation of parliament or the council on wars in general, there was the question of gaining consent to particular kinds of military levy. The parliaments of Edward II did not, apparently, discuss particular measures except in the case of the levy of men from the vills—a levy which was considered as the equivalent of a tax. The parliament summoned to discuss the 1311 levy (*inter alia*) was cancelled, but in 1316 the supply of one man per vill for sixty days was conceded in the Lincoln parliament by the lords and knights of the shire, and cancelled by the consent of the latter.[1] The consent of the *proceres* was claimed, with questionable honesty, in the writ of 1318 levying specially armed foot at local expense. The York parliament of 1322 was consulted on the campaign and agreed to the muster; it is likely that the commons shared in the disastrous decision to call out one man from each vill to serve at local expense. A postscript to this practice of Edward II was provided, ironically enough, by Mortimer. In a charge too circumstantial and too soon after the event to be doubted, he was accused of endeavouring to deceive the Winchester parliament of 1330 into granting a man-at-arms from each vill to serve in Gascony at local expense. In this action, both of the objectionable features of Edward II's measures were present: the levy itself and the bullying of parliament.

IV

Edward III's succession brought the possibilities of dramatic change.[2] Possibly following up the latent 'popularism'

[1] *Rot. Parl.* i. 351; *Parl. Writs*, ii. 166.
[2] See especially M. McKisack, 'Edward III and the Historians', *History*, xlv (1960), 1–15; Michael Powicke, 'The Commons in Scotland and the Deposition of Edward II', *Speculum* xxxv (1960).

of Lancastrian propaganda the revolution was depicted as the triumph of the people. For the first time parliamentary statutes based on common petitions regulated the limits of the general military obligation. They did this in such a highly conservative way that they were incapable of enforcement. But the possibility now arose that they could be defended or modified in parliament. Was parliament, which now included the commons at all its sessions, to prove a more effective instrument of consultation than it had yet been?

On the other hand, the complete disappearance of the feudal military summons and the triumph of the system of indentured contracts in the raising of armies might be expected to have weighed heavily against the continuation of parliamentary consultation on a large scale. However, the lords had survived the critical period as a political body, and their right to be consulted in matters of war was soon reinforced by their whole-hearted absorption in the profitable business of fighting under the king's banner in France. Moreover, Edward III with his lofty ideas about nobility and chivalry did not underestimate the role of the baronage in his political settlement.[1]

Parliamentary writs reflected the co-operation of king and lords in this reign in a way they had not done before. In place of the sporadic consultations of the previous century, there now emerged a practice of almost annual negotiations about war. The role of the council, also, became increasingly clear, and a great variety of conciliar bodies afforced by special urban or other groups were called to advise on defence. For our present purpose, it is enough to note that the phrase *de avisamento consilio* appeared from 1338 intermittently, and from 1372 regularly, in parliamentary writs. In the latter year appeared the phrase 'to treat on our business and [the] military expedition'.[2] In the last century of the Middle Ages the regular term was 'to treat by advice of our council on the state and defence of our realm'.[3]

The consent of the earls and barons to big expeditions like

---

[1] Well evidenced in the events of 1331–2, when the advice of the barons to turn to Ireland rather than France was heeded. *Foedera*, ii. 825, 828, 842; *Rot. Parl.* ii. 60; *Dignity of a Peer*, i. 492.

[2] Ibid., vol. iv; cf. Stubbs, *Constit. Hist.* iii. 403–10.

[3] Ibid.

those of 1327 or 1355 to Scotland, of 1338 to Flanders, or
the preparations in 1344–6 for the Crécy campaign, need
occasion no surprise. Edward's policy was to work with parliament, and for thirty years after 1341 there was a fine
record of co-operation.[1]

The most striking, if not the most essential, aspect of
parliamentary consultation was Edward's effort to draw the
commons into these discussions. This was a matter of some
urgency after 1327, if they were indeed to be conscripted for
service. So in 1332 the advice of the commons was asked,[2]
and, in the writ of 1338 for the naval force, the opening
campaign of the Hundred Years War was attributed to the
urgent request of the commons:

> Because of the defence and safety of our kingdom, and of our other
> lands, and of the rights of our crown, with the consent of the prelates,
> earls and *proceres* of our kingdom who were at our last parliament held
> at Westminster, and also at the urgent request of the community of our
> kingdom made to us in that same parliament, we plan to undertake an
> overseas expedition. . . .[3]

Ten years later came the famous exchange between king
and commons which may be taken as typical of their second
thoughts on the subject of their responsibility for military
policy:

> Most redoubtable lord, as to your war and the array for it . . . we are
> so ignorant and foolish that we neither know (how to), nor can, give
> advice about it; wherefore we pray . . . to excuse us and that it please
> you, by the counsel of the lords and wise men of your council to ordain
> . . . what seems necessary to you for the honour and profit of the Realm.
> And whatever is finally ordained by the assent and accord of you and
> the above mentioned lords, we gladly assent to and hold firm and
> established.[4]

This statement, it should be noted, accepts the right to
assent, but rejects any duty to share in the ordaining of

[1] H. G. Richardson and G. O. Sayles, 'The King's Ministers in Parliament',
E.H.R. xlvii (1932), 390 f.
[2] *Rot. Parl.* ii. 65.
[3] *Foedera*, ii. 1015. Cf. Miss McKisack's comment: 'Edward's plan was to present
war as a national enterprise undertaken in defence of his lawful claim to the French
Crown', 'Edward III and the Historians', p. 9.
[4] *Rot. Parl.* ii. 165.

policy. It did not renounce such requests as had been made in the 1338 petition, but it represented the more considered emphasis of the commons as members of parliament. It is noteworthy, too, that the advice of lords and council, and the consent of the lords, was firmly desiderated. The consultation of lords and commons in council and in parliament had become an almost regular practice.

It has been observed that the commons' real influence on war policy lay in their right of consent to money grants. Requests for such grants could be met by refusal or by bargaining, and at least from the end of Edward III's reign by appropriation or even appointment of war treasurers. Bargaining took the form of petitions for redress of grievances amongst which might be included the nature of military levies. Where such levies were concerned, the commons inherited from the barons the attitude of clause 16 of Magna Carta. They insisted on the limits of tenurial obligation, on the Statute of Winchester, on pay for service outside their counties except in times of invasion, and specifically on repeal of those levies on the rich whereby, for example, a man with £100 income from rent would be responsible for four men-at-arms instead of one. In spite of Edward's occasional inclination to ignore these regulations, he was probably influenced by them to encourage a more rapid transition to contractual forces for foreign campaigns. Further regulations were made by parliament in the reigns of Richard II and of Henry IV, while the control of the purse continued to make the consultation of both sections of parliament an essential prerequisite for any major campaign.

We may now turn from the question of parliamentary discussions about war to the question of consultation regarding specific kinds of military levy. As had been the case before, defence measures occasioned the widest discussions. The rolls of parliament and chancery offer many examples of consultation about military levies, especially about those for defence against invasion.[1] Nor was the consent of subjects

---

[1] Cf. *Rot. Parl.*, Index, svv. 'army' and 'array'. On the arguments for the use of justices of the peace, cf. B. Putnam, *Proceedings before the Justices of the Peace*, pp. xliv f. Note especially the intensive debates of the years 1369–77, culminating in the article of Latimer's impeachment, discussed by C. C. Bayley, 'The Campaign of 1375 and the Good Parliament', *E.H.R.* lv (1940), 370–83.

confined to parliament. As the 'advisory' council became administrative, and as it came to include a larger body of lords (and, in special circumstances, to be nominated in parliament), the direct share of a large group of subjects in organizing war was increased. Almost equally important, consultation of local or regional bodies in matters of defence developed considerably in the fourteenth and fifteenth centuries.

Defence against invasion was undoubtedly the most constant subject of consultation. The history of negotiation on this topic goes back at least to William Rufus's defence against Robert, and it is officially documented from 1205. It could take all manner of forms, from bargaining with individual towns, through county and regional assemblies, to full-scale parliamentary planning. So numerous are all these types of consultation that, even at the risk of suggesting a non-existent uniformity or consistency, one or two examples of each must suffice.

The Scottish wars necessitated constant military preparations in the years after the Treaty of Northampton; these might range from supply of garrison troops to the assembly of relief or punitive expeditions. They were marked by very extensive consultation with differing groups of subjects. These negotiations were intensified at times of large French expeditions—when the French and Scottish threats tended to unite. A series of consultations in the years 1336 to 1369 may serve to illustrate the vigour of negotiation at the centre. In October 1336 a great council at Nottingham was stated to have agreed to a revised defence plan involving the supply of foot by vills and a new arms scale.[1] A *tractatus* of the king's deputies, lords, and coast-town representatives, at London in January 1337, appears to have refused defence aid.[2] In February 1338 a *colloquium* of three to five knights from each county was summoned 'to hear and to do' on defence.[3] In the following February parliament agreed on a scheme to be administered by local assemblies, by which the wealthy would contribute according to their means.[4] Later that year the regular clergy were asked to take part 'by the advice and

[1] *Rot. Scot.* i. 459.   [2] Ibid., pp. 472, 474, 475, 478.
[3] *Foedera*, ii. 1013.
[4] C. 76/14 m. 16d, m. 15; *Foedera*, ii. 1070.

consent of the lords of the realm and others of the council'. Two knights from each county were summoned in February 1347 to treat with the council on coast defence.[1] In November 1359 a council of prelates and magnates ordained concerning the defence duties of richer subjects.[2] Ten years later, on the resumption of the French war, the array of clergy and laity against invasion was ordained by the consent of prelates, magnates, and *communitas regni*, in parliament.[3] An assembly of representatives from coastal towns, and from one or two inland cities, was called in October of that year to come before king and council to discuss defence measures.[4]

Similar discussions frequently preceded the mounting of Scottish expeditions. In 1337 parliamentary consent was obtained for the leading of chosen men-at-arms and archers from the northern counties to Berwick at the cost of the counties,[5] and in 1339 parliamentary agreement was obtained to numbers and terms of service in Scotland and to the names of the arrayers.[6] It would appear from the record that there had been some dispute as to where pay should begin. In the event, the crown conceded that it should start at Newcastle rather than Berwick. This measure represented an important advance in co-operation between king, lords, and commons. That the model for this plan was the defence scheme of the early spring referred to earlier is borne out by the fact that the agreement on Scotland was similarly followed by orders to arrayers to carry out their instructions with the consent of local assemblies of lords, knights, and men-at-arms.[7] In the following January another parliament led to still wider negotiating powers being given to commissioners. A date for the county assemblies was named. There the commissioners were to expound parliament's decisions, to negotiate on wages from leaving Newcastle, and to raise wages and supplies for the journey to that town.[8] This was as far as parliamentary direction of war was to go in the fourteenth century; that it went so far may well have been due to the king's absence in Flanders.

[1] Ibid. iii. 106.
[3] 6 July 1369; ibid. iii. 876.
[5] *Rot. Scot.* i. 495–6.
[7] *Rot. Scot.* i. 573–5, 577–8.

[2] Ibid. iii. 455–8.
[4] Ibid. iii. 880–1.
[6] *Rot. Parl.* ii. 110.
[8] Ibid. i. 583.

More frequent than parliamentary or conciliar consultation on defence and war was the assembling of regional
groups to prepare defence plans. Such assemblies appear in
the north of England as early as the twelfth century, and may
be regarded as a natural product of geography and communications. By the end of the thirteenth century the influence of national institutions came to be reflected in more
elaborate assemblies. Of key importance was that of 1296,
wherein the knights and two men from each vill of the
northern counties were to assemble before the defence wardens of the north (the bishop of Durham and the Earl
Warenne) in their respective counties 'to hear and to do' their
will on defence.

In 1335 the northern assembly, in one of three regional
sets of negotiations, agreed that all of a certain age should
be armed.[1] The terms of the Yorkshire commissioners for
defence appointed in June 1337, who may have been principally concerned with Scotland, included the assembling of
all Yorkshire knights and men-at-arms 'to hear and carry out'
instructions.[2] Two years later the above-mentioned commission of six northern notables (including the archbishop of
York) were ordered, on parliamentary authority, to bring
together at York and elsewhere all the lords, knights, and
men-at-arms, together with coast wardens, to expound the
parliamentary decision and to order the array and selection
of troops for coast defence. This northern commission was
part of a general parliamentary defence plan.[3]

This scheme of 1339 was clearly the basis of the defence
plans of 1345, when the king himself was again busily engaged in preparing for foreign war.[4] A purely ecclesiastical
commission was appointed, consisting of the archbishop of
York and his two suffragans; they were to assemble the earls,
barons, knights, and other nobility, and the 'communities' of
the clergy of the northern counties, in an assembly where the
defence of the northern March could be treated of, agreed
on, and ordained. A similar commission was given to the

1 *Rot. Scot.* i. 366–7.   2 Ibid. i. 494.
3 Ibid. i. 573–5, 577–8; *Foedera*, ii. 1070; cf. C. 76/14, mm. 8–17, 18d–3d, *passim*;
and H. G. Richardson, 'The King's Ministers in Parliament', p. 393.
4 *Rot. Scot.* i. 670, 671, 674.

archbishop of York, bishop of Durham, and two others in March 1346, to supervise the array of the *jurati* with the aid of a similar northern assembly. Maurice de Berkeley was appointed to convey the king's intentions to this body and the assembly's decisions back to the king. Later that year the wardens of the eastern and western Marches were instructed to hold *tractatus*, if feasible, on defence.[1]

These northern assemblies, as has been noted, were sometimes part of wider defence consultations. Some of the other regional discussions may now be briefly alluded to. At the end of Edward II's reign, when frantic efforts at defence against Isabella and Mortimer were being made, a meeting of all the Norfolk high constables of hundreds and constables of vills with two men from each seaport was ordered to take counsel for coast defence, and a scheme similar to the coast-defence plan of 1296 was drawn up.[2] Mention has been made of other regional consultations than the northern one in 1335; Sir Ralph Basset was to report the measures taken by Welsh Marcher lords, and the Channel Isles' wardens were to ordain on defence with the counsel of the Islanders.[3] In August 1337 various county assemblies of clergy and wealthy laity (*divitiis potentes*) as well as diocesan assemblies were charged with provision for defence.[4]

Consultation with particular towns also developed considerably during the reign of Edward III. It has its origin in town self-government, and became more important as the monarchy sought to increase the size of the infantry levies. Many of the larger towns must have won the right to be consulted, but nowhere was the success so great as in the case of London.[5] Taken in conjunction with conciliar and parliamentary discussions, the evidence suggests that, in mid-fourteenth century, England deserved the name of 'constitutional monarchy'.

[1] R. L. Storey, 'The Wardens of the Marches', pp. 593–615, shows how the Percies and Nevilles took over this role of negotiation.
[2] H. M. Cam, in *The English Government at Work*, iii. 167.
[3] *Cal. Plea and Memoranda Rolls, 1327–64*, pp. 92–93; *Foedera*, ii. 916.
[4] Ibid., ii. 989–90. This example may suffice for many such assemblies.
[5] The evidence for London is gathered in a Note at the end of this chapter. Cf. also W. Hudson, *Records of the City of Norwich*, i. 404–6.

V

The consent of parliament to war and peace continued to be a major aim of royal government in the final century of the Middle Ages. The rolls of parliament contain the speeches of the chancellors or other spokesmen of the crown who argued the case for the royal intentions. Moreover, through the expression of firm opinions backed up by the appropriation, withholding, or grant of supplies, the lords and commons had a real influence on whether war should be waged, and if so, on the scale and nature of the operations. Failure in military matters was included in the counts against both the third and sixth earls of Suffolk.[1] Occasionally, parliament entered directly into the regulation of armies and the planning of expeditions, as it had done in Edward III's reign. It may even be maintained that parliamentary support was as necessary for success in war as was effective royal leadership. The contrast between the considerable (if qualified) support of parliament for Henry V and its almost consistently negative attitude (if we apply the principle of 'by their fruits ye shall know them') to the regents and person of his son goes some way towards explaining the reversal of England's fortunes in the Hundred Years War.

It would be tedious to record all, or even a large fraction, of the requests for support in war made by the king's representatives at the opening of parliaments. The exposition of foreign policy and needs followed by a request for aid became the normal, if not the only, form of the opening of parliamentary proceedings. Almost as frequent was the request for advice on war.[2] In 1371 Chancellor Wykeham asked for advice on how the realm might be preserved from French invasion; in 1382 parliament was asked to express its view of the three 'ways' of Flanders, Portugal, and Spain; in 1402 the chancellor, in asking for an ordinance on the defence of

---

[1] Rot. Parl. iii. 216; v. 177–82. The former had failed to implement provisions made in parliament. See also the impeachment of Bishop Despenser, ibid. iii. 151–3.

[2] e.g. 'to ordain on defence of French and Scottish lands', or to consider their defence; Rot. Parl. iii. 228, 403, 485, 522, and passim. There are useful comments on these points in S. B. Chrimes, English Constitutional Ideas in the Fifteenth Century (Cambridge, 1936), pp. 142–5; J. H. Ramsay, Genesis of Lancaster and Lancaster of York; W. Longman, Life and Times of Edward III; J. H. Wylie, Henry IV and Henry V; and W. Stubbs, Constitutional History, vol. iii, esp. pp. 267 f., 405 f.

Aquitaine, Ireland, and Wales, warned that in past times the commons had put particular interest before the common good, drawing dire comparisons with the fall of the Roman Empire.[1] The council, at least in the form of great councils, had inherited the outlook of the baronial opposition to Edward II that parliamentary consent was necessary for a royal expedition, a factor of undoubted importance for the increased regularity of consultation.[2] On the other hand, Richard II made a sharp defence of his right to control military affairs (in reply to criticism of his proposed joint expedition with Charles VI to Lombardy):

Et dist outre notre Seignur le Roy, q'il voet estre a large et liberte de comander ses Gentz, pur eux envoier en aide de ses Amys, et pur disposer de ses Biens propres a sa volente, ou, et a tant des foitz, qe luy plerra.[3]

In 1414 the chancellor put the king's war proposals before parliament, but only wanted their 'counsel' in this matter (bracketed with military aid of his lords and copious money from his subjects), the classical references preferred by his father's spokesmen giving place to the crude appeal that as the king's lands increased, his lieges' payments could be lessened.[4] However, in appeals for money on later occasions, the king's representative did not hesitate to state that the king's voyage had been with the consent of all the Estates of parliament.[5]

The English stand at Arras in 1435 was presented, and military arrangements for the defence of the French territories made, in parliament.[6] These arrangements took the form of an indenture between the king and Gloucester. More active measures for the defence of England and of the seas were initiated by parliament as the war turned against her.

[1] Rot. Parl. ii. 303; ibid. iii. 114–47, 485. For another classical allusion, see ibid. iii. 622.   [2] Ibid. iii. 144–6, 215; Proceedings, i. 210.

[3] Rot. Parl. iii. 338; cf. the charge regarding domestic misuse of troops at home, ibid. iii. 418. Edward II had been told that parliament's claim to regulate war was against his rights, for 'solius principis est bellum indicere', Annales Londonienses, p. 214.

[4] Rot. Parl. iv. 34.   [5] e.g. ibid. iv. 94, 106–7.

[6] Ibid. iv. 481–4; on parliament's attitude to the war, cf. Jocelyn Dickinson, The Congress of Arras (Oxford, 1957), pp. 24–25 and notes; cf. also K. MacFarlane, 'England, the Lancastrian Kings', Cambridge Medieval History, viii. 397.

In 1442 the commons not only granted supplies, but put forward a definite scheme to be ordained by the king 'by the authority of this parliament', which would have constituted a standing naval defence.[1] At last, after turning a deaf ear to Somerset's desperate plea for aid in 1449, addressed to king, lords, and commons, parliament enacted an elaborate, but abortive, defence measure as the last bastion in Gascony finally crumbled.

This measure of March 1453 was the most drastic and detailed intervention of parliament in defence yet to be made. Twenty thousand archers were to be raised for six months 'per ipsos qui portarent onus . . . in qualibet patria', from every county, city, town, and vill by equal assessment; this number was reduced to 13,000 in April, and detailed proposals for the form of array propounded by the commons.[2] A quota was established for each county and ten cities, ranging from 1,137 for London to 56 for Westmorland and 30 for Nottingham. Commissioners were to be appointed to subdivide these quotas among the hundreds, lesser towns, and vills, and to assess the inhabitants according to lands and revenues. These subdivided quotas were to be raised by the local authorities—mayors, bailiffs, constables, or lords (where the former were not in existence). The whole force was to be ready to serve at royal summons under royal captains, at a rate of sixpence per day for each archer. Although this scheme was jettisoned for eleven years in exchange for the promise of aid for Gascony, unless the king should in the meantime take the field in person, commissions were issued in December 1457 to allocate to each hundred, borough, vill, &c., its quota of the county assessment and to assess the revenues and goods of the inhabitants to their support.[3] Taken in conjunction with the pettifogging aid actually accorded to the lost cause in France, both in this and previous years, the scheme reveals the pretentious futility of the commons when they finally turned to an active role in military planning.

---

[1] *Rot. Parl.* v. 59–60.

[2] Ibid. v. 230–1. The grant was by the commons with the assent of the lords. Of the reduction, 6,000 were by reason of the commons' 'grete kyndenesse', and 1,000 'of oure speciall grace and mere motion' with the assent and authority of the lords.

[3] *C.P.R. 1452–61*, pp. 406–10.

This scheme was revived when Edward IV obtained a parliamentary grant of 13,000 archers for his expedition of 1474, to be paid this time out of specially appropriated subsidies.[1] This grant, however, was essentially not a scheme of array but an elaborate appropriation of a series of money grants for the levy of archers. The individual counties were assessed not for the archers themselves, but for their wages.[2] Not a word was said about the form of levy of the men except that they were 'to be chosen and reteyned by such persones as youre Highnes for that cause shall depute and ordeyn'.[3]

The most persistent initiative by the commons was in the effort to circumscribe conscription and regulate the working of military contract. However, commons' petitions were sometimes put forward for the defence of particular parts of the realm. In 1404 the commons asked for three measures of defence against Wales: the enforcement of the *Ordinances faites pur les Guerres*, the strengthening of garrisons, and the appointment of specified arrayers of men-at-arms and archers in Hereford and Shropshire.[4] In 1421 the northern counties asked for reinforcements against Scottish raiders and for stricter arrangements for keeping the peace. In 1450 the defence of the Isle of Wight aroused anxiety; only one esquire and 1,200 fencibles were available, and a popular request for the appointment of the esquire as king's lieutenant was rejected.[5]

The terms of obligation under commissions of array was a subject of continued petition and parliamentary legislation. In 1384 the commons petitioned against recent arrays of men (*gentz*) of the counties to go to Scotland at their own cost or the cost of their counties, and secured the re-enactment of the Statute 1 Edward III.[6] Henry IV's vigorous domestic musters led to the extension of these demands in 1402, when parliamentary petition led to the reaffirmation of the Statutes of 1344 and 1352, and in 1404 when a 'model'

---

[1] *Rot. Parl.* vi. 4, 39–41, 111–19.
[2] Cf. the special arrangement for the levy of money for 590 archers by the northern counties, ibid., pp. 115 f.
[3] Ibid., p. 4. The muster for the first quarter's pay shows that the archers served in troops of great miscellaneity; *Foedera*, xi. 843–4.
[4] *Rot. Parl.* iii. 552.   [5] Ibid. iv. 143; v. 204.
[6] Ibid. iii. 201; above, p. 216.

form of commission of array was given parliamentary approval.[1]

In March 1406 the commons nominated a committee to work with the Council in negotiating a defence plan with the 'Merchants of England', as parliament would be over before an agreement had been reached.[2] In addition, the commons made many requests concerning the defence of Wales. When parliament resumed two months later, the commons asked the king to ordain a remedy for the heavy defence burden in France, Ireland, Scotland, and Wales, as many lords and commoners, towns and counties, had supported heavy charges and duties of finding (*impositions pur trover*) men-at-arms and archers for service in various places. It was replied optimistically that the king would charge the Council to provide remedy.[3] Further requests followed concerning defence measures—against muster padding, for example.[4] In 1407 the commons attempted to deny all responsibility for the war in Wales, asking that the lords marcher be ordained to carry out that duty—a request which was met with a polite refusal; a modified request that the lords keep up their castles in the Marches without cost to the realm received assent.[5]

The regulation of captaincies, indentures, billeting, ship levies, and archery (the list could be extended) occupied a fair proportion of parliamentary time in the last century of the Middle Ages.[6] Perhaps the most important regulation was the Statute of 1439 which made it felonious for a man to leave his company without the leave of the captain. In this way the possibility of bringing the contracted armies under parliamentary supervision was significantly advanced.[7]

Less overt, but more persistent, than direct proposals and requests regarding defence, was the appropriation of funds to particular defence projects. Some of these measures have been alluded to. As early as 1310 the lords had complained

[1] *Rot. Parl.* iii. 501, 526–7; above, p. 217.
[2] Ibid. iii. 569. The demands of the Merchants and subsequent decisions are in ibid. iii. 570.
[3] Ibid. iii. 573.   [4] Ibid. iii. 576–7.
[5] Ibid. iii. 610 (cl. 17—the king would seek the lords' advice), 612.
[6] Cf. W. Prynne, *Soveraigne Power*, pp. 10–11; *S.R.* ii, and *Rot. Parl.* iii–vi, *passim*.
[7] *S.R.* ii. 314–15, in R. A. Newhall, *Muster and Review*, pp. 150 f.; the enactment is based on *Rot. Parl.* v. 32–33.

that spending of war grants had been *par noun convenable consail*, but the remedy, as has been noted, was an attempt to set up parliamentary sanction for military undertakings. The development of conciliar supervision of war is discussed briefly below; more direct measures by parliament itself were also put in motion in the following century. Frequently the money grants of Edward III's parliaments were made with the stipulation that they be spent on some particular object: defence against the Scots, coast defence, the sending of troops abroad; and in 1377 the lords and commons asked for treasurers to be appointed to see that the money be applied only to war expenses, a precedent which came to be widely followed. In the fifteenth century, apart from the appropriation of specific subsidies such as that of 1465, the yields of tonnage and poundage were directed by parliament to the defence of the sea, and that of part of the wool custom to the defence of Calais.[1]

VI

The association of the council with the king in the issues of military summons and commissions may be traced in the authorization of the writs which embodied them.[2] The rise of the council to an administrative role naturally brought military affairs even more emphatically within its purview, so that a large part of the *Proceedings and Ordinances* is occupied with discussion of peace and war, defensive and offensive plans and musters, or the preparation of proposals for parliamentary consideration.[3] The varying contributions of conciliar debate, and the element of wide consent involved when the council met in fuller sessions than usual, would require a separate study; some of the more notable features, however, demand attention even in a survey of this kind.

'Great Councils' of varying composition met frequently in

---

[1] Stubbs, *Constitutional History*, ii. 596–9; iii. 271–2. Cf. Bedford's request in 1434, *Proceedings*, iv. 226–7.

[2] In 1335, for example, writs for the great Scottish expedition were issued variously *per ipsum regem*, *per ipsum regem et consilium*, and *per consilium*; *Rot. Scot.* i. 320–69. The classes of Chancery and Exchequer Warrants in the Public Record Office are the best guide to conciliar control (C. 81; E. 28).

[3] B. Wilkinson, *Studies*, chap. v; S. B. Chrimes, *Administrative History*, chap. vi; T. F. T. Plucknett, 'The Place of the Council in the Fifteenth Century', *R.H.S. Trans.*, 4th series, i. 157–89.

the fifteenth century to consider the needs of defence and of war. It may even be argued that, at least in Henry VI's minority, king and council, rather than the king himself, took over executive tasks, including the administration of war; moreover, councils might make plans at times when parliament was likely to be either unreceptive or inconvenient, or as a supplement to parliament. Such were the schemes of February 1400 (against Scottish invasion), 1403 (against the French and Welsh), 1411 (for the relief of Calais), 1414–15, 1425, and 1427–35 (almost annually).[1] As has been pointed out, supervision by council as well as by arrayers limited the element of free contract in the raising of military forces by the indenture system.[2] The principle of consultation was occasionally formulated, as in 1414, when the lords and knights in council went on from endorsing the royal claims in France to express their general trust that 'alle the werks of redynesse that may be to your viage thought or wrought that hit be doo by the hie avis of yow and of youre noble conseil', adding that on this condition they were prepared to serve in person as was customary.[3]

That council continued to be aware of a distinction between its own and parliament's powers in matters of peace and war is shown by such decisions as that of 1427 to the effect that the troops authorized for the defence of Gloucester's inheritance in Hainault should not engage in further conquest 'sanz le consentement des trois estatz de son royaume Dengleterre'.[4] Where the lords in council favoured a project, however, they would attempt to circumvent the possible opposition of parliament.[5] On the other hand, as we have seen, parliament might protest against conciliar as well as other military measures, and seek to revise them.

The military activities of council during the minority of

---

[1] Proceedings, i. 102–6, and Ad. Usk, Chronicon, p. 67 (1400); Foedera, viii. 342–3 (1403); Proceedings, ii. 140–55 (1414–15); iii. 274, 322–44, 349; iv. 28–36, 141, 222–32 (1425–35).

[2] Above, p. 169.

[3] Proceedings, ii. 141–2; cf. ibid., pp. 150–2. Parliament was, of course, extensively consulted in 1414 and 1415, though in the former year the commons advised against war (Rot. Parl. iv. 34).

[4] Proceedings, iii. 272. This council was the great council, afforced by 'certains notables chivalers et esquires' (ibid., p. 271). For parliamentary assent to Gloucester's undertakings, cf. Rot. Parl., iv. 289.   [5] Ibid. i. 102–6.

Henry VI are nowhere better illustrated than in the discussions, or perhaps bargaining, which were involved in the preparation for Henry's personal expedition to France in 1430.[1] The lords going to France asked for assurances on the matter of the army, the aims and duration of the expedition, the support to be expected of the allies, financing, its termination, and subsequent defence plans. Most of the replies reserved the discretion of the king and Gloucester and other lords of the council abiding at home. Apart from such extraordinary debates, however, council was for ever concerned with scraping together the small forces which could be sent, arranging for their financing, confirming appointments of commanders and divisions of authority, or preparing schemes for parliamentary consideration.[2] Even this desultory and inadequate activity dwindled in the decades after the minority.[3] Discussion of any major decision, in fact, seemed to produce a strange paralysis of the will.[4] Only occasionally did the council intervene directly in the raising of men, as in the case of Bristol in 1442, of Lincolnshire and other counties in 1443, and of Cheshire and Lancashire in 1450,[5] except by the now traditional method of encouraging and supervising the assembly of a lord's or lords' forces.

As the fifteenth century wore on, local consultations dwindled almost as much as did effective parliamentary debate. The limits of county obligation were so narrowly confined by statute and precedent that there remained little room for discussion. Only where king and parliament together sought to raise a big force, as in 1453, did negotiation occur. In the towns it was different, at least after civil war had broken out. Then, like the lords, they occupied strategic positions, so that their support became the subject of bargaining. The York records show that this 'tradition' was alive in 1481 when the city deliberated on Edward's request for troops and decided to send 120 for two months, paying each

1 *Proceedings*, iv. 35, 38–39, 91–97; *Rot. Parl.* v. 416b. The political significance of these sessions is well summarized in K. B. MacFarlane, 'England, the Lancastrian Kings, 1399–1461', *C. Med. H.* viii. 393–4.

2 *Proceedings*, iv, *passim*.

3 See Ibid., v. 5, 8, 14, 26, 42, &c.; vi. 16–18, 52–54, 152 f.

4 Ibid. v. 223–4.

5 Ibid. v. 194, 234, 412–16; cf. ibid. v. 245, 265; vi. 95–96 (cf. ibid., pp. 130–1).

man ten shillings wages in advance.[1] In Richard III's reign, at least, such negotiations were conducted with vills and hundreds as well as with towns.[2]

We may conclude from this survey of consultation in recruitment and war that even in matters which were pre-eminently the king's business there was a tendency to extend steadily the principle of consultation. Although such consultation achieved its greatest vigour at a time when public obligation to serve in war was still clearly dominant over contracted service, it did not die out thereafter. Public exhortation, to say the least, remained as important as ever; the negotiation and enforcement of contracts was brought under parliamentary supervision. Consent to both war and to service had become a real prerequisite for a successful campaign.

NOTE. THE LONDON LEVIES

THE fact of urban and, above all, of London autonomy in defence calls for some observations. London's self-government in the supply of troops cannot be regarded as typical, but it represents the most extreme example of a very widespread phenomenon. The organization of London levies, which already played an important role in twelfth-century warfare, was by wards and parishes under the aldermen.[3] The organization can be seen at work in 1215 and again in 1296, when the aldermen and citizens with the warden decided how many horsemen, cross-bowmen, and foot were to be sent to defend Kent.[4]

In Edward II's reign London found itself negotiating with the king for reduction of service on several occasions. At the end of 1314 Edward II asked for 300 cross-bowmen; he got 120, armed and paid at a cost to the city of over £178.[5] When in 1318, immediately following the Treaty of Leake, Edward asked for 500 armoured foot for service in Scotland, to serve for forty days at the city's expense, the mayor summoned a special assembly of aldermen and community 'to consider'

---

[1] R. Davies, Records, pp. 106–9, 116; cf. ibid., pp. 149–56, 216.
[2] J. H. Ramsay, Lancaster and York, ii. 529.
[3] Cf. the Anglo-Saxon origins in Athelstan's Iudicia Civitatis Lundoniae.
[4] Calendar of Letters of the City of London, Letter Book 'C.', printed in extenso in Parl. Writs, i. 278–9, and H. T. Riley, Memorials of London, pp. 31–32. Watch and ward arrangements are to be found throughout Riley's collection.
[5] Riley, Memorials, pp. 114–15.

the order. These agreed to provide 200 foot at the expense of the commonalty, and that the 200 should be levied by causing each of the more powerful and better citizens to find one armed soldier.[1] Edward's first notable distraint of arms after the Treaty of Leake, constituting as it did a serious challenge to the rights of England's cities and towns, was thus responsible for London's first recorded debate on military matters. Although he got 200, not 500, Edward sent a letter expressing his satisfaction, and paid the wages of the troops for their return journey from York.[2]

In 1321 London negotiated with the king on its contribution to defence. The occasion was, of course, exceptional, the king being in no position to speak in the voice of majesty. On 7 July the mayor and aldermen appeared before the king and council at Westminster and were asked if they would preserve London for the king in view of the current civil war. They replied that they were unwilling to refuse! Hence they were told to draw up and report their defence plans. These plans, which included the assessment of all to be assessed to arms by wards and a mobile night guard of 200, were duly drawn up, reported, and accepted.[3] In the meantime, the barons under Hereford had been negotiating with London, but were easily put off.[4]

Later in 1321 the king wanted troops for the attack on Leeds Castle and for his campaign in the Marches. These demands precipitated something of a crisis. On the one hand, the king pointed out that 500 men had been common, even customary, service from London in the past and appears to have demanded some agreement in writing on this.[5] On the other hand, while the 'commonalty' of London felt their promise to defend the city was adequate, they agreed (so reported the mayor) to send 300 men (they had apparently sent 400 to Leeds; the king's attempt to recover their pay, which had been advanced by the king's clerk, appears to have had a part in the flare-up). They begged that the service of the mayor and citizens might be excused. The king stood by his demands, and the citizens agreed to try to find 500, who would serve at the city's expense for forty days.[6] The farce of a letter granting that this would not prejudice their rights or be a precedent was demanded and reluctantly granted.[7]

The triumph of Edward at Boroughbridge was assisted by a small

---

1 *Cal. Letter Book 'E'*, p. 93.
2 Riley, *Memorials*, p. 128.
3 Ibid, pp. 142–4 (from Letter Book 'E').
4 R. Sharp, *London and the Kingdom*, p. 150 [henceforward Sharp].
5 Cf. *Chroniques de London*, ed. G. J. Aungier (Camden Society, 1844), p. 43.
6 According to the *Chroniques* they sent 380; ibid.
7 The above account is constructed from the *Cal. Letter Books 'E'*, pp. 153–5. Cf. Sharp, p. 151.

London contingent. Afterwards Edward asked for troops for Scotland, and received an offer from the 'Mayor and good folks' offering 500 men or 2,000 marks in money and supplies. He accepted the latter, and showed his new confidence by demanding in addition 100 men at the city's expense as a bodyguard. This demand led to a special assembly of all aldermen and twelve men from each ward. The assembly met on 15 May and, although the account breaks off abruptly at this point and is not resumed, there is evidence of discontent led by the high officials.[1]

The new power of the 'commonalty' was again demonstrated when they rejected a request for fifty arbalesters for the siege of Wallingford, on the grounds that defence taxed all their impoverished resources.[2] Similar bargaining, though not recorded directly, must have been behind the reduction of London's quota from 300 to 140 for the expedition to France in June 1325.[3]

In the first Scottish campaign of Edward III's reign the numbers were left to the city, as indeed to all the cities and towns addressed, and London sent a mixed force of militia and hirelings.[4] From this year dates the service of 100 men-at-arms and 100 foot as the London contingent. In 1334 there is fuller evidence of negotiation. An assembly in late October of the mayor, sheriffs, aldermen, and 'a great multitude of citizens', discussed the financing of the contingent and, later, the punishment of the recalcitrant by 'distresses, sequestrations, and all manner of coercion'.[5] After the selection of the troops, they were 'again chosen and surveyed' by mayor and aldermen.[6] The following year, the year of the great expedition, the mayor, aldermen, and sheriffs replied to the royal order for 200 hobelars in terms which made it clear that this was a grant from the city; they noted that nothing was said of costs, and as a sign of goodwill were ready to supply the men for a hundred days at the cost of the city.[7] Later, along with the representatives of many cities and counties, the mayor of London went to York parliament and negotiated the commutation of the levy into

---

[1] Cal. Letter Books 'E', p. 169. For Boroughbridge, Chroniques, p. 43, and for the service of the hundred guards, ibid., pp. 44–45. On the discontent, Riley, Memorials, pp. 147–8.

[2] Cal. Plea and Memoranda Rolls, 1327–64, p. 1.

[3] Parl. Writs, ii. 688, 698. Cf. these 137 served: Nicholas Hugate's account book, B.M. Add. MS. 7967, fols. 45–52d.

[4] Foedera (Rec. Comm.), ii. 705 (Cl. R.); Cal. of Plea and Memoranda Rolls, 1323–64, pp. 22, 28, 41; Cal. Letter Book 'F', p. 206. Other authorities are cited by V. B. Redstone, 'Some Mercenaries of Henry of Lancaster', T.R.H.S. (1931), p.151, who states incomprehensibly that Londoners' service outside London was due to 'sheer love of fighting'.

[5] Riley, Memorials, pp. 187–8.

[6] Ibid., pp. 189–90.

[7] Cal. Letter Book 'E', p. 5.

a money grant.[1] (Some towns, however, were content with the reduction obtained on complaint to the king in the preceding month.[2]

In 1337 London was to send 500 armoured foot to Gascony, but the number was reduced to 200 in order to secure better quality, the remainder being remitted at the request of Mayor Pulteney.[3] The 200 were later described as sent by the mayor, aldermen, and commonalty.

There were important negotiations in 1338 on the subject both of defence and of London's contribution to the French war. In April the mayor and aldermen were summoned before king and Council and asked to undertake the defence of the city in the king's absence. On this, they withdrew and prepared a scheme which, as it involved the arming and taxing of all householders, may well have been drawn up in the common council.[4] Certainly an assembly ('Congregation') was summoned a few months later to ordain on beacons and enforcement,[5] while in October a 'Congregation of Mayor, aldermen and an "immense commonalty" ' ordained on river defence.[6]

Parallel with these assemblies, negotiations were conducted on the subject of service in France. On 11 May the mayor and aldermen again appeared before the king and Council, this time being asked how many men they were prepared to send to France. To this they replied that they desired to consult the commonalty. The scheme drawn up had to be modified as many went on service with lords in their retinues. What the original scheme was is nowhere disclosed, but the one adopted involved the assessment of each ward to part of the total contingent of a hundred. Later in the year the king's Council was petitioned by mayor, aldermen, and commonalty to allow the aldermen and citizens summoned for service abroad to stay at home for defence of the city.[7]

In 1339–40, a great year for parliamentary and local consultation on defence and on Scotland, the mayor and aldermen are to be found organizing 'in Congregation' the watch and ward, and sending, with the commonalty, the names of men-at-arms being provided by the wealthier citizens.[8] In this latter assembly, Congregation agreed to the fine of those who defaulted (in providing men) a sum of fifty shillings.

In 1341 representation of the wards in Congregation by two commoners was first mentioned in connexion with levies—this time naval ones.[9] Naval impressment, in fact, became the chief military charge on

---

[1] *Rot. Scot.* i. 350. Some of this grant was later assigned to the levy of ships and marines; *Foedera*, ii. 920.

[2] e.g. Colchester; ibid., p. 345.   [3] *Cal. Letter Book 'F'*, p. 10.

[4] Ibid., pp. 20–23; *Cal. Plea and Memoranda Rolls*, p. 189.

[5] Ibid., pp. 167–8.

[6] Ibid., pp. 176–7; cf. also ibid., pp. 100–2, and Riley, *Memorials*, pp. 202–3.

[7] *Cal. Plea and Memoranda Rolls*, i. 170, 179, 190; *Cal. Letter Book 'F'*, pp. 25–27.

[8] *Cal. Plea and Memoranda Rolls*, pp. 102, 132–3.   [9] Ibid., p. 140.

the city as time went on. As on several previous occasions, the royal demands in 1344 had to be modified from the 300 first required; the city regulations for the 80 archers eventually conceded for the Crécy campaign are recorded.[1]

In the following year, the Calendars show London issuing defence orders and organizing the levy of garrison troops armed at the expense of wards, but there was no substantial change. Volunteers tended to replace conscripts, so negotiation with the king was no longer really necessary.[2] In 1377, on the other hand, citizens were summoned to Westminster to discuss the threat of war and the dangers to commerce.[3] In the same year the Common Council elected a committee to keep the peace, and 200 of the more reputable citizens agreed on a far-reaching defence scheme.[4]

The last century of the Middle Ages brought little change in the system of London array. It may be surmized that the hiring of troops with moneys raised by ward assessments was the normal way in which the city disposed of the few calls it received to supply troops. One new factor was the livery companies, which raised troops for the defence of Calais in 1437.[5] Beginning with the heavy assessment of 1453, there was a marked revival of military readiness during the Wars of the Roses, but it was not until the sixteenth century that arrays from among the citizens again reached, and surpassed, the level of the early fourteenth century.[6]

---

[1] *Cal. Letter Book 'F'*, p. 100; *Cal. Plea and Memoranda Rolls*, pp. 221-2.
[2] Cf. the call for volunteers in 1372—*Cal. Letter Book 'G'*, p. 294.
[3] *Cal. Letter Book 'H'*, pp. 72, 31 July.
[4] *Cal. Plea and Memoranda Rolls*, p. 243; Riley, *Memorials*, pp. 409-10. The record of other towns varies, but they clearly valued and fought for the right to make their own arraying arrangements. For Oxford, Cambridge, and Lincoln, see A. E. Prince, 'Army and Navy', 364; *Rot. Scot.* i. 212, 252, 339; for Colchester see ibid. i. 345; for Portsmouth and Lincoln, see P.R.O. C. 76/37, m. 20.
[5] Sharp, pp. 279-80.
[6] Ibid., pp. 294, 297-8, 477-8.

INDEX

PRINTED IN GREAT BRITAIN
AT THE UNIVERSITY PRESS, OXFORD
BY VIVIAN RIDLER
PRINTER TO THE UNIVERSITY